TASTING THE WORLD . . . ONE DESSERT AT A TIME

TASTING THE WORLD

...ONE DESSERT AT A TIME

NICOLE J. O'DONNELL

Fathead & Edmund, LLC
Birmingham, AL

Printed in the United States of America

First Printing, November 2021

ISBN 9798773352914

Front cover photograph by Sklo Studio
Back cover photographs by (clockwise from top left) Anna Shepulova,
Julia Bogdanova, Jehangir Hanafi, Tatiana Bralnina, Alla Koval,
Alexander Prokopenko, Viktoria Hodos
Book design by Nicole O'Donnell
Edited by Patrick O'Donnell
Typography: Mango Tango and Avenir Next Condensed

Fathead & Edmund, LLC
5260 Goldmar Drive
Irondale, AL 35210

www.fatheadandedmund.com

TABLE OF CONTENTS

INTRODUCTION

Let's get one thing out of the way: dessert is a European thing. (And to a lesser degree, a Middle Eastern thing. And maybe an Indian thing.) The very title of this cookbook is bound to offend a few purists who will read it and exclaim, "Hey wait! They don't eat desserts in (insert name of country where they don't eat desserts)!" And it's true. They probably don't.

The term itself developed from the French word *desservir*, which means "to clear the table." Around the seventeenth century, when this word first entered the English language, it was customary to change the table linens before the final course of a large formal meal. That final meal was usually a light fruit dish. Did Europeans eat heavier sweet dishes at all? They actually did, just not at the ends of meals. An aristocratic meal with twelve or more courses was not unheard of, and in some cases several of these included what we would today call desserts—cakes, custards, mousses, or puddings. Interestingly, in China—one of the countries where they don't eat desserts—a typical dim sum meal includes sweet dishes eaten alternately with savory ones.

The first sweetener known to humankind was honey. (Concentrated fruit juice, agave nectar, and maple syrup followed closely behind.) While bees are native to much of the world, in prehistoric times sugarcane was found in only one place, Papua New Guinea. Once the people of ancient Southeast Asia began developing trade routes, sugar made its way to India, where it was first refined. The earliest dish using sugar might have been rice pudding, a recipe for which was recorded in India around 400 BCE. But for the most part, sugar was used in Ayurvedic medicine. And when sugar first made its way to Greece and Rome, it was valued primarily as a treatment for headaches and stomach ailments.

Around 650 CE, sugar was introduced to the Arab world. It was there that it became the valuable commodity that it would remain for centuries after. Arab confectioners blended sugar with ground almonds to create marzipan, which was used to make the first actual desserts. (So yes, we can say that desserts really started off as a Middle Eastern thing.) The expansion of Islam and later the Crusades increased the diffusion of sugar, but it didn't change its status as a luxury good for the wealthy.

Sadly, it was colonialism—and the ills that it brought forth—that made sugar a worldwide phenomenon. Sugar plantations in the Americas helped feed the European appetite for refined sugarcane. But many other ingredients made their way from the New World to the Old World. Chocolate and vanilla, both native to Central America, were chief among these. Other seasonings like cinnamon and nutmeg made their way from the East. But it was the newfound abundance of sugar and the drop in price associated with it that opened the doors for the end-of-meal sweet dish to become a regular course. The Industrial Revolution helped speed this process along, and by the end of the nineteenth century sweets were found in all corners of the world.

But not desserts, though. In Mali, for example, if you're eating dessert at the end of dinner, you're probably dining in one of Bamako's fine French restaurants. But afternoon tea (something that most Americans don't do) is an important daily ritual in Mali, and at tea you're bound to encounter meni-meniyong (page 179) or another sweet treat. In the United States, peanut butter cookies (page 193) and coconut candy (page 269) are eaten as snacks. Waffles (page 22) and pancakes (page 59) are typical breakfast items, no matter how sweet they may be. But I can promise you that if you want to satisfy your sweet tooth, every recipe in this cookbook will do the trick.

Many of the African, Latin American, and Asian dishes in this cookbook are based on European equivalents, and they're usually the result of colonialism. I apologize in advance if this offends anyone. But today, these desserts are enjoyed and beloved by the cultures and people whom they represent in this cookbook. The fact that cocada amarela (page 140) was based on a Portuguese custard doesn't make it any less Angolan; guava duff (page 289) is a Bahamian dessert *par excellence*, even if it closely resembles the British plum pudding. While I do believe that a cookbook made up of recipes that were only eaten in the past is a promising idea, this one focuses on the world's present.

These recipes are desserts. They're also great for snacks, tea time (if that's your thing), and breakfast (you only live once, right?). So cook, eat, and enjoy!

GETTING READY TO COOK

If you're an experienced baker or confectioner, feel free to skip this section. But if you're still in the process of equipping your kitchen, here are a few helpful tips.

APPLIANCES

Blender: An essential appliance for any kitchen. Get a good one! Make sure to choose a blender with a Pulse button; it's what you'll use most often.

Food processor: Food processors can perform a wider range of tasks than blenders. Most come with multiple types of blades and can chop, shred, slice, or grate. But a good blender can take the place of a food processor in most kitchens It's your choice whether to invest in both appliances.

Handheld electric mixer: Another kitchen essential. Tasks like making meringue aren't easy to do by hand (at least not without wearing your arms out). Choose a handheld electric mixer with at least three speeds.

Ice cream maker: The four ice cream recipes in this book can all be made without an ice cream maker, but the results won't be as smooth or creamy. It's still a luxury item if you don't plan on using it often.

Stand mixer: Stand mixers are expensive and do the same job as electric mixers. So why do you need one? The stand mixer is your kitchen workhorse. A good quality stand mixer will mix dough, beat batter, and whisk meringue for a lifetime and provide more consistency than you might find with a handheld mixer. If you make this investment, choose a stand mixer with separate whisk, paddle, and dough hook attachments.

COOKWARE

Cast iron skillet: Every cook needs one! Cast iron is a material that holds heat evenly, which is useful in any type of cooking. What's even better is that it can be used in the oven as well as on the stovetop. If you only have one, get a 10-inch skillet. (And never put it in the dishwasher!)

Double boiler: A double boiler is made up of two pots, one of which fits inside the other. Water is boiled in the larger, bottom pot, while the top, smaller pot uses the steam from the boiling water to cook. It's a great way to cook custard or melt chocolate without burning. If you don't have one, a bowl set on top of a saucepan of boiling water will do the same job.

Heavy skillet: You should have at least one large, heavy-duty skillet for deep frying. It should be at least 2 inches deep. A Dutch oven will work for this purpose as well.

Non-stick skillet: It's always useful, but especially for cooking crepe-like dishes such as nalistniki (page 20) or pfannkuchen (page 59). It can be very irritating when these stick to the pan!

Saucepans: You will need them in all sizes—small, medium, and large. A complex recipe may require you to use several at once.

Steamer basket: Steaming is a popular method for cooking many desserts, especially East Asian cakes and puddings. If you can, get both a large and sturdy bamboo steamer (at least 12 inches wide) and a smaller metal steamer basket.

Stockpot: A six-quart or larger stockpot will prove very useful when boiling dumplings or making large batches of syrup.

BAKEWARE

Baking sheets: It's a good idea to have at least two rimmed half-sheet pans. The best quality pans will hold up to heat without warping or bending.

Bundt pan: The shape of a Bundt pan isn't just decorative. It is actually specially designed so that the maximum surface area of the cake is in contact with the pan, and this allows it to cook more evenly. If you only have one, get a large 12-cup Bundt pan.

Cake pan: You will need 8-inch and 9-inch round cake pans, and at least two of each (three is better). Ten-inch cake pans are good to have as well.

Covered baking dish: Very useful for baked goods; a Dutch oven or iron skillet with a lid will work as well.

Loaf pan: A "standard" loaf pan is 8-½ x 4-½ inches and 2-½ inches deep. It's helpful to have at least a couple of these.

Muffin tin: If you only have one, a regular-sized 12-cup nonstick muffin tin is great. A mini-muffin tin can be used to make candies and other treats as well as muffins.

Pie dish: You should have pie dishes in 9-inch and 10-inch sizes. A tart dish, which is shallower than a pie dish, is an added bonus.

Springform pans: When many people think of springform pans, they think of cheesecake (for which this type of pan is a requirement), but they are far more versatile than that. Some people use them in place of regular cake pans because they make removing the cakes from the pans easier. When you buy a springform pan, look for one that is leak-proof. (Leaky springform pans can cause a lot of frustration!)

Square baking dishes: If you make desserts frequently, a good 9 x 13-inch glass baking dish will get a lot of use. Ideally, you should also have square dishes in 8-inch, 9-inch, and 10-inch sizes.

Tube pan: Like a Bundt pan except without the fluted sides, a tube pan is also effective in transmitting heat evenly through a cake. You should have one 8-inch tube pan in your kitchen.

UTENSILS

Disher scoop: Much like an ice cream scoop, only smaller. A disher scoop is great for balling up cookie dough or nougat. They come in several sizes, but if you only have one make it a two-tablespoon scoop.

Dough cutter: This little tool consists of a spinning wheel on a handle, like a small pizza cutter. It provides a lot of control, but a sharp knife can be used in its place.

Dough scraper: This tool has a wide, rectangular blade and resembles a window squeegee. It can be used for chopping butter, frosting cakes, or, as you would expect, scraping dough.

Icing spatula: A small, flat tool that makes icing a cake easy (and maybe even fun).

Ladle: Don't try to pour hot syrup directly from a big unwieldy stockpot! Use a ladle!

Mallet: When you have to crack open a fresh coconut (and you will if you want to make any of the recipes in the Oceania section), a mallet will prove indispensable.

Pastry brush: You can use a knife or spoon to coat your bread or pie crust with egg, butter, or milk, but you'll have much better luck with the tool designed to do it.

Potato masher: Great for mashing many things–not just potatoes.

Sharp knife: If you've ever worked in a kitchen in any capacity, I shouldn't have to explain this one. Ideally, you should have several sharp knives (paring, carving, serrated, etc.).

Slotted spoons: Metal spoons are preferable, as they'll hold up a lot better when you're lifting fried dough out of hot oil. For this purpose, a spider ladle is a great choice.

Wire cake cutter: A sharp knife will do, but when you need to cut a cake into two layers, precision is key. (If you mess up, you'll have to bake the cake all over again!)

Wire whisk: If all you need to do is lightly beat or combine ingredients (rather than aerate them), a simple wire whisk will keep you from having to pull out the electric or stand mixer.

Wooden spoon: No, it doesn't *have* to be wood. It can be plastic, metal, or some other material. But if a recipe calls for mixing with a wooden spoon, mix with a spoon. Using an electric or stand mixer will overmix.

FOR SERVING

Cake stand with dome: Makes it easier to decorate a cake–and to keep it fresh for longer afterwards.

Gelatin mold: It's not just for gelatin! You can use it for molded desserts like halvaitar (page 228) or thue (page 259).

Ramekins: Custard, mousse, pudding, and many other single-serve treats need their own small dishes. A fully stocked kitchen should have six to eight matching 8-oz. ramekins in a material strong enough to stand up to heat or steam (porcelain or stoneware, for example).

Serving platter: For serving your finished desserts, of course!

Trifle bowl: You can use a simple large bowl to serve layered desserts, but a tall glass trifle bowl will show your guests how much effort you put into each layer.

OTHER NECESSITIES

Box grater: You can use a blender or food processor to grate, but a standard box grater gives you better control and has three different types of shredder holes for different purposes.

Cake rings: A cake ring is basically a cake pan without a bottom and with higher sides. It's used for assembling cakes or other desserts with multiple layers, including those that will need to be refrigerated or frozen. They're helpful to have in 8-inch, 9-inch, and 10-inch widths.

Candy thermometer: It's not just for candy! Use it to test the temperature of syrup or frying oil. They're available in mercury form or in battery-powered instant read versions. Make sure your candy thermometer can read temperatures up to at least 350 degrees.

Colander: For straining larger pieces from liquid.

Cookie cutters: At the very least, you should have round cookie cutters in a few different sizes.

Food mill: Used to prepare purees, sauces, jams, and jellies. A hand-cranked food mill can produce a thicker puree than a blender or food processor can.

Freezer containers: You'll need a few lidded containers to hold frozen desserts.

Jelly bag: When the finest particles need to be strained, use a jelly bag instead of a sieve. It's also great for straining the liquid from yogurt or cheese curd.

Microplane grater: Far finer than a box grater, a microplane grater is good for grinding spices such as nutmeg.

Mixing bowls: You'll need several in different sizes. Stainless steel is the best for most purposes, while a copper bowl is a superior choice for beating egg whites.

Mortar and pestle: For grinding smaller spices and seeds, especially peppercorns. It's much easier to clean and less messy than a spice grinder.

Parchment paper: Every baker's best friend! You can avoid the mess of greasing and flouring pans by cutting pieces of parchment paper to coat the bottom and sides instead. You'll find many more uses for this oven-safe, non-stick material.

Pastry blender: A great handheld tool for cutting butter into flour. It can also be used in place of a sifter.

Pie weights: These metal or ceramic balls are spread over the bottom of an unbaked pie crust while baking to keep it from "puffing up." Dry beans can be used in their place.

Piping/pastry bag: Very useful for decorating, even though a plastic bag with one corner cut can usually do a decent job. A pastry bag with a star-shaped tip is essential for making churros or their Balkan cousin, tulumba (page 53).

Rolling pin: If you plan to make pies, cookies, or pastry dough, this is something you'll need.

Sieve: For separating larger pieces from smaller ones. A well-equipped kitchen has several sieves of varying fineness.

Sifter: Most baking recipes call for sifted flour. A flour sifter can do that, and it can also seamlessly blend flour with baking powder, salt, or other ingredients.

Toothpicks: The best way to test a cake to see if it is done is by inserting a toothpick in the center. If it comes out clean (or with a few crumbs, if it's a moist cake) then you're good to go.

Wire rack: The best tool for cooling cookies and cakes. By setting them on a wire rack, air can circulate around them completely, allowing them to cool faster.

NOT SO NECESSARY

Since this is an international cookbook, you're bound to find a few unfamiliar dishes, ingredients, and cooking methods. The same goes for equipment. Here's a few things you might (or might not) need along the way.

Bahulu mold: The traditional Malaysian pastries known as bahulu (page 248) use a distinctive star-shaped mold. You can use a mini-muffin tin in its place.

Portuguese tart pan: It's essential if you want to make pastéis de nata (page 76) the right way. But a regular muffin tin will yield a fairly equitable result.

Pullman loaf pan: With steep, flat sides and a lid that pulls back, the Pullman loaf pan is different from a regular loaf pan in that it produces a perfectly squared-off loaf. Kasutera (page 242), the only recipe in this book that requires it, can be made using a standard loaf pan as well.

Savarin mold: This shallow, ring-shaped mold is traditionally used to make crema volteada (page 330) and can also be used in place of a standard gelatin mold.

Shaved ice maker: To make Taiwanese-style shaved ice (page 256), you'll need a shaved ice maker, and ideally one that can shave the ice in ribbon shapes.

Silicone baking cups: A regular muffin tin won't do in a steamer. Muffin-sized desserts like pichi-pichi (page 275) need a more flexible cup.

Waffle iron: If brunch at home is your thing, then you probably already have one. Otherwise, you'll need it to make gaufres de Lièges (Belgian waffles).

EUROPE

ALBANIA
RAVANI

EASY · COOK TIME: 45 MINUTES · ACTIVE PREP TIME: 15 MINUTES

This simple sponge cake, to which semolina gives a slightly coarse texture, came to Albania from Turkey and Greece. Albanian ravani is not made with coconut (a chief ingredient in Greek ravani) and uses lemon rather than orange juice in its delicately scented syrup.

3 eggs
3 c. white sugar, divided
¼ c. plain yogurt
2 Tbsp. olive oil
1 tsp. vanilla extract
2 tsp. baking powder
1 c. semolina
1-½ c. all-purpose flour
Oil or shortening, for greasing baking dish
3 c. water
3 Tbsp. lemon juice

In a large bowl, beat eggs and 1 c. sugar with an electric mixer on Medium speed until pale and foamy. Add yogurt, olive oil, vanilla extract, baking powder, semolina, and flour, in that order, mixing after each addition.

Preheat oven to 350 degrees. Grease a 9-inch square baking dish. Pour batter into pan and bake for 40 minutes or until cake is golden on top and a toothpick inserted in center of cake comes out clean. Remove cake from oven and allow to cool completely.

Combine remaining sugar and water in a small saucepan. Cook over Medium-High heat until sugar is completely dissolved (do not bring to a boil). Add lemon juice and stir.

Once cake is completely cooled, gently pour hot syrup evenly over top of cake. Slice into diamond shapes and serve.

MAKES 12 SERVINGS

Per serving: 318 calories, 4 g fat, 1 g saturated fat, 23 mg sodium, 69 g carbohydrates, 5 g protein.

SERVING SUGGESTIONS: Garnish with a thin layer of chopped pistachios or finely grated coconut and serve warm, at room temperature, or chilled. Many Albanians eat refrigerated ravani for breakfast.

VARIATIONS: Substitute lemon juice with orange juice. Stir chopped or small chocolate chips into batter before baking.

TIP: When making syrup-drenched cake desserts, it is very important not to pour hot syrup onto a hot cake. Wait until the cake cools and pour the syrup while hot, or wait until the syrup cools and pour onto hot cake.

ANDORRA
CREMA ANDORRANA

MEDIUM · COOK TIME: 40 MINUTES · ACTIVE PREP TIME: 20 MINUTES · INACTIVE PREP TIME: 6 HOURS, 45 MINUTES

There are a number of custard-based desserts that are popular in western Europe. The best-known of these are the French crème brûlée (burnt cream), which is flavored with vanilla, and the Spanish crema Catalana (Catalan cream), flavored with lemon and cinnamon. Both types have a crisp top crust made from caramelized sugar. The version of this dessert eaten in Andorra, a small nation sandwiched between Spain and France, is flavored with vanilla, lemon, and cinnamon and topped with a dollop of meringue and a drizzle of caramel sauce instead of burnt sugar.

1 qt. whole milk, divided
Peel of 1 lemon, pith removed
1 stick cinnamon
1 vanilla bean, split open
2-½ c. white sugar, divided
6 eggs, separated
¼ c. plus 1-½ tsp. cornstarch, divided
1 c. cold water, divided

In a medium saucepan, heat 3 c. milk over Medium heat until it reaches a temperature of 180 degrees, stirring constantly to avoid scalding (use a candy thermometer to monitor temperature). Add lemon peel, cinnamon stick, and vanilla bean and remove from heat. Cover and allow to sit for 45 minutes to infuse milk, and then remove lemon peel, cinnamon stick, and vanilla bean.

Combine 1 c. sugar, remaining 1 c. milk, egg yolks, and 3 Tbsp. cornstarch and whisk vigorously until smooth, about 5 minutes. Add egg mixture to infused milk. Warm custard over Medium heat, whisking constantly, until thickened. (Do not allow the custard to become hot enough to cook the egg yolks.)

Divide mixture between six 8-oz. ramekins. Cover each serving with plastic wrap and refrigerate for at least 6 hours (overnight is preferable).

In a small saucepan, combine ¾ c. sugar and ¼ c. water. Heat over High heat, whisking constantly, until sugar has dissolved, about 3 minutes. Continue to boil syrup over High heat for about 3 minutes longer or until it turns a golden amber color. Slowly add another ¼ c. of water and reduce heat to Medium. Continue to cook until syrup has reduced slightly and is thick and sticky, about 5 minutes longer. Remove from heat.

Combine remaining cornstarch and ½ c. water and stir until cornstarch is dissolved. With an electric mixer, beat egg whites on High until soft peaks form. Slowly add ¾ c. sugar, a little at a time. Once all sugar is dissolved, add cornstarch mixture and beat until meringue is glossy.

Top each custard with a spoonful of meringue and drizzle with caramel sauce.

MAKES 6 SERVINGS

Per serving: 431 calories, 10 g fat, 4 g saturated fat, 128 mg sodium, 79 g

carbohydrates, 11 g protein.

SERVING SUGGESTION: Serve with fresh fruit.

VARIATIONS: Orange peel can be used in place of lemon peel for a distinctly different flavor. To make this dessert with a burnt sugar crust, sprinkle chilled custards with a layer of turbinado sugar. Caramelize sugar using a small kitchen torch or by placing under a broiler until sugar is golden brown and bubbling.

AUSTRIA
SACHERTORTE

HARD · COOK TIME: 1 HOUR, 20 MINUTES · ACTIVE PREP TIME: 30 MINUTES · INACTIVE PREP TIME: 30 MINUTES

In 1832, Prince Klemens von Metternich of Vienna was preparing for a visit from an important guest when his court pastry chef became ill. The task of making a dessert for this special dinner fell to the chef's 16-year-old apprentice, Franz Sacher, and he met the challenge with a decadent two-layer chocolate and apricot cake that instantly made him a celebrity in Austria's culinary world. He went on to own several restaurants and cafes, and his son and daughter-in-law opened one of Europe's grandest hotels. This recipe comes very close to that served at the Hotel Sacher, the only place in the world where one can enjoy Franz Sacher's authentic Sachertorte (which after two centuries remains a tightly kept secret).

²/₃ **c. butter, at room temperature, plus more for greasing pan**
1 c. powdered sugar
½ vanilla bean, split open and scraped
7 eggs, separated
½ c. white sugar
7 oz. dark chocolate, chopped and divided

Water, for boiling
1 c. all-purpose flour, sifted
Apricot jam (see recipe)
Chocolate glaze (see recipe)

Combine butter, powdered sugar, and vanilla bean scrapings and mix together with an electric mixer on Low speed until thick and creamy. Fold in egg yolks one at a time. Set aside.

In a separate bowl, beat egg whites and ½ c. sugar with an electric mixer on High until stiff peaks form. Set aside.

Bring water to a boil in the bottom of a double boiler. Melt chocolate in the top of the double boiler. Gently fold the chocolate into the egg yolk mixture, a little at a time, followed by the egg white mixture and the flour.

Preheat oven to 350 degrees. Coat the sides of a 9-inch springform pan with butter. Pour batter into pan and bake for 1 hour.

Remove cake from oven and loosen wall belt from pan. Allow cake to cool for about 30 minutes. With a long, sharp knife or wire cake cutter, slice cake crosswise to make two equal halves. Spread a thick layer of apricot jam on top side of bottom half. Set other half on top and spread more jam in a thin layer on top and sides.

Pour glaze on top of cake (this is best done if the cake is placed on a wire rack beforehand). Working quickly, spread glaze over entire cake in an even layer using an icing spatula. Allow glaze to solidify at room temperature before slicing cake.

For apricot jam:
5 apricots, peeled and cut into small pieces
$^2/_3$ c. white sugar
1 tsp. pectin
2 Tbsp. rum (optional)

Sift sugar and pectin together. Combine apricots and sugar-pectin mixture in a medium saucepan. Bring to a boil over High heat, stirring constantly. Reduce heat to Medium-Low, cover, and simmer 15 minutes.

Pass the mixture through a food mill or sieve to reach a jam-like consistency and stir in rum (if using). Spread onto cake while still warm.

For chocolate glaze:
7 oz. dark chocolate, chopped
1 c. white sugar
$^2/_3$ c. water

Combine sugar and water in a small saucepan and bring to a boil over High heat, stirring constantly. Remove from heat and allow to cool for about 5 minutes. Add chocolate and stir until chocolate is melted. Pour over cake immediately.

MAKES 8-12 SERVINGS

Per serving: 648 calories, 27 g fat, 17 g saturated fat, 162 mg sodium, 94 g carbohydrates, 9 g protein.

SERVING SUGGESTIONS: Serve with whipped cream. Sachertorte is typically garnished with raspberries and sliced almonds.

VARIATION: The cake can be sliced into three or more layers to make a multi-layered Sachertorte (more apricot jam will be required).

TIPS: Premade apricot jam or preserves can be used in this recipe (you will need about 7 oz.). Leftover Sachertorte should be stored at room temperature, as refrigerating it will cause condensation to form on the glaze's surface.

BELARUS
NALISTNIKI WITH STRAWBERRY KISSEL

MEDIUM · COOK TIME: 1 HOUR, 25 MINUTES · ACTIVE PREP TIME: 15 MINUTES

Nalistniki are a staple of Belarusian cuisine. These thin crepe-like pancakes form the centerpiece for both sweet and savory dishes, the latter often including meat, sauerkraut, and mushrooms. Sweet nalistniki are eaten at breakfast as well as for dessert. Kissel is a thick fruit-based sauce that can be enjoyed either hot or cold. In

Belarus, kissel is served with pudding, over ice cream, or even by itself as a sweet beverage.

1-¼ c. whole milk
2 eggs
1 Tbsp. vegetable oil
1 dash salt
1 c. all-purpose flour, sifted
Butter, for frying and brushing
1-½ c. cottage cheese
½ c. cream cheese, softened
3 Tbsp. white sugar
¼ tsp. vanilla extract

In a medium bowl, combine milk, eggs, oil, and salt and beat with an electric mixer on Medium speed for 1 minute. Gradually add flour and continue to mix until smooth. Batter should be viscous but still runny.

Melt a small amount of butter in a large non-stick skillet over Medium-High heat. Add about ¼ c. of batter to skillet and swirl to make a thin layer. Cook about 1 minute, flip, and cook 1 minute longer and remove from pan. Repeat with remaining batter.

In a separate bowl, combine cottage cheese, cream cheese, sugar, and vanilla and beat with an electric mixer on Low speed until combined.

Preheat oven to 350 degrees. To assemble nalistniki, spread one large spoonful of cottage cheese mixture on one side of each pancake and roll from one end. Cut each rolled pancake in half, brush with melted butter, and place in a 9 x 13-inch baking dish (stack if necessary). Cover dish with foil and bake for 45 minutes.

Divide nalistniki between plates and drizzle generously with kissel.

For strawberry kissel:
1 lb. strawberries, hulled and sliced
Zest of ½ lemon
¼ tsp. ground cinnamon
1 c. water, divided

½ c. white sugar
¼ c. cornstarch

Puree strawberries in a blender along with lemon zest and cinnamon. In a small bowl, dissolve cornstarch in ½ c. water.

In a medium saucepan, heat strawberry puree, ½ c. water, and sugar over Medium heat for 10 minutes. Add cornstarch slurry and continue to cook for about 3 minutes longer or until thickened. Allow to cool or refrigerate before serving.

MAKES 4-6 SERVINGS

Per serving: 500 calories, 20 g fat, 11 g saturated fat, 364 mg sodium, 67 g carbohydrates, 15 g protein.

SERVING SUGGESTIONS: Nalistniki can be served with other toppings, such as chocolate sauce, maple syrup, or whipped cream.

TIP: To make ahead, assemble nalistniki and refrigerate until ready to bake. Kissel can also be made ahead and refrigerated.

BELGIUM
GAUFRES DE LIÈGES

MEDIUM · COOK TIME: 25 MINUTES · ACTIVE PREP TIME: 25 MINUTES · INACTIVE PREP TIME: 1 HOUR, 50 MINUTES

What Americans know as "Belgian waffles" are much different from those actually eaten in Belgium. There are two main varieties of *gaufres* (waffles): Brussels-style and Liege-style. Brussels waffles are light and crisp, with a well-defined square or rectangular shape and deep pockets. Liege waffles, such as these, have uneven edges and are rounder in shape. They are made from a thick, chewy dough and a special type of sugar called pearl sugar, which comes in granules too large to dissolve. The chunks of pearl sugar in a Liege waffle caramelize and form a crispy golden coating.

2 c. all-purpose flour
½ c. whole milk, at room temperature
1 Tbsp. plus 1 tsp. yeast
1 Tbsp. plus 1-½ tsp. brown sugar
1 egg
½ c. salted butter, at room temperature
½ c. Belgian pearl sugar

Combine milk and yeast in the bowl of a stand mixer with a paddle attachment. Add flour, brown sugar, and egg and blend on Low speed for 5 minutes. Add butter and blend for 10 minutes longer. Cover bowl with plastic wrap and allow to stand for 1 hour, 30 minutes or until dough is doubled in size.

Fold the pearl sugar into the dough with a wooden spoon until thoroughly incorporated. Form dough into ¼ c. balls and set on a sheet of parchment paper. Allow to stand at room temperature for 20 minutes longer.

Preheat a nonstick waffle iron to Medium. Place a ball of dough in the center of the iron plate, close the waffle iron, and cook for 1 minute. Rotate iron and cook for 2 minutes longer. Remove cooked waffle with a spatula and set on a wire rack to cool. Repeat with remaining dough.

MAKES ABOUT 8 WAFFLES
Per waffle: 279 calories, 13 g fat, 8 g saturated fat, 96 mg sodium, 37 g carbohydrates, 5 g protein.

SERVING SUGGESTIONS: The possibilities for serving gaufres de Lièges are endless. Top with whipped cream, powdered sugar, maple syrup and butter (American style), fresh fruits such as bananas and berries, jam, fruit compote, or chocolate, strawberry, or caramel syrup. They are also tasty by themselves.

VARIATIONS: While pearl sugar should be used if at all possible, it can be substituted with coarse turbinado sugar. Vanilla or cinnamon can be added to batter.

TIPS: Gaufres de Lièges can be stored for several days and eaten at room temperature or reheated in the microwave.

BOSNIA AND HERZEGOVINA
TUFAHIJE

EASY · COOK TIME: 30 MINUTES · ACTIVE PREP TIME: 45 MINUTES · INACTIVE PREP TIME: 30 MINUTES

Like many Balkan dishes, tufahije made its way northward from the Ottoman Empire. Its name comes from the Arabic word tuffāḥa, meaning "apple." When choosing apples for this consummate autumn dessert, select a variety that is firm enough to withstand poaching. While tart apples such as Granny Smith are typically used in Bosnia, sweeter varieties like Honeycrisp and Rome are also good choices.

4 large, firm apples, peeled and cored (reserve peel)
3 c. water
2 c. plus 2 Tbsp. white sugar, divided
½ c. chopped walnuts, divided
2 Tbsp. honey
Juice and zest of 2 lemons, divided
1 tsp. ground cinnamon
Whipped cream, for serving (see recipe)
Candied cherries, for serving

For whipped cream:
1 c. cold whipping cream
2 Tbsp. white sugar
½ tsp. vanilla extract

Combine water and 2 c. sugar in a lidded pot large enough to hold all 4 apples. Bring to a boil, reduce heat to Low, and stir until all sugar is dissolved. Add juice and zest of 1 lemon and peel from 1 apple. Carefully lower apples into pot, cover, and simmer for 10 minutes. (If apples are not completely submerged in water, turn after 5 minutes.) Remove apples from pot and set aside to cool. Add remaining apple peel to pot and continue to simmer until reduced by half.

Using a mortar and pestle, grind ¼ c. of chopped walnut pieces to make a fine powder. Mix walnuts (both ground and not ground) with remaining sugar, honey, and juice and zest of remaining lemon. Stuff poached apples with walnut filling. Chill for at least 30 minutes.

To make whipped cream: Combine all ingredients and beat with an electric mixer on High speed until stiff peaks form. Refrigerate until ready to use.

When ready to serve, place each apple in an individual serving dish. Divide warm syrup between apples. Top each apple with a dollop of whipped cream and a candied cherry.

MAKES 4 SERVINGS

Per serving: 757 calories, 19 g fat, 6 g saturated fat, 18 mg sodium, 155 g carbohydrates, 5 g protein.

SERVING SUGGESTION: Serve with a strong cup of coffee.

VARIATION: Tufahije can be baked instead of poached. Instead of poaching apples, prepare syrup alone and bake apples at 325 degrees for 60 minutes (or 400 degrees for 30 minutes), and serve warm.

BULGARIA
TIKVENIK

MEDIUM · COOK TIME: 40 MINUTES · ACTIVE PREP TIME: 30 MINUTES · INACTIVE PREP TIME: 30 MINUTES

Pumpkin spice lovers, rejoice! Tikvenik is one of many variations on the traditional

Bulgarian banitsa, a pastry dish that can be either sweet or savory depending on its filling. Named for its chief ingredient, tikva (pumpkin), tikvenik is enjoyed in the autumn months and on holidays. At Christmas, coins and other small metal objects are sometimes hidden in the tikvenik as kusmeti (lucky charms) to bring good fortune to the recipient.

One 1-lb. package uefka dough (about 24 leaves)
Melted butter, for brushing and greasing pan
1 lb. fresh pumpkin, grated (roughly one-third of a medium-sized sugar pumpkin, peeled and seeded)
3-¼ c. white sugar, divided
½ c. chopped walnuts
1 Tbsp. ground cinnamon
2 c. water

Spread out two leaves of the uefka dough and brush with butter. Spread about 2-3 Tbsp. of grated pumpkin over one dough leaf, followed by about 1-2 Tbsp. of chopped walnuts and 1-2 Tbsp. sugar. Sprinkle with a dash of cinnamon. Cover with second dough leaf. Starting on one short side, roll the leaves and filling into a log. Twist log into the shape of a spiral and place in center of metal pan.

Repeat with remaining dough leaves and filling, arranging rolled logs in a spiral shape until the pan is filled and all dough and filling is used.

Preheat oven to 350 degrees. Grease a 10-inch round metal pan or cast iron skillet. Bake for 30-40 minutes or until golden brown in color. (Watch carefully, as uefka dough burns easily.) Remove from oven and allow to cool.

Combine remaining sugar and water in a small saucepan and bring to a boil. Reduce heat and simmer until all sugar has dissolved and mixture is thick and syrupy, stirring frequently. Once the tikvenik has cooled, pour the syrup over its surface. Slice tikvenik into wedges after all syrup has been absorbed and serve.

MAKES 8 SERVINGS

Per serving: 409 calories, 11 g fat, 4 g saturated fat, 57 mg sodium, 82 g carbohydrates, 3 g protein.

SERVING SUGGESTIONS: If desired, sprinkle with powdered sugar before serving.

VARIATIONS: Nutmeg, cloves, raisins, or lemon zest can be added to the pumpkin filling if desired. Butternut squash may be used in place of pumpkin. While not recommended, one 14-oz. can of pumpkin puree can be used in place of fresh pumpkin.

TIPS: Phyllo dough is almost identical to uefka dough and can be used in its place. When making syrup-drenched cake desserts, it is very important not to pour hot syrup onto a hot cake. Wait until the cake cools and pour the syrup while hot or wait until the syrup cools and pour onto hot cake.

CROATIA
ZAGREBACKA KREMSNITA

MEDIUM · COOK TIME: 30 MINUTES · ACTIVE PREP TIME: 45 MINUTES · INACTIVE PREP TIME: 2 HOURS, 30 MINUTES

Croatia has many varieties of kremšnita, a dessert consisting of a puff pastry base topped with layers of custard and whipped cream. The version included here originated in the city of Zagreb in the early 1980s. Zagrebačka kremšnita is distinguished by a thin top layer of chocolate icing and remains the most popular offering at Slastičarna Vincek, the café where it was invented (and where one can still enjoy a slice prepared by the same pastry chefs who invented it).

8 oz. frozen puff pastry (1 sheet), thawed
10 eggs, separated
1-¾ c. white sugar, separated
3 Tbsp. vanilla sugar
2 qt. whole milk

1-½ c. all-purpose flour
1 Tbsp. plus 1 tsp. cornstarch
3 c. heavy cream
7 oz. baking chocolate
¾ c. butter, plus more for greasing baking dish
Water, for boiling

Preheat oven to 350 degrees. Roll out puff pastry onto a floured surface. Grease a 9 x 13-inch baking dish with butter. Spread puff pastry sheet in the bottom of dish and prick with a fork. Bake for 15 minutes.

With an electric mixer, beat egg whites on High speed until light and fluffy. Set aside.

Pour milk into a large pot and slowly bring to a boil over Medium heat. Reduce heat to Low. In a separate bowl, combine egg yolks, 1-½ c. sugar, and vanilla sugar. Beat on Medium speed, gradually adding flour and cornstarch. Slowly add egg yolk mixture to milk and cook over Medium heat, stirring constantly, until a thick custard is formed Remove from heat and add egg whites. Pour custard over puff pastry in baking dish and refrigerate for 15 minutes.

Combine remaining ¼ c. sugar and heavy cream. Beat on High speed until very light and fluffy. Spread whipped cream on top of custard.

Prepare a double boiler. In the top, combine butter and chocolate and stir until melted. Use an icing spatula to spread molten chocolate on top of whipped cream layer.

Allow chocolate layer to set for about 15 minutes, and then refrigerate for at least 2 hours. Cut into squares to serve.

MAKES 12 SERVINGS

Per serving: 648 calories, 44 g fat, 24 g saturated fat, 270 mg sodium, 51 g carbohydrates, 14 g protein.

VARIATIONS: To make a Samoborska kremšnita, omit the chocolate layer. Bake a second sheet of puff pastry at the same time as the first and set aside. After spreading the whipped cream layer, set the second sheet on top and sprinkle with powdered sugar.

TIPS: If you wish to make your own puff pastry, you can follow the same recipe used in šampita (page 67). Since kremšnita only requires one sheet of puff pastry rather than two, the ingredients will need to be halved. Kremšnita is often cooked in a rectangular cake ring instead of a baking dish. This allows for cleaner cutting when it is time to serve.

CYPRUS
PALOUZES

HARD · COOK TIME: 1 HOUR, 15 MINUTES · ACTIVE PREP TIME: 10 MINUTES

Grape juice, boiled to make a thick syrup, was at one time the only sweetener used in Cypriot cooking. Palouzes, a sweet jelly-like grape pudding, is traditionally made using the grapes from the end of the wine harvest. These grapes are crushed to produce must (moustos), or "young wine." In Cyprus, the freshly squeezed grape juice is combined with asproyi, a type of white soil from the island, to remove impurities before using the juice to make palouzes.

3-¾ qt. freshly-squeezed white grape juice, divided
½ c. all-purpose flour
2 Tbsp. cornstarch
3 arbaroriza leaves
3 Tbsp. rosewater
2 Tbsp. almonds, crushed
2 Tbsp. walnuts, crushed
½ tsp. white sugar
¼ tsp. ground cinnamon

In a large pot, bring 10 c. of grape juice to a rapid boil over High heat. Continue to boil for 1 hour or until reduced to 1 c. (it should reach the consistency of thick honey). Set aside.

In a separate pot, bring 4 c. of grape juice and arbaroriza leaves to a boil. Reduce heat and simmer for 5 minutes.

Whisk together flour, cornstarch, and remaining 1 c. of grape juice. Combine flour mixture with reduced grape juice. Remove arbaroriza leaves from pot and add flour mixture. Stir vigorously with a large whisk until pudding begins to set.

Add ½ tsp. rosewater to each of 6 small serving bowls. Swirl to coat the inside of each bowl. Divide pudding between bowls.

Mix together almonds, walnuts, sugar, and cinnamon. Sprinkle nut mixture on top of pudding and serve.

MAKES 6 SERVINGS

Per serving: 463 calories, 3 g fat, 0 g saturated fat, 20 mg sodium, 106 g carbohydrates, 6 g protein.

SERVING SUGGESTION: Palouzes can be served warm, but it is more commonly served chilled or at room temperature.

VARIATIONS: Some variations of palouzes use juice from black grapes instead of white. If arbaroriza leaves cannot be found, a sprig of rosemary is an acceptable substitute. Vanilla or ginger may also be substituted for a distinctly different flavor.

TIPS: Xynisteri, Sultana, and Málaga grapes are the best choices for this recipe. If using bottled grape juice (not recommended), be sure to choose juice that is pure and not from concentrate.

CZECH REPUBLIC
BUBLANINA

EASY · COOK TIME: 45 MINUTES · ACTIVE PREP TIME: 15 MINUTES

Most Czech recipes, desserts included, are very complex. Bublanina, or "bubble cake," is an exception. This light, airy coffee cake, which celebrates summer fruit, requires a short list of ingredients and only a few steps to make. The drobenka (streusel) topping, which is ubiquitous in Czech baked goods, gives the light dessert an indulgent punch.

3 c. all-purpose flour, divided, plus more for flouring pan
1-¼ c. white sugar, divided
1 Tbsp. baking powder
1 c. whole milk
½ c. vegetable oil, plus more for greasing pan
4 eggs
1 Tbsp. vanilla sugar
1 dash salt
Zest of 1 lemon
2 c. fresh fruit (cherries, blueberries, raspberries, strawberries, or a combination)
¼ c. plus 2 Tbsp. butter

Sift together 2 c. flour, 1 c. sugar, and baking powder in a bowl. In another bowl, whisk together milk, vegetable oil, eggs, vanilla sugar, salt, and lemon zest. Combine wet and dry ingredients and stir until a smooth batter is formed. Pour batter into pan and delicately drop pieces of fruit evenly into batter.

Use your fingers to mix together 1 c. flour, butter, and ¼ c. sugar in a small bowl until crumbly and completely moist. Sprinkle mixture over top of cake.

Preheat oven to 350 degrees. Grease and flour a 9-inch round baking dish or springform pan. Bake cake for 45 minutes or until a toothpick inserted in center comes out clean. Cut into slices to serve.

MAKES 8-10 SERVINGS

Per serving: 495 calories, 26 g fat, 10 g saturated fat, 113 mg sodium, 60 g carbohydrates, 8 g protein.

SERVING SUGGESTIONS: Bublanina may be served warm or at room temperature, and as a breakfast pastry or a dessert.

VARIATIONS: Any fruits can be used to make bublanina. In the Czech Republic, the fruit included often varies by the season. Berries, peaches and apricots are most commonly used in the summer; currants, apples, and pears are used in the fall and winter. Dried fruits or nuts may be added as well. If desired, replace drobenka topping with a light dusting of powdered sugar after baking.

DENMARK
WIENERBRØD

HARD · COOK TIME: 15 MINUTES · ACTIVE PREP TIME: 55 MINUTES · INACTIVE PREP TIME: 2 HOURS, 15 MINUTES

The Danish word *wienerbrød* means "Viennese bread." Wienerbrød was introduced to Denmark in the 1850s by bakers from Austria. Yet this sweet treat is so quintessentially Danish that in other parts of the world it's known as a "danish." The danishes sold in gas stations and vending machines in the United States cannot be compared to the freshly baked variety.

3 c. white bread flour, divided, plus more for kneading
¾ c. whole milk, divided
1 Tbsp. plus ½ tsp. active dry yeast
¼ c. white sugar
1-¾ c. butter, divided, plus more for greasing baking sheet

2 eggs, separated and divided
1 tsp. salt
1 c. fruit preserves
1 c. powdered sugar
½ tsp. almond extract

Combine milk and yeast and whisk together. Cover and let stand for 15 minutes. Add ½ c. plus 2 Tbsp. milk and yeast mixture to the bowl of a stand mixer, followed by sugar and ¼ c. butter.

Sift together 2-¾ c. flour and salt. Add flour mixture to bowl a few spoonfuls at a time while mixing on Medium speed. Add one egg plus one egg yolk to bowl after half the flour has been added. Continue to mix for 5 minutes after all flour has been added. Cover bowl and let stand for 1 hour or until dough is doubled in size.

On a floured surface, knead dough until smooth and flexible. Roll out the dough into a 12-inch square.

Using your hands, combine remaining 1-½ c. butter and ¼ c. flour to form a dough with a similar consistency to the pastry dough. Place butter dough in center of pastry dough square and fold each corner over to cover it completely.

Carefully roll dough into a rectangle about 12 inches wide and 18 inches long, making sure that the butter and pastry layers remain as separate as possible. Fold the long sides of the dough towards the center to form a rectangle that is about 4 inches wide. Place dough on a greased baking sheet, cover with plastic wrap, and refrigerate for 15 minutes.

Remove dough from refrigerator and repeat process twice. Each time, roll the dough into a rectangle 12 inches wide, fold long sides towards the center to form a rectangle 4 inches wide, and refrigerate for 15 minutes. The end result should have many thin, alternating layers of pastry and butter.

Once again, roll dough into a rectangle 8 inches wide and about 14 inches long. Spread preserves down the center of dough, leaving about 2-3 inches on each side. Cut the sides of the dough rectangle into strips. Fold the strips in an alternating pattern over the center so that the preserves form a filling for the pastry. Place pastry on greased baking sheet and allow it to rest at room temperature for at least 15 minutes.

Preheat oven to 400 degrees. Brush pastry with remaining egg white. Bake for 12-15 minutes or until golden.

Place remaining 2 Tbsp. milk in a small bowl and heat in microwave until warm. Add powdered sugar and almond extract to milk and whisk until combined. Drizzle icing over pastry and allow to set before serving.

MAKES 10-12 SERVINGS

Per serving: 426 calories, 18 g fat, 11 g saturated fat, 358 mg sodium, 61 g carbohydrates, 5 g protein.

SERVING SUGGESTIONS: Sprinkle with sliced almonds or chopped walnuts.

VARIATIONS: For a cheese wienerbrød, beat together 1 c. cream cheese with ¼ c. sugar, 1 egg yolk, and ½ tsp. vanilla extract. Use in place of (or in addition to) fruit preserves in recipe.

ENGLAND
STICKY TOFFEE PUDDING

EASY · COOK TIME: 1 HOUR · ACTIVE PREP TIME: 20 MINUTES

The term "pudding" is used to refer to desserts in general in England, but the most well-known ones are moist cake-like confections such as the famous sticky toffee pudding (known in the British Commonwealth by its acronym, STP). Like its cousins, plum pudding and figgy pudding, sticky toffee pudding uses fruit as its base—in this case, dates. Unlike those other well-known puddings, it was introduced to English cuisine only recently, in the 1960s. While no one is certain, many experts believe that STP made its way to the British Isles from Canada.

1 c. dates, pitted and chopped
1-½ c. water

1-¼ c. firmly packed dark brown sugar, divided

¾ c. butter, divided, plus more for greasing pan

1 Tbsp. plus 1 tsp. vanilla extract, divided

3 eggs

¼ c. molasses, divided

¼ c. dark corn syrup, divided

1-¾ c. all-purpose flour, plus extra for flouring pan

1-½ tsp. baking powder

¼ tsp. salt

1 tsp. baking soda

½ c. heavy cream

Bring dates and water to a boil over High heat in a small saucepan. Reduce heat to Low and simmer for about 3 minutes. Remove from heat, cover, and set aside.

In a large bowl, combine 1 c. brown sugar, ½ c. butter, and 2 tsp. vanilla extract. With an electric mixer, beat on Medium speed until creamy. Add eggs one at a time, followed by 3 Tbsp. molasses and 2 Tbsp. dark corn syrup.

Sift together flour, baking powder, and salt. Add flour mixture to wet ingredients one spoonful at a time until fully incorporated.

Place date mixture in a blender and puree until smooth. Add baking soda to date mixture and mix into batter.

Preheat oven to 325 degrees. Grease and flour a medium-sized Bundt pan with butter. Pour batter into prepared Bundt pan and bake in oven for 55 minutes or until a toothpick inserted in the center comes out mostly clean. (Sticky toffee pudding is better slightly undercooked than overcooked.)

Shortly before pudding has finished baking, prepare toffee sauce. Combine heavy cream, ¼ c. butter, ¼ c. brown sugar, 2 Tbsp. dark corn syrup, 1 Tbsp. molasses, and 2 tsp. vanilla extract in a medium saucepan. Bring to a boil over Medium-High heat, stirring constantly. Slice pudding and serve with sauce.

MAKES 12 SERVINGS

Per serving: 313 calories, 15 g fat, 9 g saturated fat, 258 mg sodium, 46 g carbohydrates, 3 g protein.

SERVING SUGGESTIONS: Top with a scoop of vanilla ice cream if desired.

VARIATION: Sticky toffee pudding can be made without dates. Cooking time may need to be reduced.

TIP: Pudding can also be made in a 12-cup muffin pan. If using a muffin pan, bake for 20 minutes at 350 degrees.

ESTONIA
KRINGEL

EASY · COOK TIME: 25 MINUTES · ACTIVE PREP TIME: 20 MINUTES · INACTIVE PREP TIME: 1 HOUR, 15 MINUTES

Kringels are popular throughout the Baltic states and Scandinavia, but the Estonian kringel is distinguished by its round wreath-like shape, sometimes called a "Russian rose." This simple sweet bread is served on special occasions in Estonia, such as birthdays and christenings. Traditional Estonian kringels are spiced with saffron and cardamom, but this more modern recipe is flavored with cinnamon and almond extract.

1 c. whole milk, lukewarm
2 Tbsp. plus 1 tsp. active dry yeast
¼ c. white sugar, divided
2 egg yolks
2 c. butter, at room temperature, divided, plus more for greasing baking sheet
4 c. all-purpose flour, plus more for flouring surface
1 tsp. salt
1 Tbsp. ground cinnamon
1 tsp. almond extract

Combine milk, yeast, and 1 Tbsp. sugar in a bowl. Cover and let stand for 15 minutes. Whisk in egg yolks and ½ c. butter.

Sift together flour and salt. Slowly combine flour and milk mixture until a dough is formed. Cover bowl and let stand for 1 hour or until doubled in size.

On a floured surface, knead dough until smooth and flexible. Roll out the dough into a 12-inch square.

In a small bowl combine 1 c. butter, cinnamon, and almond extract. Spread filling in an even layer over the dough. Starting at one of the long ends, roll the dough to form a log. Use a sharp knife to cut the log lengthwise into two halves, stopping just before the end so that the halves are still connected (layers of cinnamon and butter mixture should be visible on each cut side).

Preheat oven to 400 degrees. Grease a baking sheet with butter and place kringel on baking sheet. Twist the two halves together to form a "braid," and then pull the two ends together to form a round "wreath." Brush the surface of the kringel with remaining butter. Bake kringel for 20-25 minutes or until golden brown.

MAKES 6-8 SERVINGS

Per serving: 792 calories, 56 g fat, 35 g saturated fat, 725 mg sodium, 64 g carbohydrates, 10 g protein.

SERVING SUGGESTIONS: If desired, make an icing by whisking together 1 c. powdered sugar, 2 Tbsp. lukewarm milk, and ½ tsp. almond extract and drizzle over kringel while warm.

VARIATIONS: Raisins or other dried fruits can be added to the kringel with the filling. Melted chocolate or hazelnut spread can be used as a filling in place of the cinnamon butter.

FINLAND
RUNEBERG CAKE

MEDIUM · COOK TIME: 30 MINUTES · ACTIVE PREP TIME: 45 MINUTES · INACTIVE PREP TIME: 20 MINUTES

Runeberg Cake was invented not by one of Finland's great pastry chefs, but by one of its great historical novelists, Frederika Runeberg (1807-1879). Frederika's husband, Finnish national poet Johan Ludwig Runeberg (1804-1877), was especially fond of these cakes. For this reason they are most frequently served on his birthday, February 5, which in Finland is a national holiday (Runeberg's Day). But in the Runebergs' hometown of Porvoo, they are enjoyed year-round. This recipe uses a muffin pan, but in Finland Runeberg cakes are baked in individual cylinder-shaped ring forms.

2-¼ c. all-purpose flour, plus more for flouring pan

½ c. water

½ c. white sugar

2 Tbsp. dark rum

2 tsp. baking powder

1 tsp. salt

¾ c. gingersnaps, finely crushed

¼ c. almonds, finely ground

2-½ tsp. ground cardamom

Zest and juice of 1 large orange

½ c. plus 1 Tbsp. whole milk, divided

2 Tbsp. molasses

1-¼ tsp. almond extract, divided

¾ c. butter, softened, plus more for greasing pan

1 c. brown sugar

3 eggs

¾ c. powdered sugar

¾ c. raspberry jam

Begin by preparing syrup. Heat water and sugar over Medium heat until sugar is completely dissolved. Remove from heat and stir in rum. Let syrup stand until it has reached room temperature.

Sift together flour, baking powder, and salt. In a large bowl, combine flour with gingersnaps, almonds, cardamom, and orange zest. In another bowl, whisk together orange juice, ½ c. milk, molasses, and 1 tsp. almond extract.

In the bowl of a stand mixer with a whisk attachment, combine butter and brown sugar and mix on Medium speed until creamy, about 5 minutes. Gradually add the eggs one at a time. Add flour mixture, one spoonful at a time, until fully incorporated. Follow with milk and orange juice mixture, mixing only until all ingredients are combined.

Preheat oven to 350 degrees. Grease and flour a 12-cup muffin tin (preferably one with deep, narrow cups). Divide batter between 12 muffin cups. Make sure that cups are no more than three-quarters full. Bake in oven for 20 minutes or until a toothpick inserted in center of cake comes out clean. Allow cakes to rest in pan for 5 minutes, remove from pan, and cool on a wire rack with widest end facing down.

While cakes are still warm, pour cooled syrup over cakes. They should absorb most of the syrup. Allow cakes to cool completely.

In a small bowl, whisk together powdered sugar, 1 Tbsp. milk, and ¼ tsp. almond extract. Pour icing into a piping bag or plastic bag with one corner cut. Pour raspberry jam into another bag. Decorate cakes by piping icing in a circle around the rim of the top of each cake. Fill the center of the circle with raspberry jam.

MAKES 12 CAKES

Per cake: 418 calories, 15 g fat, 8 g saturated fat, 348 mg sodium, 67 g carbohydrates, 5 g protein.

SERVING SUGGESTION: Serve with spiced tea. Johan Runeberg is said to have enjoyed these cakes with a glass of punsch (Finnish spiced tea with rum), even when having them for breakfast.

VARIATIONS: Gingersnap crumbs can be replaced with an equal amount of

breadcrumbs and 1 tsp. of ground ginger. Orange or lemon juice can be used in place of rum in syrup.

TIP: When making syrup-drenched cake desserts, it is very important not to pour hot syrup onto a hot cake. Wait until the cake cools and pour the syrup while hot, or wait until the syrup cools and pour onto hot cake.

FRANCE
MOUSSE AU CHOCOLAT

EASY · COOK TIME: 15 MINUTES · ACTIVE PREP TIME: 10 MINUTES · INACTIVE PREP TIME: 4 HOURS

Chocolate was introduced to France in 1615, with the marriage of Louis XIII to a Spanish princess, and it did not take long for French chefs to find creative uses for this New World delicacy. Although they are much lighter and usually richer, mousses are often confused with puddings. The more technical difference between the two is that a mousse is traditionally made without milk or cream and is not cooked. Instead, beaten egg whites are folded into the chocolate to give it an airy texture, while egg yolks are incorporated for a rich mouthfeel.

6 oz. bittersweet baking chocolate (60-70 percent cacao), broken into pieces
¼ c. plus 1 Tbsp. butter
Water, for boiling
4 eggs, separated
½ c. powdered sugar, divided

Bring water to a boil in the bottom of a double boiler. Heat chocolate and butter in the top of the double boiler over the boiling water, stirring frequently, until completely melted. Remove from heat and allow to cool.

In a medium bowl, beat egg whites and 1 Tbsp. powdered sugar on High with an electric mixer until stiff peaks form. Set aside.

Whisk together egg yolks and remaining sugar in a separate bowl. Stir into chocolate mixture until smooth. Slowly fold egg white mixture into chocolate mixture, about 2 Tbsp. at a time.

Once all of the egg white mixture has been added, spoon mousse into 6 medium-sized ramekins. Chill for 4 hours before serving.

MAKES 6 SERVINGS

Per serving: 307 calories, 24 g fat, 14 g saturated fat, 44 mg sodium, 19 g carbohydrates, 5 g protein.

SERVING SUGGESTIONS: Garnish with whipped cream, raspberries or strawberries, and mint leaves.

VARIATIONS: Other flavorings may be added along with chocolate, such as vanilla, cinnamon, espresso, lemon extract, or brandy.

TIP: The longer the mousse is chilled, the flatter and denser it will become. Keeping this in mind, it can be made up to 3 days in advance.

GERMANY
SCHWARZWÄLDER KIRSCHTORTE

HARD · COOK TIME: 30 MINUTES · ACTIVE PREP TIME: 35 MINUTES · INACTIVE PREP TIME: 3 HOURS, 30 MINUTES

Some European desserts have been enjoyed for so long that their origins cannot be determined; others are recent inventions whose roots can easily be traced. Schwarzwälder kirschtorte (Black Forest cherry cake) is among the latter. This famous cake was first made by German pastry chef Josef Keller in 1915. Keller was from a small village near Cologne, far from southwestern Germany's Black Forest, but his cake got its name from its use of sour Morello cherries, a Black Forest specialty, and the cherry brandy made from them (kirschwasser).

7 eggs, divided
1-¼ c. white sugar, divided
2 tsp. vanilla extract, divided
¼ tsp. salt
1-¼ c. all-purpose flour, plus more for flouring pan
½ tsp. baking powder
¾ c. cornstarch, divided
½ c. cocoa powder
¼ c. butter, melted, plus more for greasing pan
One 14-oz. jar dark sour cherries
1 Tbsp. lemon juice
¼ tsp. ground cinnamon
½ c. cherry schnapps or kirsch, divided
1 Tbsp. water
1 qt. heavy whipping cream, divided
¾ c. powdered sugar
6 oz. dark chocolate, shaved, for garnish
12 fresh cherries, with stems, for garnish

In a small bowl, beat egg whites and salt with an electric mixer on Medium speed until soft peaks form. Set aside.

In another bowl, combine egg yolks, 1 c. sugar, and 1 tsp. vanilla extract and beat on High speed until light and fluffy. Sift together flour, baking powder, ¼ c. plus 2 Tbsp. cornstarch, and cocoa powder. Mix together egg yolk and flour mixtures until incorporated, then gradually fold in egg white mixture followed by melted butter.

Preheat oven to 375 degrees. Lightly grease and flour a 10-inch springform pan. Pour batter into pan and bake for 25 minutes or until a toothpick inserted in center comes out clean. Allow cake to cool in pan for 15 minutes before loosening wall belt and transferring cake to a wire rack to cool completely.

Drain cherries, reserving liquid. Place cherry liquid in a small saucepan with lemon juice, remaining sugar and cornstarch, and cinnamon. Once the sauce begins to thicken, remove from heat and stir in cherries and 3 Tbsp. schnapps.

Using a wire cake cutter or sharp knife, horizontally cut the cake into three equal layers. Mix together remaining cherry schnapps and water and brush onto cake layers until absorbed. Place the first cake layer inside a 10-inch cake ring and cover with cherry filling. Refrigerate for 15 minutes.

Beat together 2-½ c. whipping cream, ¼ c. plus 1 Tbsp. powdered sugar, and ½ tsp. vanilla on High speed until stiff peaks form. Spread half of whipped cream mixture over cherry filling and top with another cake layer. Spread remaining whipped cream over top of second cake layer and top with third layer. Refrigerate for 1 hour.

Beat together remaining whipping cream, powdered sugar, and vanilla on High speed until stiff peaks form. Remove ring and spread whipped cream evenly on top and sides of cake. Sprinkle with a thick, even layer of chocolate shavings and place cherries in a circle around edge of cake. Refrigerate for at least 2 hours longer before serving.

MAKES 12 SERVINGS

Per serving: 504 calories, 26 g fat, 16 g saturated fat, 165 mg sodium, 62 g carbohydrates, 7 g protein.

VARIATIONS: One option is to decorate as a "naked" cake, with no icing on the sides. Another is to cover the cake with a thick layer of ganache instead of the whipped cream icing.

GREECE
PORTOKALOPITA

EASY · COOK TIME: 2 HOURS, 15 MINUTES · ACTIVE PREP TIME: 10 MINUTES

Portokalopita belongs to a category of syrup-soaked Mediterranean desserts called siropiasta, which also includes ravani (page 15) and baklava (page 133). Like baklava, this orange-flavored cake gets much of its bulk from paper-thin sheets of phyllo dough. But in this recipe, the phyllo dough is broken into small pieces, which makes it much less of a challenge to make than desserts that use full sheets.

One 1-lb. package phyllo dough
Juice and zest of 3 oranges, divided
2-¼ c. white sugar, divided
1-½ c. water
1 stick cinnamon
4 eggs
1 c. plain Greek yogurt
1 tsp. vanilla extract
1 tsp. baking powder
1 tsp. baking soda
¼ tsp. salt
1 c. sunflower oil, plus more for greasing pans
All-purpose flour, for flouring pan
8 orange slices, for garnish

In a small saucepan, combine juice and zest of 1 orange, 1-½ c. sugar, water, and cinnamon stick. Bring to a boil over Medium-High heat. Reduce heat to Low and simmer for 15 minutes. Remove from heat and set aside to cool.

Preheat oven to 250 degrees. Grease a rimmed baking sheet with oil. Fold up each sheet of phyllo dough in an accordion pattern, one at a time, so that all of the dough fits on the baking sheet. Toast phyllo until dry and crispy but not burned, about 1 hour. Use your hands to break each piece of toasted phyllo into small pieces.

Combine eggs and remaining ¾ c. sugar in the bowl of a stand mixer with a whisk attachment and beat for 3 minutes. Add yogurt, vanilla extract, baking powder, baking soda, salt, and the zest of the third orange. Once combined, add oil and juice from third orange. Using a wooden spoon or spatula, gradually fold phyllo pieces into batter.

Raise oven temperature to 350 degrees. Grease and flour a 9 x 13-inch baking dish. Pour batter into dish and garnish with orange slices. Bake for 50-60 minutes or until golden.

Pierce the top of the cake with a fork several times. Pour cooled syrup on top of cake, a little at a time, until fully absorbed. Allow to cool completely before slicing and serving.

MAKES 8-10 SERVINGS

Per serving: 438 calories, 27 g fat, 3 g saturated fat, 260 mg sodium, 48 g carbohydrates, 5 g protein.

SERVING SUGGESTIONS: Serve with yogurt, whipped cream, or vanilla ice cream on the side.

TIP: When making syrup-drenched cake desserts, it is very important not to pour hot syrup onto a hot cake. Wait until the cake cools and pour the syrup while hot, or wait until the syrup cools and pour onto hot cake.

HUNGARY
ESTERHÁZY TORTA

HARD · COOK TIME: 1 HOUR · ACTIVE PREP TIME: 1 HOUR · INACTIVE PREP TIME: 8 HOURS

Are you a baker seeking a challenge? Then try the Esterházy torta, one of Europe's great aristocratic desserts. The identity of the nineteenth-century Budapest confectioner who invented this cake has not survived history. It was probably named for Prince Paul III of Hungary (of the Esterházy dynasty), who was said to be a fan of rich and complex foods. While it's not known whether this cake was among his favorites, there's no denying its richness and complexity.

3-½ c. almonds, divided
5 eggs, separated, plus 5 egg whites
1-½ c. white sugar, divided
2 Tbsp. all-purpose flour
1 c. whole milk
1 tsp. vanilla extract
Cooking spray, for spraying parchment paper
1-¼ c. butter, at room temperature
2 Tbsp. rum or cognac
2-¾ c. powdered sugar
¼ c. hot water, plus more for boiling
1 Tbsp. lemon juice
2 tsp. almond extract
2 oz. dark chocolate (70 percent cacao or higher)

Preheat oven to 375 degrees. Pulse 2-½ c. of almonds in a food processor until finely ground. Spread ground almonds on a parchment-lined baking sheet and toast in oven for 10-12 minutes, turning halfway through cooking time. Remove almonds from oven, allow to cool slightly, and then grind once again in food processor.

Beat egg yolks and ½ c. sugar with an electric mixer on Medium speed until pale and creamy. Heat milk and vanilla in a small saucepan over Medium heat until nearly boiling and reduce heat to Low. Slowly add egg yolk mixture to milk, stirring constantly until custard reaches a temperature of 185 degrees (this may require you to raise the heat slightly; use a candy thermometer to monitor temperature). Remove custard from heat and refrigerate until ready to use.

Preheat oven to 350 degrees. Cut six 8-inch circles from parchment paper and set on three large baking sheets. Spray each circle with cooking spray.

Beat the egg whites with an electric mixer on High speed. Add 1 c. sugar and flour and continue to beat until stiff peaks form. Fold 2 c. of ground almonds into egg white mixture with a wooden spoon or spatula.

Spoon an equal amount of batter into the center of each parchment paper circle and spread in an even layer so that it reaches the edges. Bake the cake layers two at a time for 12 minutes each. Remove cake layers from oven, trim if necessary, and allow to cool on a wire rack.

Pour the custard mixture into the bowl of a stand mixer. Beat on Medium speed and add butter, 1-2 Tbsp. at a time, until custard is light and fluffy. Add remaining ½ c. of ground almonds and rum or cognac.

Place a cake layer in the bottom of an 8-inch cake ring. Spread one-fifth of the custard on top of first layer, then top with second layer. Continue to alternate layers and custard, leaving the top layer bare. Place in refrigerator and chill for 8 hours or overnight.

To make the icing, whisk together powdered sugar, 2 Tbsp. hot water, lemon juice, and almond extract. Continue to add water until icing has reached a thick but spreadable consistency (you may need more water than is called for here). Spread icing in an even layer on top and sides of cake.

Bring water to a boil in the bottom of a double boiler. Heat chocolate in the top of the double boiler over the boiling water, stirring frequently, until completely melted. Pour chocolate into a piping bag or plastic bag with corner cut while hot. Pipe chocolate on top of cake in a striped pattern of vertical lines (make lines about 1 inch apart). Turn the cake 90 degrees and with a toothpick or knife, score the top of the cake to make vertical lines to cross the chocolate lines (also about 1 inch apart). Rotate cake again 180 degrees and score lines in between the ones just made going the opposite direction. The result should be an elaborate black and white spiderweb-like pattern.

Coarsely chop the remaining almonds. Toast chopped almonds in a dry skillet for 2-3 minutes or until brown. Allow almonds to cool, then pack onto sides of cake. Slice thinly and serve.

MAKES 12-16 SERVINGS

Per serving: 526 calories, 33 g fat, 15 g saturated fat, 142 mg sodium, 52 g carbohydrates, 9 g protein.

SERVING SUGGESTIONS: Serve with strawberries or chocolate wafers.

VARIATIONS: Add ¼ c. cocoa powder to batter for a chocolate Esterházy torta. Hazelnuts or walnuts may be used in place of almonds.

TIP: Esterházy torta does not keep well, so try to finish it on the day it is served. (It shouldn't be hard.)

ICELAND
HJÓNABANDSSÆLA

EASY · COOK TIME: 3 HOURS, 8 MINUTES · ACTIVE PREP TIME: 15 MINUTES · INACTIVE PREP TIME: 8 HOURS

The Icelandic word *hjónabandssæla* translates to "marital bliss." The origin of this name probably has less to do with literal marriage and more to do with the perfect "marriage" of its ingredients, which include oats and rhubarb. While rhubarb did not arrive in Iceland until the late nineteenth century, as one of the few fruits that thrives in the island country's frigid environment it has become an important part of its cuisine.

3 c. rolled oats
2-½ c. all-purpose flour
2 c. brown sugar
1 tsp. baking soda
1 tsp. baking powder
½ tsp. ground cardamom
¼ tsp. salt
1-½ c. butter, melted, plus more for greasing baking dish
1 egg

1-¼ c. strawberry-rhubarb jam (see recipe below)

Combine oats, flour, brown sugar, baking soda, baking powder, cardamom, and salt. Add butter and egg and mix well with a wooden spoon until mixture is completely moist.

Preheat oven to 350 degrees. Grease an 8-inch square baking dish with butter. Add about two-thirds of oat mixture to pan and press with your fingers until it forms an even layer that fills pan. Spread jam over the oatmeal layer. Sprinkle the remaining oat mixture over the jam.

Bake in oven for about 8 minutes or until browned. Slice into squares and serve.

For strawberry-rhubarb jam:
1 lb. fresh strawberries, hulled
1 lb. fresh rhubarb, cut into pieces
2-½ c. white sugar
½ tsp. salt

Place fruit in a large stainless steel pot and coat with sugar. Add salt, cover pot with lid, and allow to stand for 8 hours or overnight. The sugar should draw the moisture out of the fruit.

Bring pot to a boil over High heat. Reduce heat to Low and simmer for about 3 hours, stirring frequently. Pour jam into sterile jars and refrigerate until ready to use.

MAKES 8-10 SERVINGS

Per serving: 709 calories, 23 g fat, 14 g saturated fat, 500 mg sodium, 122 g carbohydrates, 8 g protein.

SERVING SUGGESTIONS: Serve warm, cold, or at room temperature with coffee or a glass of cold milk.

TIPS: One 10-oz. jar of jam may be used in place of homemade jam in this recipe. For a larger batch, double ingredients and bake in a 9 x 13-inch baking dish.

IRELAND
PORTER CAKE

EASY · COOK TIME: 1 HOUR, 10 MINUTES · ACTIVE PREP TIME: 10 MINUTES · INACTIVE PREP TIME: 1 HOUR

While most of the desserts in this cookbook are best on the day they are prepared, porter cake is said to taste better the longer it is allowed to stand, as its flavors become stronger and deeper over time. As the ingredient that gives it its name, porter beer lends this cake most of its flavor. Its alcohol evaporates during boiling, but its toasty flavor is infused into the raisins as they soak in the sweet and buttery syrup before the cake is baked.

3-½ c. all-purpose flour, plus more for flouring pan
1 c. plus 2 Tbsp. white sugar
1 c. butter, plus more for greasing pan
1-½ c. dark beer (porter or stout), divided
2 c. raisins (preferably a mix of purple and golden raisins)
Zest of 4 oranges
1 tsp. baking soda
1 tsp. baking powder
½ tsp. ground cinnamon
½ tsp. ground nutmeg
½ tsp. ground allspice
¼ tsp. ground cloves
¼ tsp. salt
3 eggs

Combine butter, sugar, and 1-¼ c. beer in a medium saucepan. Heat over Medium-High heat until sugar is completely dissolved. Add raisins and orange zest. Reduce heat and simmer for 5 minutes. Remove from heat and allow to stand for about 1 hour.

Preheat oven to 350 degrees. Grease and flour an 8-inch springform pan. Sift together flour, baking soda, baking powder, cinnamon, nutmeg, allspice, cloves, and salt. Slowly fold in beer mixture, then add eggs one at a time. Pour batter into pan and bake for 1 hour or until toothpick inserted in center comes out clean.

Drizzle warm cake with remaining ¼ c. beer. Allow cake to cool completely before loosening wall belt.

MAKES 10 SERVINGS

Per serving: 500 calories, 20 g fat, 12 g saturated fat, 349 mg sodium, 74 g carbohydrates, 7 g protein.

SERVING SUGGESTIONS: Serve with strong coffee or tea.

VARIATIONS: Chopped cherries may be added to cake batter if desired. Other alcohols such as whiskey or brandy may be used in place of beer.

TIPS: This cake is usually best 1-2 days after it is baked, and it can be kept much longer. In Ireland, a porter cake is usually made in November and eaten on Christmas Day. To keep the cake moist and fresh, a small amount of porter is drizzled on the cake every few days and allowed to absorb ("feeding" the cake).

ITALY
TIRAMISÙ

MEDIUM · ACTIVE PREP TIME: 20 MINUTES · INACTIVE PREP TIME: 2 HOURS

Tiramisù's name means "pick me up," a reference to the espresso that gives it one of its dominant flavors. The earliest records state that this dish was first served in Le Beccherie restaurant in Treviso in the 1960s. But according to legend, its origins can be found in a nineteenth-century Treviso brothel, where it was served as an aphrodisiac. Tiramisù is undoubtedly a native dessert of Treviso, also the home of one of its key ingredients, mascarpone.

1-½ c. espresso or strong black coffee, at room temperature
¼ c. amaretto or other liqueur (see Variations section), divided
½ c. heavy whipping cream, very cold
½ c. powdered sugar, divided
4 eggs, separated
1 lb. mascarpone cheese
One 1-lb. package savoiardi (ladyfingers)
Cocoa powder, for garnish

Combine espresso and 3 Tbsp. liqueur in a small bowl and set aside. In another bowl, whisk together whipping cream and 2 Tbsp. powdered sugar with an electric mixer on High speed until stiff peaks form, about 5 minutes, and set aside.

In a third bowl, combine ¼ c. plus 2 Tbsp. sugar and egg yolks and beat on High speed for 3 minutes or until mixture is pale and sugar has dissolved. Add mascarpone and beat for 1 minute longer. Gently fold in whipped cream, a little at a time, with a wooden spoon or spatula.

In a fourth bowl, beat egg whites on Medium speed until soft peaks form. Fold egg white mixture into mascarpone mixture and add remaining 1 Tbsp. liqueur.

Soak savoiardi in espresso mixture for only a few seconds (do not allow them to become soggy and oversaturated). Place a layer of savoiardi in the bottom of an 8 x 8-inch glass baking dish and top with a layer of mascarpone mixture to fill the dish halfway. Repeat the process with another layer of soaked savoiardi and another layer of mascarpone mixture. Use a flat knife to smooth the surface and refrigerate for 2 hours. Dust with a thick, even layer of cocoa powder and serve.

MAKES 8 SERVINGS

Per serving: 415 calories, 18 g fat, 9 g saturated fat, 754 mg sodium, 43 g carbohydrates, 15 g protein.

VARIATIONS: Marsala wine is traditionally used in tiramisù. Dark rum, brandy, or hazelnut, coffee, or chocolate liqueurs can all be used in place of amaretto. For a chocolate tiramisù, add ½ c. melted chocolate (cooled) along with mascarpone.

TIP: Since tiramisù contains raw eggs, it is best not served to people who are pregnant or in compromised health. Choose another dessert from this cookbook instead—there are nearly two hundred others!

KOSOVO TULUMBA

MEDIUM · COOK TIME: 30 MINUTES · ACTIVE PREP TIME: 10 MINUTES · INACTIVE PREP TIME: 10 MINUTES

In a region that culturally balances between Eastern Europe and the Middle East, tulumba lean more towards the latter than the former. The origins of these tiny bites of sticky and sweet fried dough have been claimed by Turkey and Greece, but they are hugely popular throughout the Balkans. Tulumba are formed using a star-shaped pastry tip, giving them a distinctive shape reminiscent of Latin American churros.

2-½ c. all-purpose flour, sifted
3 c. plus 2 Tbsp. white sugar, divided
1 qt. plus 1 c. water, divided
Juice and zest of 1 lemon
2 Tbsp. butter
3 eggs
3 Tbsp. semolina
2 Tbsp. cornstarch
1 Tbsp. white wine vinegar
Sunflower oil, for frying

Combine 3 c. sugar and 3 c. water in a large saucepan. Bring to a boil over Medium-High heat, stirring frequently. Reduce heat and simmer for 15 minutes. Stir in lemon juice and zest. Remove from heat and set aside.

In another saucepan, add 2 c. water, 2 Tbsp. sugar, and butter. Heat over Low heat until butter is melted. Add flour and stir with a wire whisk until a loose dough is formed. Remove from heat and set aside until cooled.

Use a wooden spoon to slowly fold eggs, semolina, cornstarch, and vinegar into dough. Once all ingredients are fully incorporated, transfer the dough to a pastry bag fitted with a ½-inch star-shaped tip.

Heat about 2 inches of oil in a heavy skillet to a temperature of 350 degrees. Use the pastry bag to squeeze 1- to 2-inch sections of dough into hot oil (it may help to cut the dough with wet scissors to make pieces of correct length). Fry tulumba in small batches for 2-3 minutes, turning them over halfway through. Remove from pan and set on paper towels to drain.

While tulumba are slightly warm, add to the cooled syrup and soak for about 3 minutes longer. Remove from syrup with a slotted spoon and serve.

MAKES 8-10 SERVINGS

Per serving: 630 calories, 29 g fat, 5 g saturated fat, 41 mg sodium, 92 g carbohydrates, 5 g protein.

SERVING SUGGESTION: Sprinkle tulumba with finely chopped pistachios or walnuts before serving.

VARIATIONS: Add vanilla extract or cinnamon to dough if desired.

LATVIA
KLINGERIS

MEDIUM · COOK TIME: 45 MINUTES · ACTIVE PREP TIME: 30 MINUTES · INACTIVE PREP TIME: 1 HOUR, 15 MINUTES

In Latvia, klingeris is usually made to celebrate birthdays. While a giant pretzel-shaped sweet bread may be much different from a typical American birthday cake, at a Latvian birthday party a kliņģeris is festively decorated–usually with candles, which the birthday person blows out after making a wish.

9-½ c. all-purpose flour, divided, plus more for kneading
1-¼ c. raisins
Boiling water, for soaking
2-½ c. white sugar, divided
½ c. whole milk
2 Tbsp. plus 2 tsp. active dry yeast
2 c. plus 2 Tbsp. butter, divided, plus more for greasing baking sheet
7 eggs
1 c. sour cream
Zest of 1 lemon
1-½ tsp. ground cardamom
Powdered sugar, for garnish

Place raisins in a large bowl and cover with boiling water. Allow raisins to soak for at least 10 minutes. Drain raisins and set on a clean towel to dry.

Combine milk, 1 Tbsp. sugar, and yeast in a small bowl. Stir until dissolved and allow to stand for 5 minutes. Meanwhile, sift 8 c. flour into a large bowl and add 1 c. plus 2 Tbsp. butter. Use your hands to mix flour and butter until a crumbly dough is formed. Set aside.

In another bowl, beat together 1 c. sugar and 6 eggs with an electric mixer on Medium speed until pale and foamy. Add sour cream, lemon zest, and cardamom. Whisk in milk and yeast mixture.

Fold raisins into flour mixture. Combine wet and dry ingredients in the bowl of a stand mixer with a dough hook attachment and mix until a soft dough is formed, about 5 minutes. Return dough to bowl, cover with plastic wrap, and allow to rise for 1 hour.

As dough is rising, prepare crumb topping. Combine remaining flour, sugar, and butter in a bowl and use your fingers to mix them together until dry crumbs are formed, adding more flour if needed.

Preheat oven to 350 degrees. Turn dough onto a floured surface and knead until pliable. Form the dough into a log about 3 feet long and 4 inches in diameter. Grease a large rimmed baking sheet, place dough log on baking sheet, and twist the log into a pretzel shape. Beat remaining egg and brush surface to glaze. Sprinkle kliņģeris generously with crumbs. Bake in oven for 45 minutes or until golden. Sprinkle with powdered sugar before serving.

MAKES 24 SERVINGS

Per serving: 437 calories, 20 g fat, 12 g saturated fat, 142 mg sodium, 58 g carbohydrates, 7 g protein.

SERVING SUGGESTIONS: Serve warm with jam or butter.

VARIATIONS: If desired, top kliņģeris with sliced almonds instead of crumbs. Other dried fruits, such as apricots or dates, or candied ginger may be added in place of or in addition to raisins.

LIECHTENSTEIN PFANNKUCHEN

MEDIUM · COOK TIME: 40 MINUTES · ACTIVE PREP TIME: 10 MINUTES · INACTIVE PREP TIME: 15 MINUTES

The word *pfannkuchen* means "pancake" in German. As in most of Europe, Liechtensteiner pancakes lack the baking powder that makes American pancakes thick and fluffy. They are generally not quite as thin as the French crêpes, but are similar in that they are served with a sweet filling. These pfannkuchen are served stacked rather than rolled up in the French style, with sweet raspberry preserves spread between layers.

1 c. all-purpose flour
2 Tbsp. white sugar

½ tsp. salt
4 eggs
2 c. whole milk
1 tsp. vanilla extract
Juice and zest of 1 lemon
Butter, for frying
1-½ c. raspberry preserves (see recipe below)

Sift together flour, sugar, and salt. In another bowl, whisk together eggs, milk, vanilla, and lemon juice and zest. Combine wet and dry ingredients and stir until batter is completely smooth and moist. Allow to stand for 15 minutes.

Heat butter in a nonstick skillet over Medium heat. Add ¼ c. batter to pan and spread with the back of a spoon to coat pan. Cook pancake until batter starts to bubble and edges become crisp; flip and cook other side until fully cooked but not brown, about 30 seconds. Transfer to serving tray and repeat with remaining batter.

To serve, spread about 2 Tbsp. of raspberry preserves on top of one pancake. Top with another pancake and spread another layer of preserves on top. Repeat with as many pancakes and preserve layers as desired, leaving the top pancake bare.

For raspberry preserves:
4 c. frozen raspberries
¾ c. white sugar
¼ c. cornstarch
¼ c. water
2 Tbsp. lemon juice

Whisk together sugar and cornstarch in a medium saucepan. Stir in raspberries, water, and lemon juice. Heat pan over Medium heat, stirring constantly, for 10 minutes or until mixture bubbles and thickens.

Pour preserves into a separate bowl and allow to stand at room temperature (or refrigerate) until cooled.

MAKES 4-6 SERVINGS

Per serving: 664 calories, 17 g fat, 9 g saturated fat, 389 mg sodium, 122 g carbohydrates, 12 g protein.

SERVING SUGGESTIONS: Serve with fresh mint and strawberries, blueberries, or other fruit.

VARIATIONS: Other fillings can be used in place of preserves, such as applesauce, fruit compote, hazelnut spread, or cinnamon sugar.

TIP: One 12-oz. jar of preserves may be used in place of homemade preserves in this recipe.

LITHUANIA
TINGINYS

EASY · COOK TIME: 5 MINUTES · ACTIVE PREP TIME: 10 MINUTES · INACTIVE PREP TIME: 4 HOURS, 10 MINUTES

How much easier can a recipe get when its name literally means "lazy"? These no-bake cookies have a short prep time, an even shorter list of ingredients, and an interesting origin. The first tinginys was made in 1967, when a Lithuanian woman accidentally added too much sugar when cooking chocolate syrup. She mixed shortbread crumbs into the syrup to reduce its sweetness, and when the product solidified the result was a delicious cookie.

One 1-lb. package shortbread cookies, broken into small pieces
One 14-oz. can sweetened condensed milk
¾ c. plus 2 Tbsp. butter, melted
¼ c. plus 1 Tbsp. cocoa powder

Combine condensed milk, butter, and cocoa powder in a small saucepan. Heat over Medium heat until mixture begins to thicken, about 5 minutes.

Pour milk mixture over shortbread pieces. Stir until shortbread is completely coated. Allow to cool for about 10 minutes.

Wrap shortbread mixture in a long piece of plastic wrap and shape into a log. Refrigerate for at least 4 hours (preferably overnight). When tinginys has fully solidified, slice the log with a sharp knife or a wire into ¼-inch thick cookies and serve.

MAKES ABOUT 20-30 COOKIES

Per cookie: 203 calories, 13 g fat, 9 g saturated fat, 124 mg sodium, 19 g carbohydrates, 3 g protein.

VARIATIONS: Dried cherries or nuts such as hazelnuts or walnuts may be added along with shortbread. Add a dash of cinnamon, vanilla extract, or other flavoring. Any other types of cookies (e.g., chocolate or vanilla wafers, butter cookies, or gingerbread) may be used in place of shortbread.

TIP: When wrapping the tinginys, it may be helpful to line a small loaf pan with plastic wrap before pouring the shortbread mixture into the pan.

LUXEMBOURG QUETSCHENTAART

MEDIUM · COOK TIME: 55 MINUTES · ACTIVE PREP TIME: 30-45 MINUTES · INACTIVE PREP TIME: 1 HOUR, 30 MINUTES

One of the many national dishes of Luxembourg, quetschentaart is made with a variety of plum (quetschen) not frequently found outside the small country. Damson plums, which have a lower water content and looser stones than common varieties, can be used instead. Quetschentaart is a beloved Luxembourger tradition during plum season, which falls in the autumn months.

1-½ lbs. Damson plums, pitted and sliced into wedges
½ c. butter, plus more for greasing dish

¼ c. plus 2 Tbsp. white sugar, divided
1 egg
2 c. all-purpose flour, plus more for flouring pan
¼ tsp. salt

Beat butter and ¼ c. sugar with an electric mixer on High speed until pale. Add the egg and continue to beat until fluffy. Sift together flour and salt and add to the bowl of a stand mixer with a paddle attachment. Add wet ingredients and mix on Medium speed until a firm dough is formed. Cover with plastic wrap and refrigerate for 30 minutes.

Preheat oven to 350 degrees. Grease and flour a 9- or 10-inch pie or tart dish. Roll the dough into a flat circle and press into dish, fluting the edges with your fingers, and prick the base of the crust with the tines of a fork. Bake crust for 15 minutes.

Arrange plum wedges on top of the crust in a circular pattern, making sure to pack them tightly together with the skin side down (this will keep the plum juice from saturating the crust). Sprinkle with remaining 2 Tbsp. sugar. Bake tart for 40 minutes longer. Allow tart to cool for 1 hour before serving.

MAKES 8 SERVINGS

Per serving: 347 calories, 13 g fat, 8 g saturated fat, 164 mg sodium, 57 g carbohydrates, 6 g protein.

SERVING SUGGESTIONS: Serve with whipped cream or vanilla ice cream and coffee.

VARIATION: Sprinkle cinnamon over plums along with sugar.

MALTA
PUDINA TAL-HOBZ

MEDIUM · COOK TIME: 1 HOUR, 50 MINUTES · ACTIVE PREP TIME: 20 MINUTES · INACTIVE PREP TIME: 2 HOURS, 30 MINUTES

Malta is a former British colony, and pudina tal-ħobż ("bread pudding" in Maltese) was most likely made as a variation of the traditional English pudding (page 34), with its moist texture and inclusion of dried fruit. But many Americans might agree that this Maltese dessert more resembles chocolate brownies than bread pudding.

1 day-old loaf Maltese bread (see recipe below), sliced
1 c. golden raisins, chopped
Zest and juice of 1 orange
3 c. whole milk
2 eggs, beaten
¼ c. dark baking chocolate, chopped, or dark chocolate chips
¼ c. brown sugar
3 Tbsp. cocoa powder
1 tsp. ground cinnamon
Cooking spray, for spraying pan

Combine raisins and orange juice and set aside to soak. Place bread slices in a large bowl and cover with milk, making sure that bread is completely saturated. Allow bread to soak in milk for 20 minutes.

Squeeze bread slightly to remove excess milk. Drain raisins and add to bread mixture, stirring to combine. In a separate bowl, whisk together orange zest, eggs, chocolate, brown sugar, cocoa powder, and cinnamon. Fold egg mixture into bread mixture until fully incorporated.

Preheat oven to 425 degrees. Spray an 8 x 8-inch baking dish with cooking spray. Pour pudina into dish and spread to make an even layer. Bake for 30 minutes or until firm and crisp on the top. Allow pudina to cool, then cut into squares to serve.

For Maltese bread:
3 c. white bread flour
1-¼ tsp. salt
2 c. lukewarm water, divided
2 Tbsp. yeast
3 Tbsp. olive oil, divided

Sift together flour and salt. In a small bowl, combine 1-½ c. water, yeast, and 2 Tbsp. olive oil and allow to stand for 10 minutes. Combine wet and dry ingredients in the bowl of a stand mixer with a dough hook attachment and mix for about 5 minutes or until a dough is formed. Cover and allow to stand for 2 hours or until doubled in size.

Preheat oven to 350 degrees. Pour remaining water into a medium-sized covered baking dish. Place dish in oven (with lid) for 30 minutes. Discard water and coat inside of dish with remaining olive oil.

Place dough in baking dish. Cover and bake for 30 minutes. Remove lid and bake for 20 minutes longer. Remove bread from dish and cool on wire rack.

MAKES 9 SERVINGS

Per serving: 346 calories, 10 g fat, 3 g saturated fat, 311 mg sodium, 57 g carbohydrates, 10 g protein.

SERVING SUGGESTIONS: Serve either warm or chilled with coffee.

VARIATIONS: Other dried fruits can be added, such as apples, dates, prunes, or candied cherries or orange peel. Nuts may be added as well. If desired, add a small amount of rum along with the wet ingredients.

TIPS: A medium-sized round loaf of white or sourdough bread may be substituted for the Maltese bread. If time is a factor, heat raisins and orange juice in microwave for 1 minute to speed up soaking process.

MOLDOVA
SMETANNIK

MEDIUM · COOK TIME: 40 MINUTES · ACTIVE PREP TIME: 40 MINUTES · INACTIVE PREP TIME: 1 HOUR

Desserts are not as popular in Moldova as they are in other Eastern European countries. Most of the ones you're likely to find there are borrowed from the cuisines of its neighbors. One example is smetannik (sour cream cake), a tribute to the favorite condiment of Russia. According to legend, smetannik was invented by the wife of a Russian dairy farmer, who wished to show that sour cream could be used not only in a sweet cake, but also in its icing.

2 c. plus 2 Tbsp. all-purpose flour, divided, plus more for flouring pans
2 c. white sugar
3 eggs
4 c. sour cream, divided
1 tsp. baking powder
Juice of 1 lemon
1 tsp. vanilla extract
2 Tbsp. cocoa powder
Butter, for greasing pans
1 c. powdered sugar
2 tsp. rum extract
1-½ c. chopped walnuts

Using an electric mixer, beat sugar and eggs together in a large bowl until pale and fluffy. Add 2 c. flour and 2 c. sour cream and continue to mix until a smooth batter is formed. In a smaller bowl, combine baking powder and lemon juice (they will fizz when combined), then stir mixture into batter along with vanilla extract.

Divide batter between two bowls. Add cocoa powder to one bowl and remaining 2 Tbsp. flour to other bowl. Mix each together until combined (chocolate batter should be a rich brown color throughout).

Preheat oven to 375 degrees. Grease and flour two 9-inch round cake pans. Pour chocolate batter into one pan and white batter into the other. Bake for 40 minutes or until cakes are golden on top and a toothpick inserted in center of each cake comes out clean. Allow cakes to cool before removing from pans.

To prepare frosting, mix remaining 2 c. sour cream, powdered sugar, and rum extract on Medium speed until smooth. Frosting will be slightly drippy.

Once cakes are completely cool, use a long, sharp knife or wire cake cutter to trim the tops of the cakes so that they are completely flat. Reserve any cake scraps that are trimmed. Use the knife or wire to slice each cake crosswise to make two equal halves (there should be a total of four layers of equal thickness when you are finished).

Place trimmed cake scraps in a blender or food processor and pulse until even crumbs are formed. Set crumbs aside.

To assemble cake, spread a layer of icing on the top of one of the chocolate layers and sprinkle with 2 Tbsp. walnuts. Lay one of the white layers on top of the chocolate layer and top with another layer of icing and 2 Tbsp. walnuts. Repeat with remaining layers. Once all four layers have been assembled, spread remaining icing over top and sides of cake in an even layer. Press remaining walnuts into sides of cake and sprinkle cake crumbs over top. Allow cake to stand at room temperature for at least 1 hour before refrigerating.

MAKES 12-16 SERVINGS

Per serving: 419 calories, 20 g fat, 9 g saturated fat, 49 mg sodium, 55 g carbohydrates, 7 g protein.

SERVING SUGGESTIONS: Serve cake chilled with berries.

VARIATION: Smettanik is often made with more than four layers. To increase the number of layers, simply slice each cake into three or four layers instead of two. The more layers the cake has, the more icing and walnuts will be needed.

MONACO GALAPIAN

HARD · COOK TIME: 3 HOURS, 20 MINUTES · ACTIVE PREP TIME: 10 MINUTES · INACTIVE PREP TIME: 6 DAYS, 9 HOURS

Joie de vivre is the name of the game in the Principality of Monaco, home of the Côte d'Azur, Monte Carlo, and the world's most expensive real estate. So even though its origins are found a few hours west of Monaco, the galapian definitely fits the bill as a national dessert. This rich and unique fruit tart was created in the Apt region of France by master pastry chef Alain Bouchard for a 1994 competition held by the Confrérie du fruit confit d'Apt, an organization founded to promote products native to the region (most specifically its candied fruit confit, which has a central place in this recipe).

3 c. plus 2 Tbsp. all-purpose flour, divided, plus more for flouring surface
1 c. white sugar, divided
2-¼ c. butter, divided, plus more for greasing pie dish
3 eggs, divided
¼ tsp. salt
1 tsp. vanilla extract
1-½ c. melon confit (see recipe below)
¾ c. maraschino cherries, drained
2 tsp. ground angelica seed (optional)
1 c. ground almonds
1 Tbsp. orange liqueur (optional)
Slivered almonds, for garnish

Sift together 3 c. flour, ½ c. sugar, and salt. Add to bowl of a stand mixer with a paddle attachment along with 1 egg, 1-¾ c. butter, and vanilla extract and mix on Medium speed until a stiff dough is formed, about 5 minutes. Refrigerate dough for 1 hour.

Grease a 9- or 10-inch pie plate. Roll the dough into a flat circle about ½-inch thick and press into dish. Prick the base of the crust with the tines of a fork. Arrange slices of melon confit inside crust in an even layer. Top with cherries and sprinkle with angelica seed (if using).

Preheat oven to 325 degrees. Combine remaining 2 Tbsp. flour, ½ c. sugar, ½ c. butter (at room temperature), 2 eggs, ground almonds, and orange liqueur (if using) and stir together until creamy. Spread almond mixture over melon and cherries and top with an even layer of slivered almonds. Bake for 30 minutes or until tart is brown on top. Brush with reserved syrup from melon confit and serve warm.

For melon confit:
1 lb. firm cantaloupe, peeled, seeded, and sliced into strips
¼ tsp. salt
1 qt. plus 2 c. water, plus more for boiling
3-½ c. white sugar
3 Tbsp. light corn syrup

Place cantaloupe slices and salt in a large nonreactive pot with enough water to cover. Bring to a boil, reduce heat to Low, and simmer for 1 hour. Drain and rinse cantaloupe.

Add water, sugar, and corn syrup to the same pot and bring to a boil. Reduce heat to Low, add cantaloupe, cover, and simmer for 20 minutes. Remove from heat and allow to stand overnight at room temperature.

Each day for the next four days, bring cantaloupe and syrup mixture to a boil, reduce heat, and simmer covered for 20 minutes before removing from heat. Stir mixture each day so that the cantaloupe slices are evenly coated (syrup will start to reduce over time).

On the sixth day, heat the cantaloupe and syrup over Medium heat until temperature reaches 235 degrees (use a candy thermometer to monitor temperature), stirring frequently. Remove from heat and allow to stand overnight.

On the seventh day, remove cantaloupe slices from syrup and arrange on a wire rack, reserving syrup. Allow slices to drain for 8 hours before using.

MAKES 8 SERVINGS

Per serving: 1002 calories, 54 g fat, 30 g saturated fat, 508 mg sodium, 123 g carbohydrates, 11 g protein.

SERVING SUGGESTION: Serve with Muscat or another sweet wine.

TIPS: If available, candied cantaloupe can be used in place of melon confit. Any leftover syrup can be used in cocktails or other desserts.

MONTENEGRO SAMPITA

MEDIUM · COOK TIME: 40 MINUTES · ACTIVE PREP TIME: 35 MINUTES · INACTIVE PREP TIME: 8 HOURS, 25 MINUTES

Šampita is one of many Balkan desserts based on the French millefeuille (Napoleon), a layered dessert made of puff pastry, custard, and whipped topping. Kremšnita (page 27) is another example. But the somewhat simpler Montenegrin šampita has the distinction of being the only one without the custard layer; instead, it consists of a single thick, marshmallow-like layer of meringue sandwiched between two sheets of puff pastry.

1-½ c. all-purpose flour, plus more for flouring surface
¼ tsp. salt
1-½ c. cold butter, cut into small cubes
½ c. cold water, plus more for boiling
7 egg whites
2 c. white sugar
1 tsp. vanilla extract
Juice of ½ lemon
Powdered sugar, for garnish

Sift together flour and salt in a large metal bowl. Place bowl in refrigerator and chill for about 10 minutes.

Using a pastry blender, combine flour with butter and water until a rough dough is formed. Wrap dough in plastic wrap and chill for 15 minutes longer.

Turn dough onto a floured surface and roll into a rectangle about 6 inches wide and 18 inches long. Fold sides over center to form a 6 x 6-inch square. Roll out into a rectangle again, and then fold sides over center again. Repeat this process at least four times. Refrigerate dough for 8 hours or overnight.

Preheat oven to 400 degrees and place rack in center of oven. Divide dough into two portions. Roll each portion into a 9 x 13-inch rectangle. Bake pastry sheets in oven (separately) for 15 minutes or until golden. Set pastry sheets aside to cool.

Bring a large saucepan of water (about one-quarter full) to a boil. While waiting for water to boil, whisk egg whites gently in a metal bowl. When water begins to boil, place egg whites in bowl above saucepan and continue to beat with whisk. Gradually add sugar and vanilla extract. Heat egg white mixture until it reaches a temperature of 150 degrees (use a candy thermometer to monitor temperature).

Transfer egg white mixture to the bowl of a stand mixer with a whisk attachment. Mix on Medium speed until meringue is completely cool and has doubled in size. Add lemon juice to meringue halfway through the process. When finished, the meringue should be completely opaque and stiff enough to impede the stand mixer's movement.

Place one puff pastry sheet in the bottom of a 9 x 13-inch dish (trim sides if necessary). Spoon meringue on top of pastry and spread evenly, then top with second puff pastry sheet. Refrigerate until ready to serve. To serve, slice into squares with a serrated knife and dust with powdered sugar.

MAKES 12 SERVINGS

Per serving: 310 calories, 16 g fat, 10 g saturated fat, 179 mg sodium, 42 g carbohydrates, 3 g protein.

VARIATIONS: Šampita can be served topped with cocoa powder, chocolate syrup, or shredded coconut instead of powdered sugar. It can also be made using only one puff pastry sheet (on the bottom).

NETHERLANDS
BOTERKOEK

EASY · COOK TIME: 25 MINUTES · ACTIVE PREP TIME: 20 MINUTES

Definitely one of the simpler European desserts, boterkoek is as rich and decadent as any. Its name means "butter cake," and while many variations on this Dutch delight include almond, vanilla, or lemon, butter is always the dominant flavor. The large amount used in this cake makes it moist, dense, and crispy all at once. This version includes an *amandelspijs* (almond paste) filling, but it can be made without it.

2 c. all-purpose flour
¾ c. white sugar
1 dash salt
3 eggs, separated and divided
1 tsp. vanilla extract
Zest of 1 lemon
1 c. cold butter, cut into small cubes, plus more for greasing dish
1 c. whole almonds
Water, for blanching
1 c. powdered sugar
1 Tbsp. almond extract

Sift together flour, sugar, and salt. Add 1 whole egg, vanilla extract, and lemon zest and stir until smooth. Cut the butter into the batter and knead with your hands until a rough dough is formed.

Bring a small saucepan of water to a boil. Add almonds and allow to boil for 1 minute. Drain almonds and quickly rinse with cold water. Remove skins of almonds and discard.

Pulse almonds in a blender or food processor to form a coarse meal. Combine almond meal, 1 egg white, powdered sugar, and almond extract and stir until combined. Gradually add egg yolk to mixture.

Preheat oven to 350 degrees. Grease a 9-inch pie dish. Divide cake batter in half and pour half of batter into pan, patting the top of the batter to make its surface smooth. Spread the almond mixture on top of batter, then top with remaining batter. Use the tines of a fork to make a lattice pattern on the top of the cake and brush with remaining egg. Bake for 15 minutes or until cake begins to pull away from sides of pan and a toothpick inserted in center comes out mostly clean. Allow cake to cool completely before slicing.

MAKES 10-12 SERVINGS

Per serving: 393 calories, 23 g fat, 11 g saturated fat, 152 mg sodium, 44 g carbohydrates, 6 g protein.

SERVING SUGGESTIONS: Serve with coffee.

VARIATIONS: If desired, top cake with an even layer of slivered almonds. To make a boterkoek without the amandelspijs filling, pour all batter into pie dish at once. Joodse boterkoek, a variation popular in Dutch-Jewish cuisine, includes ½ c. of finely chopped candied ginger in the batter.

NORTH MACEDONIA
KOZINJAK

EASY · COOK TIME: 45 MINUTES · ACTIVE PREP TIME: 35 MINUTES · INACTIVE PREP TIME: 2 HOURS, 10 MINUTES

Braided breads, both sweet and savory, are well-loved in Balkan cuisine. Kozinjak is a yeasty, airy sweet bread made with milk and dried fruit that is most often enjoyed on holidays. In Macedonia it is customary to bake two loaves of kozinjak for Easter, one for one's own family and one to share with the priest at the local church.

5 c. plus 2 tsp. bread flour, divided, plus more for flouring surface

¾ c. raisins
Zest and juice of 2 oranges
1 c. whole milk, divided
1 c. white sugar, divided
2 Tbsp. active dry yeast
4 eggs, divided
¼ c. vegetable oil, plus more for greasing pan
1 tsp. vanilla extract
Sesame seeds, for garnish

Combine raisins and orange juice and set aside to soak. Whisk together ¼ c. milk, ½ tsp. sugar, 2 tsp. flour, and yeast in a small bowl and whisk together. Allow to stand for about 10 minutes or until mixture starts to foam.

Whisk together 3 eggs, ¾ c. sugar, ¾ c. milk, vegetable oil, and vanilla extract. In the bowl of a stand mixer with a dough hook attachment, combine egg mixture with 5 c. flour, orange zest, and yeast mixture and mix on Medium speed for 5 minutes.

Turn dough onto a floured surface and knead for 5-10 minutes longer or until dough is smooth and pliable. Place dough in a bowl and cover with plastic wrap. Allow to stand for 1 hour or until doubled in size. Knead dough for 5 minutes longer and allow to stand for another 30 minutes. Drain raisins, add to dough, and knead for 5 more minutes.

Grease a 9-inch cake pan, preferably one with tall sides, or a Bundt pan. Divide dough into three portions and roll each into a 2-foot strand. Pinch the three strands together at one end and braid together, alternately overlapping the left and right strands with the center strand. Twist the braid to form a circle and set inside pan. Allow dough to stand in pan for 30 minutes.

Preheat oven to 375 degrees. Beat remaining egg and use to brush top of bread. Sprinkle with sesame seeds and remaining sugar. Bake for 10 minutes or until the top of the bread begins to brown. Remove from oven, cover with aluminum foil, and bake 10 minutes longer. Reduce heat to 300 degrees and bake 10 minutes. Reduce heat again to 225 degrees and bake 10 minutes longer. Remove foil and continue to bake until top of bread is a deep golden brown color, about 5-10 more minutes. Cool slightly before serving.

MAKES 8-10 SERVINGS

Per serving: 479 calories, 10 g fat, 3 g saturated fat, 42 mg sodium, 87 g carbohydrates, 12 g protein.

SERVING SUGGESTIONS: Serve warm with butter and a glass of milk.

VARIATIONS: For a straight loaf, place on a greased baking sheet after braiding without twisting into a circle. Garnish and bake as directed. For a different flavor, soak raisins in rum instead of orange juice. Dried plums, figs, pineapple, cranberries, or apricots may be used in place of raisins.

TIP: If time is a factor, heat raisins and orange juice in microwave for 1 minute to speed up soaking process.

NORWAY
KVÆFJORDKAKE

HARD · COOK TIME: 40 MINUTES · ACTIVE PREP TIME: 35 MINUTES · INACTIVE PREP TIME: 1 HOUR

In the 1930s, two sisters from the Kvæfjord municipality of northern Norway who owned a café on the nearby island of Hinnøya first created the kvæfjordkake, naming it for their home region. Exactly how popular is it in Norway today? In 2002, the Norwegian Broadcasting Corporation (NRK)'s Nitimen cooking program had its audience members choose Norway's national dessert. With 69 percent of the vote, kvæfjordkake emerged the winner–earning it the nickname *verdens beste* ("world's best" in Norwegian).

1-¼ c. all-purpose flour
1-½ tsp. baking powder

1-¾ c. white sugar, divided
½ c. butter, plus more for greasing pan
4 eggs, separated, plus 2 egg yolks
2-¼ c. whole milk, divided
1 tsp. vanilla extract, divided
½ c. slivered almonds
1 Tbsp. cornstarch
1-½ c. heavy cream

Sift together flour and baking powder in a large bowl. With an electric mixer, beat ½ c. sugar and butter together on Medium speed until pale. Gradually add 4 egg yolks, followed by ¼ c. milk and ½ tsp. vanilla extract. Combine wet and dry ingredients and whisk together until a smooth batter is formed. Set aside.

Add egg whites to the bowl of a stand mixer with a whisk attachment. Mix on Medium speed until foamy. Add 1 c. sugar and continue to mix until stiff.

Preheat oven to 325 degrees. Grease a large rimmed baking sheet and line it with parchment paper. Pour batter onto baking sheet and use a spatula to spread it so that the entire sheet is covered. Spread meringue over batter in an even layer and sprinkle with slivered almonds. Bake for 30 minutes or until meringue is golden on top. Remove from oven and allow to cool.

Heat 2 c. milk and ½ tsp. vanilla extract over Medium heat in a large saucepan until warm (do not bring to a boil). Remove from heat.

Whisk together ¼ c. sugar, 2 egg yolks, and cornstarch until smooth, about 5 minutes. Add egg mixture to milk. Warm custard over Medium heat, whisking constantly, until thickened. (Do not allow the custard to become hot enough to cook the egg yolks.) Remove from heat and allow to cool.

Beat heavy cream on High speed until soft peaks form. Slowly fold whipped cream into custard.

Remove cake from baking sheet and place on a cutting board. Cut cake in half, turn one half upside down, and carefully place on a serving plate with the meringue side down. Spread custard on top of inverted cake half. Top with second half of cake, with the meringue side up. Chill in refrigerator for 1 hour before serving.

MAKES 12 SERVINGS

Per serving: 275 calories, 16 g fat, 9 g saturated fat, 96 mg sodium, 29 g carbohydrates, 5 g protein.

SERVING SUGGESTION: Serve chilled with strawberries or other fresh fruits.

VARIATION: To greatly simplify this recipe, use instant vanilla pudding in place of custard.

TIP: All ingredients should be completely cooled before assembling or kvæfjordkake will not hold together. You may wish to refrigerate custard before assembling and use a piping bag to apply the custard layer.

POLAND
BABKA

MEDIUM · COOK TIME: 30 MINUTES · ACTIVE PREP TIME: 35 MINUTES · INACTIVE PREP TIME: 3 HOURS, 35 MINUTES

Jewish babka, a chewy sweet bread made from leftover challah bread dough with a cinnamon or chocolate filling, exploded in popularity in the United States in the 2010s. But traditional Polish babka is a much different product. It more resembles panettone, the dried fruit-heavy Italian dessert it is based upon. It was introduced to Poland in the early sixteenth century during the reign of the Milan-born Queen Bona Sforza. Its name (Polish for "grandmother") comes from its traditional shape, which resembles a woman's skirt. But like the more familiar babka, this recipe has a yeasty texture that walks the line between cake and bread.

4-½ c. plus 1 Tbsp. all-purpose flour, divided, plus more for flouring surface
1 c. raisins (preferably a mix of purple and golden raisins)
2 Tbsp. dark rum

1 Tbsp. plus 1-½ tsp. active dry yeast

¾ c. plus 1 Tbsp. white sugar, divided

1 c. lukewarm milk, divided

1 whole egg plus 5 egg yolks

1 dash salt

1 tsp. vanilla extract

¼ tsp. almond extract

Zest and juice of 1 lemon

½ c. butter, at room temperature, plus more for greasing pan

½ c. candied orange peel, chopped

1-¼ c. powdered sugar

1 Tbsp. light corn syrup

Combine raisins and rum and set aside to soak. Combine yeast, 1 Tbsp. sugar, and $^1/_3$ c. milk in a small bowl and stir until dissolved. Add ¼ c. flour and continue to stir until creamy. Cover with a towel and allow to stand for 20 minutes.

With an electric mixer, beat together 5 egg yolks, ¾ c. sugar, and salt on High speed until pale. Add vanilla extract, almond extract, and lemon zest and continue to beat for 1 minute. Add yeast mixture, reduce speed to Low, and beat for 1 minute longer.

Add egg yolk mixture to the bowl of a stand mixer with a dough hook attachment. Gradually add 3-¾ c. flour and remaining $^2/_3$ c. milk while mixing on Low speed for about 3 minutes. Gradually add butter and mix for 3 minutes longer.

Drain raisins from rum and pat dry with a paper towel. Dredge raisins in 1 Tbsp. flour. Using a wooden spoon, fold raisins and orange peel into the dough. Add remaining ½ c. flour. Turn dough onto a floured surface and knead for at least 5 minutes or until dough is smooth and pliable.

Grease a 12-cup Bundt pan. Form dough into a log and press into pan. Cover pan with a towel and allow to stand in a warm place for at least 3 hours or until it has risen to fill the pan.

Preheat oven to 350 degrees. Brush surface of babka with remaining egg. Bake for 30 minutes or until a toothpick inserted in center of cake comes out clean. Allow cake to cool for 15 minutes before removing from pan. Set cake on a wire rack to cool.

Whisk together powdered sugar, lemon juice, and corn syrup until thick and translucent. Once babka is completely cooled, use a pastry brush to coat surface with glaze. Cut and serve babka once glaze is dry.

MAKES 12-16 SERVINGS

Per serving: 338 calories, 9 g fat, 5 g saturated fat, 76 mg sodium, 58 g carbohydrates, 6 g protein.

SERVING SUGGESTIONS: Serve with butter or cream cheese.

VARIATIONS: Dried fruits such as cherries and cranberries may be used in addition to or in place of the raisins. Other extracts, such as lemon, may be used in place of almond extract for a different flavor.

TIP: Many bakers believe that babka has its best flavor the day after it is made.

PORTUGAL
PASTÉIS DE NATA

MEDIUM · COOK TIME: 25 MINUTES · ACTIVE PREP TIME: 15 MINUTES · INACTIVE PREP TIME: 30 MINUTES

Pastéis de nata (Portuguese for "cream puffs") can be found in all corners of the Portuguese diaspora. Fast food giant KFC even sells a version at its Macau locations. The centuries-old dessert's origins can be found in a Lisbon monastery, where the clergy invented the custard tarts as a way to raise money while also finding a use for leftover egg yolks (egg whites were used to starch clerical vestments at the time). In 1834 the recipe was sold to a sugar refinery, which opened a patisserie in the Lisbon neighborhood of Belém for the sole purpose of baking the tarts. Today, pastéis de nata are still made in the same building using the original recipe.

8 oz. frozen puff pastry (1 sheet), thawed

Melted butter, for brushing
1 whole egg plus 4 egg yolks
½ c. white sugar
3 Tbsp. cornstarch
2 c. heavy cream
2 Tbsp. light corn syrup
½ tsp. lemon extract
1 stick cinnamon
Ground cinnamon, for garnish

Roll out pastry into a 12-inch square and brush with an even coat of melted butter. Starting at one end, roll pastry into a log, wrap in plastic wrap, and refrigerate for 30 minutes.

Remove from refrigerator and cut into 12 even slices. Roll each slice into a circle roughly 3 inches wide. Press each circle into the well of a Portuguese tart pan, trimming any excess. Refrigerate pastry in pan until ready to use.

Preheat oven to 500 degrees. Combine egg and egg yolks, sugar, and cornstarch in a saucepan and stir until smooth. Add heavy cream, corn syrup, lemon extract, and cinnamon stick and bring to a boil over Medium heat. Continue to cook, stirring and scraping bottom of pan constantly, until custard is very thick. Remove cinnamon stick.

Divide custard between pastry shells in tart pan, smoothing the top of each. Bake for 15 minutes or until the top of custard has become dark brown and caramelized (you may need to broil the tarts during the last few minutes of cooking). Let cool before removing from pan. Generously dust with cinnamon before serving.

MAKES 12 TARTS

Per tart: 253 calories, 17 g fat, 8 g saturated fat, 70 mg sodium, 22 g carbohydrates, 3 g protein.

VARIATION: For a Macanese-style pastéis de nata (Macau Po egg tarts), replace lemon extract and cinnamon with 1 tsp. vanilla extract. Instead of dusting with cinnamon, coat top of tart with a simple sugar syrup (one part sugar to one part water) and broil until caramelized.

TIPS: If you wish to make your own puff pastry, you can follow the recipe used for šampita (page 67). Half the amounts of ingredients used. A 12-cup nonstick muffin tin can be used in lieu of a Portuguese tart pan; tarts will not fill cups entirely and will have a different shape.

ROMANIA
JOFFRE CAKE

HARD · COOK TIME: 35 MINUTES · ACTIVE PREP TIME: 40 MINUTES · INACTIVE PREP TIME: 1 HOUR, 30 MINUTES

In 1920, French division general Joseph Joffre took a trip to Casa Capșa in Bucharest. A visit from the commander-in-chief of France's forces on the Western Front to Romania's most exclusive restaurant and hotel required a luxurious dessert to match the occasion. This velvety ganache and buttercream delight can best be described as every chocoholic's dream come true.

10 eggs, separated
1 c. cocoa powder
½ c. plus 1 Tbsp. water, divided
3 c. white sugar, divided
1 Tbsp. all-purpose flour, plus more for flouring pan
2 Tbsp. day-old breadcrumbs
1-¾ c. butter, plus more for greasing pan
1 tsp. vanilla extract
½ tsp. rum extract
1/3 c. baking chocolate, melted
½ c. powdered sugar

    Combine 2-½ c. white sugar, cocoa powder, and ½ c. water in a saucepan. Bring to a boil, reduce heat, and simmer for 5 minutes. Transfer syrup to a bowl and allow to cool. Once cooled, fold egg yolks into syrup one at a time using an electric mixer on Low speed.

In a separate bowl, stir flour and breadcrumbs into one-third of egg yolk mixture. Beat egg whites and 3 Tbsp. of sugar in another bowl on High speed until soft peaks form and fold into batter.

Mix remaining egg yolk mixture with butter, vanilla extract, and rum extract on Medium speed until smooth and fluffy. Cover and refrigerate for 1 hour.

Preheat oven to 400 degrees. Grease and flour an 8-inch round cake pan. Pour batter into pan and bake for 30 minutes or until a toothpick inserted in center of cake comes out clean. Remove from oven and allow to cool in pan for 10 minutes before turning onto wire rack to finish cooling.

Once cake has cooled completely, use a long, sharp knife or wire cake cutter to slice cake crosswise to make three equal layers. To assemble cake, place one layer at the bottom of an 8-inch cake ring. Spread half of filling on top of cake layer, then top with second layer. Spread remaining filling over second layer and top with third layer. Refrigerate for at least 30 minutes before decorating.

To make icing, combine 1 Tbsp. water, melted chocolate, and powdered sugar in a small bowl and whip until smooth. Spread in an even layer over top and sides of cake.

MAKES 10-12 SERVINGS

Per serving: 444 calories, 21 g fat, 12 g saturated fat, 174 mg sodium, 63 g carbohydrates, 7 g protein.

SERVING SUGGESTIONS: Serve with orange slices or with vanilla ice cream.

VARIATIONS: Walnuts or almonds can be added to filling. For a sour cherry Joffre cake, spread a thick layer of sour cherry jam between the first two layers of cake and layers of filling.

TIP: Instead of cooking a single cake and cutting it after baking, you may divide the batter between three separate cake pans. Adjust cooking time accordingly.

RUSSIA
PTICHYE MOLOKO CAKE

HARD · COOK TIME: 35 MINUTES · ACTIVE PREP TIME: 30 MINUTES · INACTIVE PREP TIME: 3 HOURS, 10 MINUTES

Pre-revolutionary Russian cuisine was characterized by its use of traditional Russian ingredients (such as sour cream) and French cooking methods. Even though it wasn't invented until 1978, ptichye moloko cake would have been very popular among the aristocracy of Moscow and St. Petersburg. Its name means "bird's milk," a reference to an ancient Greek idiom indicating "something so rare that it doesn't even exist."

7 eggs, separated
1-¾ c. white sugar, divided
1 tsp. vanilla extract
1-¼ c. plus 2 Tbsp. butter, divided, plus more for greasing pan
1-¼ c. all-purpose flour, plus more for flouring pan
1 tsp. baking powder
¾ c. water, divided
2 tsp. agar agar
¾ c. sweetened condensed milk
½ tsp. citric acid
¾ c. heavy cream
1-½ c. baking chocolate, grated

With an electric mixer, beat egg yolks, ¾ c. sugar, and vanilla extract on Medium speed. Add ½ c. butter and continue to mix until mixture is light and fluffy. Sift together flour and baking powder and fold into egg yolk mixture.

Preheat oven to 400 degrees. Grease and flour a 10-inch round cake pan. Pour batter into pan and bake for 20 minutes or until a toothpick inserted in center of cake comes out clean. Allow cake to cool in pan for 10 minutes, then remove and finish cooling on a wire rack.

In a medium saucepan, combine ½ c. water and agar agar. Bring to a boil over Medium-High heat. Add remaining 1 c. sugar, stirring constantly, and continue to boil until temperature reaches 240 degrees (use a candy thermometer to monitor temperature). Set syrup aside to cool.

Add egg whites and citric acid to the bowl of a stand mixer with a whisk attachment and mix on High speed until soft peaks form. Slowly add syrup and continue to mix until stiff. Reduce speed to Medium and gradually add ¾ c. butter and condensed milk.

Using a long, sharp knife or wire cake cutter, slice cake crosswise to make two equal halves. Place one half in the bottom of a 10-inch cake ring. Top with three-quarters of egg white mixture and spread evenly. Place second cake half on top and spread remaining egg white mixture over it in an even, smooth layer. Refrigerate for 3 hours.

Bring heavy cream to a simmer over Medium heat in a small saucepan (do not bring to a boil). Pour warmed cream over chocolate in a small bowl and stir with a spoon until chocolate is melted. Add 2 Tbsp. butter and allow to cool slightly.

Remove cake from cake ring. Pour chocolate ganache on top of cake (this is best done if the cake is placed on a wire rack beforehand). Working quickly, spread ganache over entire cake in an even layer using an icing spatula. Allow ganache to solidify at room temperature before slicing cake.

MAKES 8-10 SERVINGS

Per serving: 605 calories, 38 g fat, 23 g saturated fat, 265 mg sodium, 59 g carbohydrates, 10 g protein.

SERVING SUGGESTION: Serve with raspberries or other fruits.

VARIATION: For a chocolate ptichye moloko cake, add 3 Tbsp. of cocoa powder to batter.

TIP: Vladimir Guralnik, the inventor of ptichye moloko cake, used agar agar as a thickening agent because it was capable of withstanding the high temperatures needed to ensure an airy consistency. Gelatin can be used as substitute but be careful not to allow syrup to boil.

SAN MARINO TORTA TRE MONTI

EASY · COOK TIME: 5 MINUTES · ACTIVE PREP TIME: 10 MINUTES · INACTIVE PREP TIME: 1 HOUR

For a country with a total area of less than 24 square miles, there are quite a few desserts that are unique to San Marino. The most famous is definitely Torta Tre Monti, first made to commemorate the country's famous three-peaked Monte Titano and its three Medieval towers. The Sammarinese bakery La Serenissima has manufactured and exported the cake since 1942.

Six 10-inch round tort wafers
½ c. roasted hazelnuts, chopped
1 Tbsp. powdered sugar
½ c. heavy cream
1 Tbsp. corn syrup
1-½ c. milk chocolate, chopped

Combine hazelnuts and powdered sugar in a blender or food processor and pulse to form a fine paste. Set aside.

Heat cream and corn syrup over Medium heat in a small saucepan until warm (do not bring to a boil). Remove from heat and stir in chocolate until smooth. Fold hazelnut paste into chocolate mixture. Refrigerate ganache for about 1 hour (it should be fully cooled but still spreadable).

Once cooled, spread a thin layer of ganache over the surface of one tort wafer. Top with another wafer and spread a thin layer to cover; repeat process until all six wafers are assembled. Holding the cake at a 90-degree angle, coat the edge of the cake with ganache (pouring the ganache in a shallow dish beforehand will make this easier). Set cake on top of a can or jar so that ganache can solidify without being touched. Slice into wedges and serve.

MAKES 6-8 SERVINGS

Per serving: 384 calories, 15 g fat, 8 g saturated fat, 46 mg sodium, 30 g carbohydrates, 4 g protein.

SERVING SUGGESTIONS: Serve with a scoop of ice cream or gelato and a strong cup of coffee.

VARIATIONS: To make a chocolate Torta Tre Monti, replace hazelnuts with an equal amount of additional milk chocolate. A shot of espresso or hazelnut liqueur may be added to the ganache.

SCOTLAND
CRANACHAN

EASY · COOK TIME: 5 MINUTES · ACTIVE PREP TIME: 15 MINUTES · INACTIVE PREP TIME: 8 HOURS

Cranachan is the most Scottish of all desserts because it includes the most Scottish of all ingredients: well-known ones such as whisky and oats, and lesser-known but equally beloved staples like double cream, heather honey, and raspberries. This simple but boozy fruit trifle is enjoyed year-round in Scotland. But you're most likely to find it at a Burns supper, an annual ceremony held on January 25 to celebrate the birthday of Scottish national poet Robert Burns.

½ c. steel-cut oats, divided
½ c. Scotch whisky, divided
2 c. fresh raspberries
3 Tbsp. honey, divided
2 tsp. white sugar
1-½ c. heavy cream

½ c. plain yogurt

Toast ¼ c. oats in a dry skillet over High heat just until browned. Remove from heat and allow to cool. Once oats are cooled, place in a small bowl and cover with ¼ c. whisky. Allow to stand for at least 8 hours.

Toast the remaining ¼ c. oats in a dry skillet, just as the first batch. Set oats aside to cool.

Using the side of a fork, coarsely crush raspberries in a large bowl, reserving all juice. Stir together 1 Tbsp. whisky, 1 Tbsp. honey, and sugar. Drizzle raspberries with whisky and honey mixture and set aside.

Combine cream and yogurt in another bowl. Beat with an electric mixer on High speed until thickened. Add remaining 3 Tbsp. whisky and 2 Tbsp. honey and continue to beat until stiff. Fold soaked oats into cream mixture with a wooden spoon.

To assemble cranachan, divide half the raspberries between six glasses. Top with half of the cream mixture and sprinkle with half the dry oats. Repeat with another layer of raspberries, cream, and oats. Serve immediately or refrigerate until ready to serve.

MAKES 6 SERVINGS

Per serving: 238 calories, 9 g fat, 5 g saturated fat, 23 mg sodium, 26 g carbohydrates, 4 g protein.

VARIATIONS: Oranges, plums, rhubarb, or raisins may be used in place of raspberries. If using raisins, soak in an additional ¼ c. whisky for at least 20 minutes. Spiced rum may be used in place of whisky.

TIP: The traditional way of serving cranachan is to bring the raspberries, cream, and oats to the table and allow each guest to assemble their own.

SERBIA
VASINA TORTA

HARD · COOK TIME: 40 MINUTES · ACTIVE PREP TIME: 50 MINUTES · INACTIVE PREP TIME: 5 MINUTES

Vaso and Jelena Čokrljan were married in the small town of Paraćin, Serbia in 1908. Shortly after, Jelena became pregnant with the couple's first child. Her pregnancy had many complications, and when local doctors feared that she would not survive the child's birth, Vaso took her to Vienna and spared no expense to make sure she had access to the best doctors in Europe. When the Čokrljans returned to Paraćin with their newborn daughter, Jelena's mother arranged a huge celebration complete with a decadent cake that she created just for her son-in-law. Vasina Torta (Vaso's Cake) included several ingredients that were difficult to obtain in rural Serbia, especially oranges–illustrating the gratitude with which it was prepared.

9 eggs, separated and divided
2-¼ c. white sugar, divided
⅓ c. ground almonds
1 Tbsp. all-purpose flour, plus more for flouring pan
½ c. whole milk
2 c. ground walnuts
Juice and zest of 1 orange
2 oz. dark chocolate (70 percent cacao or higher), melted
⅔ c. butter, at room temperature, plus more for greasing pan
½ c. water, plus more for boiling
½ tsp. cream of tartar
½ tsp. vanilla extract
Candied orange peel, sliced, for garnish

In a large bowl, beat 5 egg yolks and ½ c. sugar with an electric mixer on High speed until pale and fluffy. In a separate bowl, beat egg whites on Medium speed until stiff. Fold about one-quarter of the egg whites into the egg yolk mixture. Gradually add remaining egg whites as well.

Combine ground almonds and flour. Gently fold almond mixture into egg mixture, one spoonful at a time.

Preheat oven to 400 degrees. Grease and flour a 9-inch springform pan. Pour batter into pan and spread in an even layer. Bake for 20 minutes or until cake has risen and springs back when the center is pressed. Allow cake to cool in pan for 5 minutes, and then loosen wall belt and transfer to a wire rack to finish cooling completely.

Combine milk and 2 Tbsp. sugar in a medium saucepan. Bring to a boil over Medium heat. Remove from heat and stir in walnuts. Cover with lid and set aside to cool.

Bring water to a boil in the bottom of a double boiler. Reduce heat to Low and add 4 egg yolks and ½ c. plus 2 Tbsp. sugar to the top of the double boiler. Stir egg yolk mixture constantly until it forms a thick custard (this will take at least 10 minutes). Remove from heat and set aside until custard cools completely.

Using an electric mixer, whip butter at High speed for 5 minutes in a large bowl. Stir walnut mixture, orange juice, orange zest, and chocolate into custard until smooth. Slowly fold custard into butter.

Place cake inside of a 9-inch cake ring and top with an even layer of custard. Refrigerate until ready to finish assembling.

Combine 1 c. sugar and water in a saucepan and bring to a boil over High heat. Continue to boil syrup until temperature reaches 240 degrees (use a candy thermometer to monitor temperature), stirring constantly. Set aside.

Beat 4 egg whites, cream of tartar, and vanilla extract with an electric mixer at Medium speed in a large bowl until soft peaks form. Increase speed to High and slowly add syrup until the meringue is opaque, stiff, and glossy. Allow meringue to cool completely.

Remove cake from cake ring and set on a serving plate. Use a spatula to spread meringue on top and sides of cake in an even layer. Garnish with candied orange peel and refrigerate until ready to serve.

MAKES 12 SERVINGS

Per serving: 441 calories, 29 g fat, 10 g saturated fat, 127 mg sodium, 40 g carbohydrates, 11 g protein.

SERVING SUGGESTION: Vasina Torta is best served chilled.

VARIATION: Some versions of Vasina Torta include a chocolate ganache topping. To make ganache, melt together 5 oz. dark chocolate, ¼ c. whole milk, 3 Tbsp. butter, and 2 Tbsp. vegetable oil over Low heat. Once cake is completely cooled, spread ganache over top and sides with a spatula or flat knife. Refrigerate overnight before serving.

TIP: It is extremely important that each layer is completely cooled before adding the next. Particularly, the meringue layer will collapse if applied while the cake or custard is warm; applying a warm meringue will make the cake and custard soggy.

SLOVAKIA
MAKOVNÍK

EASY · COOK TIME: 30 MINUTES · ACTIVE PREP TIME: 30 MINUTES · INACTIVE PREP TIME: 1 HOUR, 10 MINUTES

Do you think you know poppyseeds? They have a distinctive nutty, fruity flavor that many Americans are not aware of. While they are usually used only as a garnish for baked goods in the United States, in Slovakia and other Eastern European countries poppyseeds take the main stage in many recipes—and are often used in copious amounts. They are a Slovak symbol of wealth and luck, which is one reason why a poppyseed-rich dessert like makovník is traditionally baked for New Year's Day.

2 c. plus 2 Tbsp. all-purpose flour, plus more for flouring surface
¹/₃ c. cold butter, cut into cubes, plus more for greasing baking sheet
¼ c. rendered lard

2 Tbsp. powdered sugar
1 dash salt
2 tsp. active dry yeast
1 whole egg plus 1 egg yolk, divided
¾ c. whole milk, divided
2 c. poppyseeds, finely ground
2 tsp. ground cinnamon
½ tsp. vanilla extract
Juice and zest of 1 small orange
1 Tbsp. honey
½ c. white sugar

In a small bowl, combine yeast, ¼ c. milk, and 1 egg yolk. Stir until smooth and allow to stand for at least 10 minutes.

Sift flour into a large bowl and add butter, lard, powdered sugar, and salt. Mix ingredients using your hands until a moist dough is formed. Add yeast mixture and continue to mix until dough is very smooth. Divide dough into two equal portions and roll each half into a ball. Cover dough with plastic wrap and refrigerate for 1 hour.

Combine poppy seeds, cinnamon, vanilla extract, orange juice, and orange zest and stir together with a wooden spoon. Set aside.

In a small saucepan, bring ½ c. milk to a boil over Medium heat. Add sugar and honey and stir until sugar is dissolved. Add milk mixture to poppy seed mixture and stir until smooth. Set aside.

Preheat oven to 350 degrees. Grease a large baking sheet. Remove dough from refrigerator. Roll each dough ball into a 9- x 13-inch rectangle. Spread half of the poppy seed mixture over each rectangle in an even layer, ending about one-half inch from each edge. Beginning with one of the longer sides, roll each rectangle into a log. Place the two logs on the baking sheet and brush with remaining egg. Bake for 25 minutes or until golden brown. Allow makovník to cool completely before slicing and serving.

MAKES 2 LOAVES

Per one-quarter loaf: 515 calories, 31 g fat, 10 g saturated fat, 100 mg sodium, 51 g carbohydrates, 12 g protein.

SERVING SUGGESTIONS: Serve with coffee or tea. Dust with powdered sugar before serving.

VARIATION: Soak ½ c. raisins in 1 Tbsp. rum and add to poppyseed filling.

TIP: To grind poppyseeds, use a food grinder with a fine grinding plate or a coffee or spice mill. They can also be ground by hand using a mortar and pestle.

SLOVENIA
PREKMURSKA GIBANICA

HARD · COOK TIME: 1 HOUR, 30 MINUTES · ACTIVE PREP TIME: 55 MINUTES · INACTIVE PREP TIME: 5 HOURS

Prekmurska gibanica is a Slovenian national treasure; it has appeared on a postage stamp and was even granted Protected Geographical Status by the European Union in 2010. Named for Prekmurje, a region of Slovenia sandwiched between Austria and Hungary, this gibanica (layered pastry) has been a part of Slovenian cuisine for centuries. Over time, it has evolved from its original form (with cabbage, turnips, and other savory ingredients) to an impossibly rich dessert. While Prekmurska gibanica has been described as "a cake with the most layers possible," this recipe only has eight.

2-¼ c. all-purpose flour, plus more for flouring surface
½ c. plus 1 Tbsp. white sugar, divided
½ c. plus 2 Tbsp. white wine
2 Tbsp. vegetable oil
1 c. poppyseeds, finely ground

½ c. whole milk, warmed

1 c. walnuts, finely ground

2 tsp. ground cinnamon, divided, plus more for garnish

¼ c. rum

4 large, tart apples (such as Granny Smith), finely chopped

Juice and zest of 1 lemon

1 c. cottage cheese or quark

½ c. sour cream, divided

2 eggs, divided

Melted butter, for greasing pan and brushing

Powdered sugar, for garnish

In the bowl of a stand mixer with a dough hook attachment, combine flour, 1 Tbsp. sugar, wine, water, and vegetable oil. Mix at Low speed until a rough dough is formed. Increase speed to Medium and continue to mix for 10 minutes. Cover dough with plastic wrap and refrigerate for 1 hour.

Combine ground poppyseeds, 2 Tbsp. sugar, and milk. Stir until a smooth paste is formed. Set aside.

Combine apples, 2 Tbsp. sugar, 1 tsp. cinnamon, lemon juice, and lemon zest. Stir until apples are coated with other ingredients. Set aside.

Combine cottage cheese, 2 Tbsp. sugar, 2 Tbsp. sour cream, and 1 egg. Stir until mixture is smooth. Set aside.

Combine ground walnuts, 2 Tbsp. sugar, 1 tsp. cinnamon, and rum. Stir until a smooth paste is formed. Set aside.

Brush sides and bottom of an 8-inch springform pan with butter. Remove dough from refrigerator and cut into 10 even pieces. Combine two of the dough pieces and roll onto a floured surface to form a 12-inch circle. Use this circle to line the bottom and sides of pan (excess will hang over the pan's edges). Brush crust with additional butter.

Roll each remaining piece of dough into an 8-inch circle. For first layer, spread half of poppyseed filling into pan and top with one 8-inch dough circle. For second layer, spread half of apple filling into pan and top with another dough circle. Do the same for the third and fourth layers, using cottage cheese and walnut fillings. Once the first four layers are assembled, repeat the process for the fifth through eighth layers. Brush each dough circle with butter before adding next layer.

Before adding final dough circle to top of cake, fold overhanging edges of cake over the top walnut layer. Place last dough circle on top and pinch edges to seal. Prick the surface of the cake a few times with the tines of a fork. Refrigerate for at least 4 hours.

Preheat oven to 350 degrees. Whisk together remaining egg and ¼ c. plus 2 Tbsp. sour cream. Spread sour cream mixture over the top of the cake, leaving a ½-inch border around the edge. Cover the cake with aluminum foil, creating a tent so that the foil does not touch the top of the cake, and bake for 1 hour. Remove foil and bake for 30 minutes longer or until edges are golden brown (center will remain pale).

Loosen wall belt and set cake on a wire rack until completely cooled. Dust cake with cinnamon and powdered sugar and serve.

MAKES 10-12 SERVINGS

Per serving: 406 calories, 20 g fat, 4 g saturated fat, 117 mg sodium, 44 g carbohydrates, 12 g protein.

SERVING SUGGESTION: Serve at room temperature.

VARIATION: Soak ¼ c. raisins in 1 Tbsp. rum and add to apple filling.

TIP: Prekmurska gibanica can also be made using phyllo dough, which will greatly reduce the time and effort required. If using phyllo dough, substitute each layer of dough with two layers of phyllo, cut to fit the pan. Brush each phyllo layer liberally with butter.

SPAIN
FLAN

MEDIUM · COOK TIME: 1 HOUR, 15 MINUTES · ACTIVE PREP TIME: 10 MINUTES · INACTIVE PREP TIME: 4 HOURS, 30 MINUTES

The egg custard that formed the basis for flan, known as flado, originated in the Roman Empire. Most flado-based dishes were savory, but a few incorporated the only sweetener known to the Romans, honey. Flado quickly made its way through the Roman world and retained its popularity long after the Empire's fall. Around 800 CE sugar was introduced to Spain by the Moors, and the modern flan (complete with caramel sauce topping) was born. While many Latin American flan varieties are very elaborate, traditional Spanish flan adheres to a simple list of four ingredients: sugar, eggs, milk, and vanilla.

1-½ c. white sugar, divided
4 eggs
2 c. whole milk
2 tsp. vanilla extract

Preheat oven to 350 degrees. Place six 8-oz. custard cups inside a deep glass baking dish and fill dish with hot (but not boiling) water. Set aside to allow water to warm cups while flan is being prepared.

Heat 1 c. sugar in a small saucepan over Medium-Low heat until a smooth, golden-brown syrup is formed, stirring constantly. It should take at least 15 minutes for the sugar to completely liquefy. Divide hot syrup between cups.

With an electric mixer, whisk together eggs and ½ c. sugar in a large bowl on Low speed. Slowly add milk and vanilla and continue to whisk to form a silky custard. Divide custard between cups and cover each cup with foil, sealing tightly around rims. Bake flan for 1 hour or until firm but not completely solid.

Remove custard cups from water and allow to sit at room temperature for 30 minutes or until completely cooled. Refrigerate for at least 4 hours.

To serve, invert each flan onto a dessert plate (run a knife around the inside of the cup to loosen it if necessary). The syrup at the bottom of the cup will create a caramel sauce to coat the flan.

MAKES 6 SERVINGS

Per serving: 220 calories, 6 g fat, 3 g saturated fat, 74 mg sodium, 37 g carbohydrates, 6 g protein.

SERVING SUGGESTIONS: Serve with raspberries or other fruit if desired.

VARIATIONS: For citrus flan, add ½ c. freshly-squeezed orange juice to sugar while cooking syrup and the zest of one orange to the custard. For flan de café, replace ½ c. milk with an equal amount of freshly-brewed espresso. For flan Napolitano, a version popular in Mexico, replace half of milk with 1 c. softened cream cheese.

SWEDEN PRINSESSTÅRTA

HARD · COOK TIME: 30 MINUTES · ACTIVE PREP TIME: 45 MINUTES · INACTIVE PREP TIME: 4 HOURS

Swedish home economics teacher Jenny Åkerström (1867-1957) is credited with inventing the prinsesstårta (princess cake), a scrumptious marriage of custard, jam, and pastry sealed inside a shell of green marzipan. Åkerström originally named her confection gröntårta (green cake), but renamed it in honor of three of her students: Margaretha, Märtha, and Astrid, the nieces of Sweden's King Gustaf V. These young women were especially fond of this cake, and it is easy to see why; it's hard to imagine a dessert more fit for royalty.

5 whole eggs plus 1 egg yolk, divided

1-¼ c. white sugar, divided
2 Tbsp. cornstarch
2 c. whole milk
2 tsp. vanilla extract, divided
1 c. all-purpose flour
1 tsp. baking powder
1 dash salt
¼ c. butter, at room temperature, divided
Cooking spray, for spraying parchment paper
¾ c. raspberry jam
1 lb. green marzipan (see recipe below)

In a small bowl, whisk together 1 egg and egg yolk, ¾ c. sugar, and cornstarch with an electric mixer on Low speed. Heat milk and 1 tsp. vanilla extract in a saucepan over Medium-High heat just until it begins to boil. Remove from heat and vigorously whisk one-third of egg mixture into milk.

Gradually add remaining egg mixture to milk mixture to form a custard. Return custard to heat and bring to a boil, stirring constantly. Allow to boil for about 1 minute (do not allow milk to scald). Pour custard into a bowl and cover with plastic wrap (so that wrap covers the actual surface of the custard). Refrigerate for at least 4 hours.

With an electric mixer, whisk together 4 eggs and ¾ c. sugar on Low speed for 5 minutes. Sift together flour, baking powder, and salt and gently fold into egg mixture until a smooth batter is formed. Fold butter and 1 tsp. vanilla extract into batter.

Preheat oven to 350 degrees. Cut three 8-inch circles from parchment paper and set on three baking sheets. Spray each circle with cooking spray. Spoon an equal amount of batter into the center of each parchment paper circle and spread in an even layer so that it reaches the edges. Bake the cake layers one at a time for 8 minutes each. Remove cake layers from oven, trim if necessary, and transfer to a wire rack to cool completely.

To assemble the cake, place one cake layer on a serving plate. Spread ¼ c. raspberry jam evenly over the surface of the cake layer. Top with one-third of the custard. Repeat with remaining two cake layers, raspberry jam, and custard.

Roll marzipan into a thin circle wide enough to completely cover cake. Carefully place the marzipan circle on top of the cake and pull edges down so that sides of cake are covered (cake should be rounded on top, like a dome). Trim any excess at the base of the cake. Cut into slices and serve.

For marzipan:
1-½ c. almonds, finely ground
1-½ c. powdered sugar
2 tsp. almond extract
1 tsp. rosewater
1 egg white
All-purpose flour, for flouring surface
Green food coloring (liquid or gel), as needed

Place almonds and powdered sugar in a blender or food processor and pulse until evenly combined. Add almond extract and rosewater and pulse to form a light paste. Add egg white and pulse until mixture resembles a thick dough.

Turn marzipan onto a lightly floured surface and knead until pliable. While kneading, add a few drops of food coloring until desired color is reached. Wrap marzipan in plastic wrap until ready to use. (Marzipan can be refrigerated, but it should be at room temperature before using.)

MAKES 10-12 SERVINGS

Per serving: 500 calories, 22 g fat, 8 g saturated fat, 232 mg sodium, 58 g carbohydrates, 20 g protein.

SERVING SUGGESTION: Prinsesstårta is traditionally dusted with powdered sugar and garnished with a red or pink fondant rose.

VARIATIONS: For a prinstårta (prince cake), use yellow marzipan and replace raspberry jam with an equal amount of lemon curd. For an operatårta (opera cake), use red or pink marzipan, replace raspberry jam with strawberry jam or preserves, and fold 2 Tbsp. cocoa powder into custard before assembling.

SWITZERLAND
ZUGER KIRSCHTORTE

HARD · COOK TIME: 50 MINUTES · ACTIVE PREP TIME: 45 MINUTES

First created in 1921 by pastry chef Heinrich Höhn, Zuger kirschtorte (cherry cake) soon became the specialty of the Swiss town of Zug. Höhn's bakery, the Conditorei Treichler, still operates in Zug and produces as many as 100,000 of these cakes every year. Audrey Hepburn, Charlie Chaplin, Winston Churchill, and Pope Francis I are among this cherry liqueur-filled confection's most well-known fans.

4 whole eggs, separated, plus 3 egg whites
1-¾ c. white sugar, divided
1 c. almonds, finely ground
1 c. all-purpose flour, divided, plus more for flouring pan
Cooking spray, for spraying parchment paper
Zest of 1 lemon
1 tsp. salt
1 tsp. vanilla extract
3 Tbsp. cornstarch
1 c. whole milk, cold
1 c. butter, plus more for greasing pan
¼ c. plus 1 Tbsp. kirsch, divided
1 drop red food coloring
½ c. water
Powdered sugar, for garnish
Slivered almonds, toasted, for garnish

Using an electric mixer, beat 3 egg whites until thick and opaque. Add ¼ c. sugar, one spoonful at a time, while beating egg whites until meringue is very stiff and glossy. In a separate bowl, whisk together ¼ c. sugar, almonds, and 1 Tbsp. flour. Gently fold almond mixture into meringue.

Preheat oven to 300 degrees. Cut two 9-inch circles from parchment paper and set on two baking sheets. Spray each circle with cooking spray. Using a piping bag or small spatula, spread meringue over parchment paper circles in an even layer. Bake for 20 minutes. Set baked meringues aside.

Whisk together 4 egg yolks, ½ c. sugar, lemon zest, salt, and vanilla extract. Sift together remaining flour and 1 Tbsp. plus 1 tsp. cornstarch and gently stir into egg yolk mixture. Using an electric mixer, beat remaining 4 egg whites until stiff peaks form. Fold egg whites into batter.

Raise oven temperature to 350 degrees. Grease and flour a 9-inch springform pan. Pour batter into pan and bake for 20 minutes. Allow cake to cool completely before loosening wall belt.

To make buttercream, mix together remaining cornstarch and milk in a medium saucepan. Add ¼ c. sugar and bring to a boil over Medium heat. Continue to cook, stirring constantly, until thickened. Remove from heat and allow to cool completely. Using an electric mixer, beat butter until pale and fluffy. Slowly add cooled milk while continuing to beat until smooth. Add 2 Tbsp. kirsch and food coloring.

To make kirsch syrup, combine ½ c. sugar and water in a small saucepan. Bring to a boil over High heat until sugar is fully dissolved. Remove from heat and stir remaining 3 Tbsp. kirsch into syrup.

To assemble cake, place one meringue circle on a serving plate, with the flat side down. Spread a layer of buttercream over top of meringue. Place cake on top of buttercream layer and brush the top with the kirsch syrup. Spread another layer of buttercream over top of cake. Top with second meringue circle, with flat side facing up. Spread remaining buttercream over top and sides of cake. Dust top of cake with powdered sugar and use a sharp knife to make a diagonal pattern in the top layer of buttercream. Press toasted almonds into sides of cake. Cut into slices and serve.

MAKES 8-10 SERVINGS

Per serving: 464 calories, 29 g fat, 15 g saturated fat, 455 mg sodium, 39 g carbohydrates, 8 g protein.

SERVING SUGGESTION: Zuger kirschtorte is best served chilled.

VARIATIONS: Ground hazelnuts may be used in place of almonds. For a blackberry Zuger kirschtorte, add ½ c. pureed blackberries or ¼ c. blackberry jam to buttercream.

UKRAINE
PAMPUSHKY WITH ROSE PETAL JAM

MEDIUM · COOK TIME: 1 HOUR, 20 MINUTES · ACTIVE PREP TIME: 1 HOUR · INACTIVE PREP TIME: 2 HOURS, 15 MINUTES

The pampushka (plural: pampushky) came to the Ukraine via German settlers in the nineteenth century. But it soon reached the status of a national dish in the Ukraine, where an annual festival is held every January (towards the end of the Eastern Orthodox Christmas season) in the city of Lviv to celebrate the treat. Pampushky filled with rose petal jam are a specialty of Kyiv, where "jam roses" are a distinct variety.

5 c. all-purpose flour, divided, plus more for flouring surface
½ c. plus 2 Tbsp. white sugar, divided
½ c. water
2 Tbsp. active dry yeast
¾ c. whole milk, lukewarm
½ c. butter, at room temperature
2 whole eggs plus 3 egg yolks
1 tsp. vanilla extract
Zest of 2 lemons
1 tsp. salt
¼ tsp. ground ginger
1 c. rose petal jam (see recipe below)
Vegetable oil, for frying, plus more for greasing baking sheet
Powdered sugar, for garnish

Combine 2 Tbsp. sugar, water, and yeast in a small bowl. Cover and let stand for 5 minutes. Add milk and ¾ c. flour, mix well, and allow to stand for 10 minutes longer.

Using an electric mixer, beat butter and ½ c. sugar on Medium speed. Add eggs and egg yolks and beat until pale and fluffy. Stir in yeast mixture, vanilla extract, and lemon zest.

Sift together remaining flour, salt, and ginger in the bowl of a stand mixer with a dough hook attachment. Add wet ingredients and mix on Low speed for 10 minutes. Cover dough and allow to stand for 1 hour or until doubled in bulk.

Grease a large baking sheet. Divide dough into 4 portions. On a floured surface, roll out one portion of dough to a ¼-inch thickness. Use a 4-inch round cookie cutter to cut circles from the dough. Place a small spoonful of jam in the center of each dough circle and pinch the edges upwards to form a ball with the jam in the center. Repeat until all of the dough has been used. Set the pampushky on the baking sheet and allow to stand for 1 hour.

Heat about 2 inches of oil in a heavy skillet to a temperature of 350 degrees. Fry pampushky in small batches for 2-3 minutes, turning halfway through. Remove from pan and set on paper towels to drain. When pampushky are completely cooled, dust with powdered sugar and serve.

For rose petal jam:
2 c. fresh or ¾ c. dried rose petals
1-½ c. water
2 c. white sugar, divided
3 Tbsp. lemon juice
1 tsp. fruit pectin

Combine rose petals and water in a large saucepan. Bring to a boil over Medium-High heat. Reduce heat and simmer for 10 minutes. Add 1-¾ c. sugar and stir until completely dissolved. Add lemon juice and simmer for 10 minutes longer.

Combine remaining ¼ c. sugar and pectin in a small bowl. Add to pan and simmer for 20 minutes longer or until mixture begins to gel (jam will become firmer upon standing). Pour into a sterilized container and refrigerate until ready to use.

MAKES ABOUT 60-75 PAMPUSHKY

Per pampushka: 115 calories, 7 g fat, 2 g saturated fat, 49 mg sodium, 11 g carbohydrates, 2 g protein.

VARIATIONS: Other types of jam can be used as a filling for pampushky. Popular choices include sour cherry, peach, plum, and blackberry.

TIP: If using fresh rose petals, clean the flowers thoroughly and make sure that they are from plants that have not been treated with pesticides. Foraged rose petals can be used; if foraging, choose flowers growing away from roads or highways.

VATICAN CITY
BIGNÈ DI SAN GIUSEPPE

MEDIUM · COOK TIME: 55 MINUTES · ACTIVE PREP TIME: 20 MINUTES · INACTIVE PREP TIME: 1 HOUR

In Vatican City, home of the Roman Catholic Church, the feast days of multiple saints are celebrated throughout the year. Some saints are commemorated with special foods on their feast days; one example is St. Joseph, the husband of Mary, legal father of Jesus, and patron saint of Sicily. St. Joseph's namesake pastries, known as zeppole outside of Rome, are such a special treat that you're only likely to find them once a year–on March 19, St. Joseph's Day.

2-½ c. whole milk, cold, divided
¹/₃ c. water
½ c. butter, plus more for greasing baking sheets
1 c. white sugar, divided
1 c. all-purpose flour
½ tsp. salt

4 whole eggs plus 4 egg yolks
½ tsp. vanilla extract
Zest of 1 lemon
¼ c. cornstarch

Combine ½ c. milk, water, butter, and 1-½ tsp. sugar in a small saucepan. Bring to a boil over Medium heat, stirring frequently. Remove from heat and set aside.

Sift flour and salt together and add to the bowl of a stand mixer with a paddle attachment. Gradually add milk mixture to bowl while mixing on Low speed. Add the 4 whole eggs one at a time and mix until batter is very smooth and shiny.

Preheat oven to 325 degrees. Grease two large baking sheets (or cover with parchment paper). Place batter in a piping bag with a ½-inch open star nozzle. Pipe 12 circles onto baking sheets, each about 3 inches apart. Each circle should have a small hole in the center. Bake bignè for 35 minutes or until golden. Turn off oven and allow bignè to sit in oven for 10 minutes longer. Remove from oven and finish cooling on wire racks.

Combine remaining 2 c. milk, vanilla extract, and lemon zest in a small saucepan and bring to a boil over Medium heat. While milk is heating, combine remaining sugar, 4 egg yolks, and cornstarch in a bowl and whisk together until fully mixed. Add half the milk to the egg yolk mixture and whisk vigorously.

Add egg yolk mixture to pot with hot milk and continue to cook over Medium heat until a thick and creamy custard is formed. Remove from heat and refrigerate for at least 1 hour.

To assemble, place custard in a piping bag with a ¼-inch round nozzle. Use a skewer to make a hole in the side of each bignè and squeeze custard into hole until the bignè is filled.

MAKES 12 PASTRIES

Per pastry: 242 calories, 12 g fat, 7 g saturated fat, 192 mg sodium, 29 g carbohydrates, 5 g protein.

SERVING SUGGESTION: Sprinkle with powdered sugar before serving.

VARIATIONS: Zeppole di San Giuseppe, popular in southern Italy and Sicily, are piped in a ring shape and topped with a maraschino cherry. Bignè can be fried instead of baked; to fry bignè, heat vegetable oil in a heavy skillet over Low heat and fry a few at a time for about 5 minutes on each side.

WALES
MONMOUTH PUDDING

EASY · COOK TIME: 1 HOUR, 5 MINUTES · ACTIVE PREP TIME: 15 MINUTES · INACTIVE PREP TIME: 20 MINUTES

Of all the great puddings of Britain, Monmouth pudding (*Pwdin Mynwy* in Welsh) is possibly the easiest to make. But don't confuse ease with humility; there's a reason why some call it the Queen of Puddings (other than the fact that it was one of Queen Victoria's favorite desserts). In the Welsh town of Monmouth, the eponymous pudding is made using leftover bread and whichever berries are available from the garden.

12 slices white bread, crusts removed
2 c. part-skim milk, divided
¼ c. plus 2 Tbsp. white sugar, divided
2 Tbsp. plus 1 tsp. butter, divided, plus more for greasing dish
Juice and zest of 1 lemon
3 eggs, separated
½ c. blackberry jam, divided

Preheat oven to 300 degrees. Place bread slices on baking sheets and toast for 15 minutes or until browned, turning halfway through cooking time. Remove from oven and allow to cool completely. (A toaster can also be used for this step.) Tear bread slices into small pieces and pulse in a blender or food processor. Place breadcrumbs in a large bowl and set aside.

Combine milk, 2 Tbsp. sugar, 2 Tbsp. butter, lemon juice, and lemon zest in a medium saucepan. Bring to a boil over High heat. Remove from heat, pour milk over breadcrumbs, and allow to stand for 20 minutes or until milk has cooled completely.

Preheat oven to 350 degrees. Grease an 8-inch round baking dish. Add egg yolks to breadcrumb mixture and whisk vigorously to form a custard. Pour half of custard into baking dish. Warm blackberry jam (you can use the microwave for this) and spread ¼ c. over custard layer. Top with remaining custard, followed by remaining jam. Bake for 35 minutes and remove from oven.

Reduce oven temperature to 300 degrees. With an electric mixer, beat egg whites on High speed until soft peaks form. Slowly add remaining ¼ c. sugar, one spoonful at a time, and continue to beat until meringue is stiff and glossy. Spread meringue over top of pudding. Bake for 10 minutes longer or until lightly browned on top.

MAKES 6 SERVINGS

Per serving: 252 calories, 8 g fat, 4 g saturated fat, 219 mg sodium, 39 g carbohydrates, 7 g protein.

VARIATIONS: Strawberry or raspberry jam may be used in place of blackberry jam. If desired, replace jam with 1 c. coarsely-mashed fresh blackberries.

The MIDDLE EAST and NORTH AFRICA

ALGERIA
MKHABEZ

EASY · COOK TIME: 15 MINUTES · ACTIVE PREP TIME: 30 MINUTES · INACTIVE PREP TIME: 2 HOURS

Like nowhere else in the Arab world, cookies are serious business in Algeria. If you like decorating cookies better than baking them, mkhabez are for you. These very fancy North African almond cookies are fragrant, delicately flavored, and richly embellished. You're likely to find them at weddings, at Eid al-Fitr celebrations, or at tea in the afternoon.

3 c. almond flour
1 c. white sugar
Juice and zest of 1 lemon
2 eggs
1 tsp. vanilla extract
All-purpose flour, for flouring surface
¼ c. whole milk
¼ c. vegetable oil, plus more for greasing baking sheet
¼ c. rosewater
1-½ c. powdered sugar, sifted
Food coloring, as needed
Edible glitter, as needed

Sift together almond flour, sugar, and lemon zest in a large bowl. In a smaller bowl, mix the eggs and vanilla extract together with a wire whisk. Slowly add wet ingredients to dry ingredients and mix together using your hands or a wooden spoon to make a moist dough. Cover dough and refrigerate for at least 2 hours.

Preheat oven to 350 degrees. Grease two large baking sheets. Roll out dough on a floured surface to a ½-inch thickness. Using cookie cutters, cut shapes from the dough and place on baking sheets. Bake for 10 to 15 minutes. Remove from oven and transfer to a wire rack to cool.

To make the icing, combine milk, oil, and rosewater in a small bowl. Add powdered sugar one spoonful at a time, whisking after each addition, until desired consistency is reached. Add lemon juice, mix well, and then add food coloring.

Dip the cookies in icing to coat and set on wire racks for icing to dry. Dust with edible glitter before icing dries completely.

MAKES 20-25 COOKIES

Per cookie: 193 calories, 11 g fat, 1 g saturated fat, 12 mg sodium, 19 g carbohydrates, 4 g protein.

SERVING SUGGESTION: Mkhabez can be very elaborate. They are usually cut in simple shapes (such as triangles and squares), decorated with several colors of icing and other adornments such as edible flowers, and presented in individual paper cups.

VARIATIONS: Orange blossom water can be used in place of rosewater in icing. For an additional sheen, add a beaten egg white to icing ingredients before adding powdered sugar.

BAHRAIN
KUNAFA

MEDIUM · COOK TIME: 40 MINUTES · ACTIVE PREP TIME: 20 MINUTES

Bahrainis know kunafa as the highlight of a typical iftar, the meal served at the end of the day during Ramadan to break the daylight fast. The kataifi dough used to make this dessert resembles rice noodles but is actually finely shredded phyllo dough. Kunafa is traditionally made with Middle Eastern cheeses such as nabulsi or akkawi; mozzarella, which is very similar to these, is a substitute that is much easier to find in the United States.

1 c. plus 2 Tbsp. white sugar, divided
¾ c. whole milk
½ c. heavy cream
2 Tbsp. semolina
½ tsp. cornstarch
12 oz. shredded phyllo dough (kataifi)
¼ c. ghee, melted, plus more for greasing pan
1 c. mozzarella cheese, grated
¼ c. plus ½ tsp. water, divided
¼ c. orange blossom water
½ tsp. vanilla extract
Chopped pistachios, for garnish

Combine milk, cream, 2 Tbsp. sugar, and semolina in a small saucepan. Whisk together cornstarch with ½ tsp. water until dissolved and add to pan. Bring to a boil over Medium-High heat, stirring constantly, and cook until thickened. Remove from heat and set aside.

Break the shredded phyllo dough into 1-inch pieces and place in a large bowl. Cover with melted ghee and toss until completely coated.

Preheat oven to 400 degrees. Grease a 12-cup muffin pan. Divide the dough between cups, pressing firmly inside each cup to make a "bowl" shape with a center indentation surrounded by higher sides.

Add mozzarella cheese to milk mixture and stir so that the cheese is slightly melted. Divide the cheese mixture between the cups, placing a heaping spoonful in each "bowl." Fold the sides of each "bowl" around the cheese mixture to enclose it. Bake in oven for at least 20 minutes or until golden brown.

Combine 1 c. sugar, ½ c. water, and orange blossom water in a small saucepan. Bring to a boil over High heat. Reduce heat to Low and simmer for 10 minutes. Remove from heat, stir in vanilla extract, and set aside.

Remove kunafa from oven and immediately pour hot syrup on top, reserving about one-quarter of the syrup. Allow to cool for about 1-2 minutes, then invert pan to remove kunafa.

To serve, place 2 kunafa on each plate. Top with remaining syrup and chopped pistachios and serve.

MAKES 6 SERVINGS

Per serving: 450 calories, 18 g fat, 10 g saturated fat, 318 mg sodium, 68 g carbohydrates, 7 g protein.

SERVING SUGGESTION: Serve warm with cardamom tea.

VARIATIONS: Rosewater with a squeeze of fresh lemon juice may be used in place of orange blossom water in syrup. Kunafa can also be made in a 10-inch cake or pie pan. When assembling, press three-quarters of the dough into the pan, spread cheese mixture over it, and top with remaining dough. Bake for 30-40 minutes or until golden.

TIP: Leftover kunafa may be stored in the refrigerator and reheated.

EGYPT
BASBOUSA

EASY · COOK TIME: 35 MINUTES · ACTIVE PREP TIME: 10 MINUTES

One of the best-known desserts of the Middle East, basbousa has many variants. In the Levant, there is hareesa; in Armenia, shamali; in the Balkans, ravani (page 15); and in Kuwait, pastūçha. But traditional basbousa has its origins in Egypt. Unlike most versions, which use semolina, traditional Egyptian basbousa is made with farina, which gives it a much coarser texture.

1-¾ c. farina
1-½ c. white sugar, divided
½ c. finely shredded coconut
1-½ tsp. baking powder
½ c. ghee, melted, plus more for greasing pan

3 Tbsp. honey, divided
½ c. plain yogurt
Tahini, for brushing pan
Whole almonds or pistachios, for garnish
1 c. water
Juice and zest of 1 small lemon
½ tsp. vanilla extract

Combine farina, ½ c. sugar, coconut, and baking powder in a large bowl and sift together with a pastry blender. In a separate bowl, stir 1 Tbsp. honey into ghee. Add ghee mixture to dry ingredients, followed by yogurt, and stir to combine.

Preheat oven to 350 degrees. Move oven rack to center of oven. Grease a 10-inch round cake pan and brush with a layer of tahini. Pour batter in pan and spread in an even layer, pressing the surface with the back of a spoon. Decorate the top of the basbousa with almonds or pistachios and bake for 10 minutes. Move oven rack to top of oven and bake for 15 minutes longer or until golden brown on top.

Combine 1 c. sugar, water, and 2 Tbsp. honey in a small saucepan. Cook over Medium-High heat for 10 minutes or until sugar is completely dissolved. Add vanilla extract and stir.

Gently pour hot syrup evenly over top of hot cake. Slice into diamond shapes and serve.

MAKES 12 SERVINGS

Per serving: 190 calories, 10 g fat, 7 g saturated fat, 75 mg sodium, 25 g carbohydrates, 1 g protein.

SERVING SUGGESTIONS: Garnish with a layer of finely grated coconut or shaved almonds. Basbousa can be served warm or cold.

VARIATIONS: Cinnamon, rosewater, or orange blossom water can be used to flavor the syrup instead of vanilla.

TIP: When making syrup-drenched cake desserts, it is usually important not to pour hot syrup onto a hot cake. But since basbousa is made from farina rather than a finer grain, this is not an issue.

IRAN
FALOODEH

EASY · COOK TIME: 20 MINUTES · ACTIVE PREP TIME: 10 MINUTES · INACTIVE PREP TIME: ABOUT 3-4 HOURS

According to legend, during an especially cold winter in the Persian Empire around 400 BCE, someone accidentally spilled syrup on the snow—and the world's first frozen treat was born. Whether this story is true or not, this tasty lime and rosewater granita is definitely one of the world's oldest desserts. Thick-walled ice houses called yakhchals were built to store the ice that provided Persians with the ice used to make faloodeh in warmer months. Thankfully, with modern refrigeration it's a lot easier to make today.

1 c. white sugar, divided
4-½ c. water, divided, plus more for boiling and rinsing
1 dash sea salt
Juice of 2 Persian limes
¼ c. rosewater
4 oz. rice noodles

Heat ½ c. sugar and ½ c. water in a small saucepan over Medium heat, stirring occasionally, for 5 minutes. Add salt and remaining sugar and continue to cook for 5 minutes longer. Remove from heat and allow to cool completely.

Once syrup is cooled, pour into a 2-qt. container along with 4 c. water, lime juice, and rosewater. Freeze for 1 hour.

Bring a large pot of water to a boil. Break noodles into 1-inch pieces. Add noodles to pot and cook for 6-8 minutes or until completely soft. Drain noodles and rinse with cold water.

Stir noodles into syrup mixture and return to freezer. (At this point the syrup mixture should be partially frozen but still "slushy.") Freeze for 1 more hour, then rake with a fork to break up any large chunks of ice that have formed and return to freezer. Repeat the process each hour until faloodeh reaches a light, sorbet-like consistency.

When ready to serve, scoop faloodeh and divide between 6 dishes or cups.

MAKES 6 SERVINGS

Per serving: 146 calories, 0 g fat, 0 g saturated fat, 47 mg sodium, 38 g carbohydrates, 0 g protein.

SERVING SUGGESTIONS: Garnish with lime wedges, pomegranate seeds, chopped pistachios, or sour cherry syrup. Faloodeh is sometimes served with a scoop of pistachio or vanilla ice cream.

VARIATIONS: Lime juice can be replaced with an equal amount of rosewater (or the reverse), or lemon juice can be used instead. For a festive presentation, add red or purple food coloring.

TIP: Be careful not to add the noodles to the frozen syrup mixture before it is sufficiently frozen. The noodles will sink to the bottom and will not be suspended properly.

IRAQ
MANN AL-SAMA

MEDIUM · COOK TIME: 15 MINUTES · ACTIVE PREP TIME: 10 MINUTES · INACTIVE PREP TIME: 12 HOURS

Nougat originated in Baghdad in the tenth century CE. Mann al-sama contains many ingredients that are native to Iraq, including pistachios, almonds, and cardamom. Its name means "manna from heaven," a reference to the celestial food provided to the Israelites in the Old Testament: "And the house of Israel called the name thereof Manna; and it was like coriander seed, white; and the taste of it was like wafers made with honey" (Exodus 16:31).

2 c. white sugar
1-½ c. corn syrup
¼ c. water
¼ tsp. salt
2 egg whites
1 tsp. ground cardamom
¼ c. butter, plus more for greasing pan
1 c. whole pistachios, roasted
½ c. whole almonds, roasted
2 Tbsp. rosewater (optional)
All-purpose flour, for flouring pan

Combine sugar, corn syrup, water, and salt in a medium saucepan. Bring to a boil over Medium-High heat. Continue to boil until temperature reaches 260 degrees (use a candy thermometer to monitor temperature), stirring frequently.

Place egg whites in the bowl of a stand mixer with a whisk attachment and mix on Medium speed until stiff peaks form. Add the syrup to the egg whites in a steady stream to form a thick nougat. Gently fold in cardamom, butter, rosewater (if using), and pistachios and almonds, in that order.

Grease and flour an 8 x 8-inch square baking dish. Spread the nougat into the dish and allow to stand for at least 12 hours. (Standing time can be shortened by refrigerating, but wait until taffy is cooled.)

Cut nougat into squares with a sharp knife and serve.

MAKES ABOUT 45 CANDIES

Per candy: 76 calories, 2 g fat, 1 g saturated fat, 29 mg sodium, 15 g carbohydrates, 1 g protein.

SERVING SUGGESTION: Serve with strong coffee.

VARIATION: In rural areas, mann al-sama is made using walnuts instead of pistachios and is dusted with flour. It can also be rolled into balls and coated with powdered sugar or cocoa.

TIP: Mann al-sama can be kept in the refrigerator for several days. If refrigerating, wrap tightly in plastic wrap.

ISRAEL
KICHLACH

EASY · COOK TIME: 20 MINUTES · ACTIVE PREP TIME: 35 MINUTES · INACTIVE PREP TIME: 3 HOURS, 30 MINUTES

The word *kichel* (plural: kichlach) is Yiddish for "cookie." But in the Jewish baking world, the kichel (or "baker's bowtie," as it is also called) has long been the subject of a controversial question: Is it a cookie or a cracker? However they are best defined, kichlach are very sweet, very crisp, and perfect when dunked in coffee or tea after dinner. As the Yiddish expression says, *azoy vert dos kichel tzekrochen* (that's how the cookie crumbles).

3-½ c. all-purpose flour
¾ c. vegetable oil, plus more for greasing baking sheets
6 whole eggs plus 3 egg yolks
3 Tbsp. white sugar, plus more for sprinkling and sugaring surface
2 tsp. vanilla extract
1 tsp. salt
1 tsp. baking powder

Place all ingredients in the bowl of a stand mixer with a paddle attachment (do not sift flour beforehand). Mix ingredients on Low speed for 20 minutes or until a smooth, stretchy dough is formed. Cover bowl with plastic wrap and allow to stand for 30 minutes.

Turn dough onto a surface coated with sugar and roll out into a ¼-inch thick rectangle. Sprinkle top of dough with more sugar. Use a pizza cutter or sharp knife to cut the dough into 1 x 2-inch rectangles.

Preheat oven to 375 degrees. Grease two large baking sheets. Twist each kichel around the center so that it resembles a bow tie and set on baking sheets. Bake for 20 minutes or until golden brown.

After baking, allow kichlach to cool on wire racks for at least 3 hours before serving.

MAKES 40 KICHLACH

Per kichel: 88 calories, 5 g fat, 1 g saturated fat, 68 mg sodium, 8 g carbohydrates, 2 g protein.

SERVING SUGGESTIONS: Serve with coffee or tea for dunking.

VARIATION: For Möhn kichel, an Ashkenazi variation on the Israeli kichel, add 2 Tbsp. poppy seeds to the dough while mixing.

JORDAN
WARBAT BIL-ESHTA

HARD · COOK TIME: 50 MINUTES · ACTIVE PREP TIME: 30 MINUTES · INACTIVE PREP TIME: 2 HOURS, 30 MINUTES

In Jordan it's unheard of to end a meal without a sweet treat, especially during the month of Ramadan. The gooey, flaky triangles known as warbat bil-eshta in Jordan and by other names elsewhere in the Levant originated here. In some ways they're much like baklava (page 133) and other syrup-drenched, phyllo-based pastries, but warbat bil-eshta include a milky custard filling that gives a nod to French and British colonial influence.

One 1-lb. package phyllo dough (about 24 sheets)
2-¼ c. white sugar, divided

1-½ c. whole milk
¼ c. plus 2 Tbsp. cornstarch
1 c. plain yogurt
1 c. water
Juice of 1 small lemon
2 Tbsp. orange blossom water
½ c. butter, melted, plus more for greasing pan
Crushed pistachios, for garnish

In a medium saucepan, combine milk and ¼ c. sugar and bring to a boil over Medium heat. Whisk in cornstarch and continue to boil, whisking constantly, until thickened. Remove from heat and fold in yogurt. Pour custard into a bowl and cover with plastic wrap (so that wrap covers the actual surface of the custard) and refrigerate for at least 30 minutes.

Combine 2 c. sugar and water in a small saucepan. Bring to a boil over Medium heat and add lemon juice. Continue boiling for 10 minutes or until sugar is completely melted and syrup is thick. Remove from heat, stir in orange blossom water, and set aside.

Spread out one sheet of phyllo dough and brush with melted butter until saturated. Top with another sheet of dough and brush with butter. Repeat until one-third of the dough (about 8 sheets) has been used. Spread one-third of the custard filling along the short end of the top sheet. Starting at that end, roll to form a log, brushing the roll with butter as you roll it. Repeat process with remaining phyllo dough, butter, and custard filling to make a total of three rolls.

Preheat oven to 375 degrees. Grease a 9 x 13-inch baking dish. Lay phyllo rolls side-by-side in the dish. Use a sharp knife to cut the rolls into triangles, cutting across at a 45-degree angle starting at the top corner of each roll. Bake for 30 minutes or until golden brown.

Drizzle syrup over warbat bil-eshta until completely moist and top with crushed pistachios. Allow to cool at room temperature for 2 hours before refrigerating.

MAKES ABOUT 18 PASTRIES

Per pastry: 229 calories, 7 g fat, 4 g saturated fat, 174 mg sodium, 39 g carbohydrates,

3 g protein.

SERVING SUGGESTION: Warbat bil-eshta are best served chilled with a cup of hot, strong coffee.

VARIATIONS: Some varieties of warbat bil-eshta include crushed pistachios, almonds, or walnuts inside the custard filling.

TIP: To significantly reduce time and effort, use 1 lb. ricotta cheese in place of custard filling.

KUWAIT
ELBA

MEDIUM · COOK TIME: 1 HOUR, 15 MINUTES · ACTIVE PREP TIME: 10 MINUTES · INACTIVE PREP TIME: 4 HOURS, 45 MINUTES

Since Kuwait is on the Persian Gulf coast and is home to people from many parts of the world, Kuwaiti cuisine reflects Arabian, Persian, Indian, and Mediterranean influences. Elba, a milk pudding specific to Kuwait, is very similar to Spanish flan (page 92). Its flavors come from saffron, a seasoning originating in Persia, and cardamom, one of the key spices in Indian cuisine.

2 c. whole milk
1-½ c. white sugar
2 Tbsp. hot water
3-4 threads saffron
4 eggs
2 tsp. vanilla extract
½ tsp. ground cardamom

Place saffron in hot water and allow to soak for at least 15 minutes. Water will become a deep yellow or orange-red color.

Preheat oven to 350 degrees. Place six 8-oz. custard cups inside a deep glass baking dish and fill dish with hot (but not boiling) water. Set aside to allow water to warm cups while elba is being prepared.

Heat 1 c. sugar in a small saucepan over Medium-Low heat until a smooth, golden-brown syrup is formed, stirring constantly. It should take at least 15 minutes for the sugar to completely liquefy. Divide hot syrup between cups.

Use an electric mixer to whisk together eggs and ½ c. sugar on Low speed in a large bowl. Add milk, vanilla, and cardamom and continue to whisk to form a silky custard. Stir in saffron water. Divide custard between cups and cover each cup with foil, sealing tightly around rims. Bake elba for 1 hour or until firm but not completely solid.

Remove cups from water and allow to sit at room temperature for 30 minutes or until completely cooled. Refrigerate for at least 4 hours.

To serve, invert each elba onto a dessert plate (run a knife around the inside of the cup to loosen it if necessary). The syrup at the bottom of the cup will create a caramel sauce to coat the elba.

MAKES 6 SERVINGS

Per serving: 220 calories, 6 g fat, 3 g saturated fat, 74 mg sodium, 38 g carbohydrates, 6 g protein.

VARIATIONS: Goat milk is traditionally used in this recipe. Kuwaitis sometimes use a combination of condensed and powdered milk in place of whole milk to make elba.

LEBANON
SFOUF

EASY · COOK TIME: 40 MINUTES · ACTIVE PREP TIME: 20 MINUTES

One of many semolina-based cakes of the Middle East, sfouf is distinguished by its simplicity. Unlike most others, it is a dry cake that is not drenched in syrup before serving. Its name is Arabic for "lines," a reference to the very simple way in which the cake is sliced. In Lebanon, sfouf is a favorite on religious holidays, birthdays, and family reunions; elsewhere in the Lebanese diaspora, it is a popular tea cake.

1-¼ c. whole milk
1 c. white sugar
1-½ c. semolina
½ c. all-purpose flour, plus more for flouring baking dish
1 Tbsp. ground turmeric
1-½ tsp. baking powder
1 tsp. ground aniseed
¼ c. butter, melted
¼ c. vegetable oil
Tahini, for brushing baking dish
¼ c. pine nuts or almonds, for garnish

In a small bowl, combine milk and sugar and stir until sugar is completely dissolved. Set aside.

Sift together semolina, flour, turmeric, baking powder, and aniseed in a large bowl. Add butter and oil to dry ingredients and stir until a crumbly dough is formed. Slowly stir in milk mixture until batter is completely smooth and without lumps.

Preheat oven to 350 degrees. Brush the bottom and sides of an 8 x 8-inch baking dish with tahini and then flour dish. Pour batter into pan and spread to make an even layer. Sprinkle with pine nuts or almonds. Bake for 40 minutes or until a toothpick inserted in center comes out clean. Once sfouf is cooled, cut into squares to serve.

MAKES 9 SERVINGS

Per serving: 330 calories, 16 g fat, 5 g saturated fat, 50 mg sodium, 44 g carbohydrates, 5 g protein.

SERVING SUGGESTIONS: Serve at room temperature with hot tea.

VARIATIONS: The earliest sfouf was made with molasses and honey instead of sugar. To make a molasses sfouf, substitute sugar with $1/3$ c. dark molasses, $1/3$ c. honey, and 2 Tbsp. brown sugar. For a moister sfouf, substitute milk with 1 c. plain yogurt.

LIBYA
KA'AK BIL-TAMR

HARD · COOK TIME: 25 MINUTES · ACTIVE PREP TIME: 1 HOUR · INACTIVE PREP TIME: 2 HOURS, 15 MINUTES

The Arabic word *ka'ak* literally means "cake," but it's most often used to describe a variety of Arab and North African cookies and pastries that have a ring-like shape. Ka'ak bil-tamr (date-filled cookies) are sometimes called "bracelet cookies." Libyan ka'ak tend to be less sweet than other types. In this recipe, which uses very little sugar, the Medjool date paste filling provides much of the cookies' sweetness.

1 lb. Medjool dates, pitted and coarsely chopped
2 c. all-purpose flour
½ c. whole milk, lukewarm
1 tsp. active dry yeast
½ c. semolina
¼ c. white sugar
1 tsp. baking powder
½ c. plus 1 Tbsp. olive oil, divided, plus more for greasing baking sheets

½ c. ghee

2 Tbsp. sesame seeds, toasted

1 Tbsp. ground aniseed

1 tsp. black cumin seeds

1 tsp. ground cardamom, divided

½ tsp. ground fennel seed

½ tsp. ground mahlab (optional)

¼ tsp. ground nutmeg

½ c. water

½ tsp. ground cinnamon

Combine milk and yeast and whisk together. Cover and let stand for 15 minutes.

Sift together flour, semolina, sugar, and baking powder. Add ½ c. olive oil and ghee to dry ingredients and stir with a wooden spoon to form a smooth, moist dough. Stir in sesame seeds, aniseed, black cumin seeds, ½ tsp. cardamom, fennel seed, mahlab (if using), and nutmeg. Add milk and yeast mixture to dough and stir once more. Cover dough with plastic wrap and allow to rest for 2 hours.

Add dates and water to a blender or food processor and pulse to make a smooth paste. Stir together date paste, 1 Tbsp. olive oil, ½ tsp. cardamom, and cinnamon.

Preheat oven to 350 degrees. Grease two large baking sheets. To assemble, divide dough into 2-Tbsp. portions and date paste into 2-tsp. portions. For each cookie, roll out one dough portion and one date paste portion into logs, each about 4 inches in length. Place the date paste log on top of dough log and pinch edges of dough over date paste so that date paste is completely encased in dough. Continue to roll so that the log is about 6-8 inches in length. Pinch together the ends of the log to form a ring. Place ka'ak bil-tamr on baking sheets and bake for 10-12 minutes. Allow to cool on wire racks before serving.

MAKES ABOUT 40 COOKIES

Per cookie: 110 calories, 6 g fat, 2 g saturated fat, 2 mg sodium, 15 g carbohydrates, 1 g protein.

SERVING SUGGESTIONS: Serve with mint, sage, or rose petal tea.

VARIATION: If desired, brush cookies with egg and sprinkle with sesame and black cumin seeds before baking.

MOROCCO MEZKOUTA

EASY · COOK TIME: 40 MINUTES · ACTIVE PREP TIME: 15 MINUTES · INACTIVE PREP TIME: 25 MINUTES

Like the nation's cuisine in general, Moroccan desserts can be very elaborate and complex. But the one dessert that is bound to be encountered in every Moroccan home and at every big or small social event, mezkouta, is a simple one. The sweet orange is not native to Morocco, but it became a major producer around the sixteenth century when the fruits were first introduced to the Mediterranean region from Asia. Mezkouta is one of many Moroccan dishes that incorporate this fruit.

Juice and zest of 2 oranges
3-4 threads saffron
2 Tbsp. hot water
4 eggs
1-½ c. white sugar
½ c. vegetable oil, plus more for greasing pan
2 c. all-purpose flour, plus more for flouring pan
1 Tbsp. plus 1 tsp. baking powder
½ tsp. salt
1 tsp. vanilla extract

Place saffron in hot water and allow to soak for at least 15 minutes. Water will become a deep yellow or orange-red color.

In the bowl of a stand mixer with a whisk attachment, mix eggs and sugar on

Medium speed until thick and pale. Slowly add oil to egg mixture.

Sift together flour, baking powder, and salt. Add flour mixture to egg mixture a little at a time, followed by orange juice, orange zest, saffron water, and vanilla.

Preheat oven to 350 degrees. Grease and flour a medium-sized Bundt pan. Pour batter into pan and bake for 40 minutes or until a toothpick inserted in center comes out clean. Allow cake to cool in pan for 10 minutes before removing from pan and transferring cake to a wire rack to cool completely.

MAKES 12 SERVINGS

Per serving: 241 calories, 11 g fat, 2 g saturated fat, 118 mg sodium, 33 g carbohydrates, 4 g protein.

SERVING SUGGESTIONS: Dust with powdered sugar and serve with tea or coffee.

VARIATIONS: For a lemon mezkouta, substitute orange juice and zest with the juice and zest of 2 lemons and ½ c. milk. To make a glaze for the cake, whisk together 1 c. powdered sugar and 2 Tbsp. fresh lemon juice.

OMAN
HALAWET AHMAD

EASY · COOK TIME: 15 MINUTES · ACTIVE PREP TIME: 10 MINUTES

Many Middle Eastern dishes are unique to Oman, a nation whose position on the Arabian Sea has long made it a cultural crossroads. Halawet Ahmad, or "Ahmad's dessert," is one of these. Made from roasted vermicelli, condensed milk, coconut, and almonds, these little nests are very sweet and exceptionally easy to make. Interestingly, vermicelli is used in several desserts in both southern Arabia and the Horn of Africa, which is located near Oman.

1 lb. uncooked rice or vermicelli noodles, broken into medium-sized pieces

½ c. butter, plus more for greasing pan
One 14-oz. can sweetened condensed milk
½ c. finely ground almonds
½ c. finely shredded coconut
Chopped pistachios, for serving

Grease the cups of a 12-cup muffin pan. Heat butter in a large skillet over Medium heat. Add noodles and fry in butter for 2-3 minutes or until golden brown (be careful not to burn them).

Pour condensed milk over noodles and stir to coat. Reduce heat to Low and simmer for 10 minutes. Remove from heat and fold in almonds and coconut. Allow mixture to cool until it can be handled easily. Divide noodle mixture into muffin cups and pack tightly.

Once completely cooled, remove from cups, sprinkle with chopped pistachios, and serve.

MAKES 4-6 SERVINGS

Per serving: 743 calories, 31 g fat, 18 g saturated fat, 240 mg sodium, 99 g carbohydrates, 17 g protein.

SERVING SUGGESTION: Serve with Oman's national beverage, coffee.

VARIATIONS: In some versions of Halawet Ahmad, the vermicelli is cooked very briefly in boiling water before roasting in butter, which significantly changes the texture. For a festive appearance, use colored vermicelli or add food coloring to vermicelli before roasting.

PALESTINE
QATAYEF

MEDIUM · COOK TIME: 45 MINUTES · ACTIVE PREP TIME: 20 MINUTES · INACTIVE PREP TIME: 40 MINUTES

According to legend, qatayef was first prepared for a ruler of the Abbasid Caliphate (750 – 1258 CE) who requested a dish that could satisfy his hunger for a long period of time during Ramadan. What is known is that their first recipe originated in the tenth century, and they have been popular in the Levant ever since. How popular? They were enjoyed both in the palaces of kings, where poets of the royal courts wrote about them, and on the streets of Levantine cities, where vendors sold them from carts. The stuffed, folded pancakes remain among the most beloved of all Ramadan treats.

1-¾ c. all-purpose flour
3 c. warm water, divided
½ c. plus 2 Tbsp. white sugar, divided
½ c. honey
Juice and zest of 1 lemon
1 Tbsp. plus 1 tsp. orange blossom water, divided
½ c. whole milk
½ tsp. active dry yeast
¼ c. semolina
1 tsp. baking powder
½ tsp. salt
Vegetable oil, for frying
1 c. finely chopped walnuts
1 c. finely chopped almonds
1 tsp. ground cinnamon

Combine ½ c. water, ½ c. sugar, and honey in a small saucepan. Bring to a boil, reduce heat to Medium-Low, and simmer for 15 minutes. Remove from heat, stir in lemon juice and zest and 1 tsp. orange blossom water, and set aside to cool.

In a medium-sized bowl, combine 2 c. water, milk, 1 Tbsp. sugar, and yeast. Stir until sugar and yeast are dissolved and allow to stand for 10 minutes. Add flour, semolina, baking powder, and salt and stir until a smooth batter is formed. Cover with plastic wrap and allow to stand for 30 minutes longer.

Mix together walnuts, almonds, 1 Tbsp. sugar, 1 Tbsp. orange blossom water, and cinnamon and stir until incorporated. Set aside.

Heat a small amount of oil in a heavy skillet over Medium heat. Pour enough batter in the pan to form a 4-inch circle (you may be able to fry several pancakes at once). Once small bubbles begin to appear and edges turn golden brown, remove pancake from pan and set on a wire rack to cool (fry one side only). Repeat with remaining batter.

Preheat oven to 350 degrees. Place 1 Tbsp. of nut mixture in the center of each pancake and fold in half to close, pinching edges to seal. Place sealed pancakes on a baking sheet and bake for 10 minutes.

Pour cooled syrup over pancakes while still warm and serve.

MAKES 6-8 SERVINGS

Per serving: 691 calories, 49 g fat, 7 g saturated fat, 179 mg sodium, 58 g carbohydrates, 11 g protein.

VARIATIONS: Other ingredients may be added to the filling, including pistachios, pine nuts, hazelnuts, raisins, vanilla extract, or rosewater. In Palestine, akkawi cheese is a popular qatayef filling. Mozzarella, ricotta, goat cheese, cream cheese, or a combination may be used in its place.

QATAR
ESH AL-ASARAYA

EASY · COOK TIME: 30 MINUTES · ACTIVE PREP TIME: 15 MINUTES · INACTIVE PREP TIME: 3 HOURS, 15 MINUTES

The name of this Qatari bread pudding translates to "bread of the royal court." Its origins are found in the Ottoman Empire, where it was a favorite of several sultans. It is understandable that this dish gravitated to Qatar, the country with the highest per-capita GDP in the world and one known for luxury, as it's definitely rich enough for the royal court.

8 thick slices white bread, cut into ½-inch cubes
3 c. white sugar, divided
2 c. water
¼ c. orange blossom water, divided
3 c. whole milk
1-½ c. heavy cream
¼ c. plus 1 Tbsp. cornstarch
1 c. chopped pistachios

Preheat oven to 350 degrees. Place bread cubes in a single layer in a 9 x 13-inch baking dish. Bake for 25 minutes or until golden brown.

While bread cubes are baking, prepare syrup. Combine 2-½ c. sugar and water in a medium saucepan. Bring to a boil over Medium-High heat and cook until sugar is dissolved and syrup is thick, about 5 minutes. Add 2 Tbsp. orange blossom water and remove from heat. Sprinkle syrup over toasted bread cubes while both are still hot (use only enough syrup to saturate the bread).

Combine milk, cream, ½ c. sugar, cornstarch, and 2 Tbsp. orange blossom water in the bowl of a stand mixer with a whisk attachment. Mix at Medium speed for 10 minutes or until cream has reached a custard consistency. Pour cream over bread cubes in pan and allow to stand for 15 minutes.

Sprinkle an even layer of chopped pistachios over surface of cream. Refrigerate for at least 3 hours (preferably overnight). Cut into squares and serve.

MAKES 12 SERVINGS

Per serving: 311 calories, 8 g fat, 4 g saturated fat, 97 mg sodium, 60 g carbohydrates, 4 g protein.

SERVING SUGGESTION: Serve chilled with karak (tea flavored with cardamom and saffron and sweetened with evaporated milk).

VARIATION: Use rosewater and lemon juice, in equal proportions, in place of orange blossom water.

SAUDI ARABIA
MUHALLEBI

MEDIUM · COOK TIME: 30 MINUTES · ACTIVE PREP TIME: 10 MINUTES · INACTIVE PREP TIME: 5 HOURS, 5 MINUTES

Muhallebi is one of the Middle East's most ancient desserts, and it is believed to be the inspiration for its European counterpart, blancmange. A simple milk-based pudding, muhallebi assumes the character of whichever flavorings are used to make it. The process of distilling rose petals originated in Iran but has spread throughout the Middle East. In Saudi Arabia, rose-flavored muhallebi is one of several popular varieties.

1-½ c. whole milk
½ c. heavy cream
1-¼ c. white sugar, divided
3 Tbsp. cornstarch or rice flour
¼ c. plus ½ tsp. rosewater, divided

¼ tsp. ground cardamom
½ c. chopped pistachios, divided
¼ c. water
Red food coloring (optional)
Dried rose petals (optional), for garnish

Combine milk, cream, ¼ c. sugar, and cornstarch or rice flour in a medium saucepan. Whisk vigorously to form a thin slurry, and then heat over Medium heat for 10 minutes or until thickened, whisking constantly. Remove from heat, add ½ tsp. rosewater and cardamom, and allow to stand for 5 minutes.

Place 1 Tbsp. of chopped pistachios in the bottom of each of four 8-oz. serving glasses or dishes. Divide milk pudding between glasses and refrigerate for at least 5 hours.

Combine 1 c. sugar and water in a small saucepan. Bring to a boil over High heat and continue to boil until sugar is completely melted. Add ¼ c. rosewater, reduce heat to Medium-Low, cover, and simmer for 15 minutes. Remove from heat and allow to stand until completely cooled. Add red food coloring (if using) until desired color is reached.

To assemble, divide rose syrup between glasses, pouring an even layer on top of each pudding. Top with remaining pistachios and rose petals (if using) and serve chilled.

MAKES 4 SERVINGS

Per serving: 339 calories, 11 g fat, 5 g saturated fat, 71 mg sodium, 61 g carbohydrates, 4 g protein.

VARIATIONS: Some versions of muhallebi use sweetened condensed milk in place of heavy cream and sugar. For an orange muhallebi, replace rosewater with orange blossom water in pudding and syrup and add the zest of one small orange to pudding. For a chocolate muhallebi, top with 2 Tbsp. melted chocolate instead of rose syrup. Other flavorings may be added as well, such as vanilla, cinnamon, or nutmeg.

TIP: If you have any extra rose syrup from this recipe, it can be combined with seltzer, club soda, white grape juice, or pear nectar to make a non-alcoholic cocktail.

SYRIA
KARABIJ WITH NATEF DIP

MEDIUM · COOK TIME: 30 MINUTES · ACTIVE PREP TIME: 1 HOUR, 10 MINUTES · INACTIVE PREP TIME: 1 HOUR, 30 MINUTES

A specialty of the Syrian city of Aleppo, karabij are delicate, nutty treats that are great for snacking. Freshly-baked batches of karabij are frequently given as gifts during Eid al-Fitr and other holidays. Karabij are usually served with natef, a creamy meringue-like dip that is traditionally made from soapwort root (shirsh al-halaweh). Since food-grade soapwort root is difficult to find in the United States, the recipe for natef dip included here uses an egg white to produce its marshmallow-like texture.

1-½ c. semolina
¾ c. farina
¼ c. plus 2 Tbsp. powdered sugar, divided, plus more for dusting
½ c. plus 1 Tbsp. butter, melted, divided, plus more for greasing baking sheets
¼ c. rosewater, divided
2 Tbsp. water
1 c. finely ground walnuts
Natef dip, for serving (see recipe below)

Sift together semolina, farina, and 1 Tbsp. powdered sugar in a large bowl. Add ½ c. melted butter and stir with a wooden spoon to form a moist dough. Cover with plastic wrap and allow to stand at room temperature for 1 hour. Add 1 Tbsp. rosewater and water and allow to stand for 30 minutes longer.

In a separate bowl, combine walnuts, ¼ c. plus 1 Tbsp. powdered sugar, 3 Tbsp. rosewater, and 1 Tbsp. melted butter. Stir until a paste is formed.

Preheat oven to 375 degrees. Grease two large baking sheets. To assemble cookies, take 1 Tbsp. of semolina dough and form a ball. Use your finger to make the ball of dough into a bowl shape with a deep impression in the center. Place 2 tsp.

of walnut paste inside and pinch shut. Gently roll the ball to form a 2-inch log. With the tines of a fork, make a linear pattern along the length of the cookie. Repeat with remaining dough and paste. Set cookies on baking sheets and bake for 25 minutes or until golden on top. Allow cookies to cool completely, dust with powdered sugar, and serve with natef dip.

For natef dip:
1-¾ c. white sugar
¾ c. water
1-½ tsp. lemon juice
1-½ tsp. rosewater
1 egg white
½ tsp. vanilla extract

Combine water and sugar in a medium saucepan. Bring to a boil over Medium-High heat, add lemon juice, and continue to cook for 5 minutes. Remove from heat and add rosewater.

Add egg white and vanilla to the bowl of a stand mixer with a whisk attachment and mix at High speed until stiff peaks form. While still mixing, slowly add syrup to egg white mixture in a steady stream. Refrigerate natef dip until chilled.

MAKES ABOUT 36 PIECES
Per piece: 88 calories, 5 g fat, 2 g saturated fat, 35 mg sodium, 10 g carbohydrates, 2 g protein.

VARIATIONS: Pistachios may be used in place of walnuts; date paste may also be used as a filling. Orange blossom water may be used in place of rosewater.

TIP: To make traditional natef dip using soapwort root, boil 2 oz. soapwort root with 4 c. water until liquid is reduced to ½ c. Use soapwort liquid in place of egg white in recipe (it will become white and fluffy upon mixing).

TUNISIA
MAKROUDH

MEDIUM · COOK TIME: 40 MINUTES · ACTIVE PREP TIME: 30 MINUTES · INACTIVE PREP TIME: 2 HOURS, 30 MINUTES

Tunisian cuisine combines influences from both North Africa and the Mediterranean, but its dishes carry a distinct spiciness that makes them its own. Unlike many desserts of the region, makroudh are "daily pastries," or treats that are enjoyed on a regular basis rather than reserved for special occasions such as weddings. Authentic Tunisian makroudh are made with Deglet Noor dates, which are light in color and have a flavor reminiscent of honey, but other varieties can be used as well.

2 c. semolina
1 c. all-purpose flour
½ c. butter, melted
¼ c. plus 3 Tbsp. olive oil
8 oz. dates (preferably Deglet Noor), pitted and coarsely chopped
1-¼ c. water, divided
½ tsp. ground cinnamon
¼ tsp. ground cloves
2 c. white sugar
1 Tbsp. lemon juice
Vegetable oil, for frying
Sesame seeds, for garnish

Sift together semolina and flour and add to the bowl of a stand mixer with a paddle attachment. Add butter and olive oil and mix on Medium speed until batter is completely moist but still slightly crumbly. Cover dough with plastic wrap and allow to rest for 2 hours.

Add dates and ¼ c. water to a blender or food processor and pulse to make a smooth paste. Set aside.

Combine sugar, 1 c. water, and lemon juice in a medium saucepan. Bring to a boil over High heat, reduce heat to Medium-Low, and simmer for 10 minutes. Remove from heat and set aside.

To assemble, divide dough and date paste each into four portions. Roll each portion into a log shape, making all dough and date paste logs the same length. Place one date paste log on top of each dough log. Fold sides of dough log over date paste log and roll it so that the date paste is completely encased in dough. Flatten log with the tines of a fork (it should be about 2 inches wide) and use a sharp knife to slice into pieces at a 90-degree angle (so that the pieces are diamond-shaped). Repeat until all dough and date paste has been used.

Heat about 1 inch of oil in a heavy skillet to a temperature of 350 degrees. Fry makroudh in small batches for 2-3 minutes, turning them over halfway through. Remove from pan and set on paper towels to drain.

Once makroudh are drained, drizzle them with syrup until they are completely saturated. Allow makroudh to stand for 30 minutes at room temperature, then sprinkle with sesame seeds and serve.

MAKES ABOUT 60 PIECES

Per piece: 123 calories, 7 g fat, 2 g saturated fat, 11 mg sodium, 15 g carbohydrates, 1 g protein.

VARIATIONS: In addition to date paste, other fillings can be used in makroudh. Algerian makroudh is made using almond paste; other varieties use fig paste or peanut butter. Makroudh may be drizzled with honey instead of lemon syrup.

TURKEY
BAKLAVA

HARD · COOK TIME: 1 HOUR, 10 MINUTES · ACTIVE PREP TIME: 30 MINUTES · INACTIVE PREP TIME: 1 HOUR, 10 MINUTES

With Americans, baklava stands as the most popular of all Mediterranean treats as well as the best-known of the siropiasta (syrup-soaked desserts). It's hard to resist adding a slice of the sticky, multilayered delight to your order when grabbing a gyro or falafel. It originated in the kitchens of Istanbul's Topkapi Palace, where the Janissaries who guarded the sultan's household were presented with trays of the rich pastry each year on the fifteenth day of Ramadan. While not the easiest recipe to make, baklava is within the skill range of most cooks who are willing to put forth a little extra time and effort.

8 oz. phyllo dough (about 12 sheets)
2 c. walnuts
1-½ c. pistachios
2 tsp. ground cinnamon
¼ tsp. ground cloves
½ c. butter, melted
1-½ c. white sugar
¾ c. water
¼ c. honey
1 Tbsp. lemon juice
¼ tsp. vanilla extract

Place walnuts, pistachios, cinnamon, and cloves in a blender or food processor and pulse until finely chopped. Set aside.

Brush the bottom and sides of an 8 x 8 x 2-inch square pan with butter. Trim phyllo sheets to fit pan. Place 4 sheets of dough on bottom of pan, brushing the top of each sheet with butter before adding another. Spread one-fourth of the nut mixture over top sheet. Add two more sheets of phyllo, brushing each with butter, followed by another one-fourth of nut mixture. Repeat until there are four layers of nut mixture and four layers of phyllo with two sheets each (top layer should be a phyllo layer). Drizzle the top phyllo layer with remaining butter. Cover with plastic wrap and refrigerate 1 hour.

Preheat oven to 350 degrees. With a sharp knife, make 4 parallel cuts in the surface of the baklava, extending to the bottom layer. Rotate pan 45 degrees and make 4 similar cuts to make diamond-shaped pieces. Bake for 1 hour or until golden brown. Allow to rest for at least 10 minutes after removing from oven.

Combine sugar, water, honey, and lemon juice in a medium saucepan. Bring to a boil over Medium-High heat and whisk until sugar is completely dissolved. Remove from heat and stir in vanilla extract.

Pour cooled syrup in an even layer over top of baklava. Allow baklava to cool completely before serving.

MAKES 12-16 SLICES

Per slice: 313 calories, 20 g fat, 5 g saturated fat, 149 mg sodium, 31 g carbohydrates, 6 g protein.

SERVING SUGGESTIONS: Sprinkle with grated pistachios and serve at room temperature.

VARIATIONS: Baklava may be made with only walnuts, only pistachios, or other nuts such as almonds. Some varieties of baklava do not use syrup at all; others are soaked in warmed milk instead of syrup.

TIP: Cutting the baklava before baking is not essential but highly recommended; refrigerating it so that the butter solidifies makes it easier to cleanly cut through the layers of nuts and phyllo.

UNITED ARAB EMIRATES
LUQAIMAT

MEDIUM · COOK TIME: 20 MINUTES · ACTIVE PREP TIME: 15 MINUTES · INACTIVE PREP TIME: 50 MINUTES

The word *luqaimat*, which means "small bites" in Arabic, is an appropriate name for these crispy, sticky morsels of dough. But it's a small snack with a long history; luqaimat were first described in cookbooks dating to the thirteenth-century Abbasid Caliphate. They also boast mentions in *One Thousand and One Nights* and in the memoirs of the Berber scholar and traveler Ibn Battuta. They're enjoyed in Greece and Cyprus as well as throughout the Middle East, but the combination of fennel seed, saffron, and cardamom is especially popular in the Emirati region.

3 c. all-purpose flour
1 c. lukewarm water (more if needed)
1 c. plus 2 Tbsp. white sugar, divided
1 Tbsp. active dry yeast
1 tsp. ground cinnamon
½ tsp. ground fennel seed
2 Tbsp. hot water
3-4 threads saffron
1 c. water, at room temperature
3 cardamom pods, lightly crushed
Vegetable oil, for frying

Combine lukewarm water, 2 Tbsp. sugar, and yeast and whisk together. Cover and let stand for 15 minutes.

Sift together flour, cinnamon, and fennel seed. Knead wet and dry ingredients together until a sticky, moist dough is formed (add more water if necessary). Cover and let stand for 20 minutes or until doubled in size.

Place saffron in hot water and allow to soak for at least 15 minutes. Water will become a deep yellow or orange-red color.

Combine 1 c. sugar, room-temperature water, and cardamom pods in a medium saucepan. Bring to a boil over High heat and continue to boil for 5-10 minutes or until syrup has thickened. Remove from heat and stir in saffron water.

Heat about 2 inches of oil in a heavy skillet to a temperature of 350 degrees. Use a spoon to scoop small balls of dough (about 2 tsp. each) and drop into hot oil until pan is filled. Fry each batch of luqaimat for 2-3 minutes, turning frequently with a slotted metal spoon, until they are dark golden brown on all sides. Remove from pan and set on paper towels to drain.

Once syrup has cooled to room temperature, add luqaimat to syrup and stir so that all sides are coated. Allow to soak in syrup for 1-3 minutes (the longer they soak, the sweeter and less crispy they will be). Stack luqaimat on a serving plate in a pyramid and drizzle with remaining syrup.

MAKES ABOUT 40-50 LUQAIMAT

Per luqaimat: 91 calories, 5 g fat, 1 g saturated fat, 0 mg sodium, 11 g carbohydrates, 1 g protein.

SERVING SUGGESTION: Garnish with sesame seeds in addition to syrup.

VARIATIONS: In the syrup, replace cardamom and saffron with the juice and zest of 1 small lemon for a much different flavor. You may also use date molasses or honey in place of sugar (use ½ c. instead of 1 c.).

TIP: A piping bag can be used to form dough balls. Fill the piping bag with dough, cut a medium-sized opening in the corner, and squeeze 2 tsp. portions of dough over hot oil (use scissors or a knife to separate dough).

YEMEN
MASOUB

EASY · COOK TIME: 5 MINUTES · ACTIVE PREP TIME: 10 MINUTES

Due to Yemen's proximity to the Horn of Africa, a region that greatly influences its culture, Yemeni cuisine is much different from that of other Arab nations. Masoub is eaten in Somalia, Ethiopia, and Saudi Arabia as well as in Yemen. As a pudding it is enjoyed at the end of a meal, but it is also often eaten at breakfast as a porridge. Like oatmeal or grits, masoub is seasoned and garnished based on personal preference.

4 very ripe bananas, peeled and cut into large chunks
9 slices whole wheat bread, torn into small pieces
1 Tbsp. plus 1 tsp. ghee
1 c. light cream or half-and-half
¼ c. honey
Raisins, for garnish
Almonds, for garnish

In a medium bowl, mash the banana chunks with a potato masher or the back of a large spoon. Place bread pieces in a blender or food processor and pulse on Low speed until even crumbs are formed.

Heat ghee in a skillet over Medium heat. Add bananas, cream, and honey and stir to combine. Add bread crumbs and continue to cook until warmed.

Divide masoub between four serving dishes. Top with raisins and almonds and serve.

MAKES 4 SERVINGS

Per serving: 502 calories, 18 g fat, 9 g saturated fat, 311 mg sodium, 80 g carbohydrates, 12 g protein.

SERVING SUGGESTION: Masoub can be served warm, at room temperature, or chilled.

VARIATIONS: Dates, pitted and pureed in a food processor, may be added to masoub in place of some of the bananas. Depending on one's personal taste, masoub is sometimes served with grated Cheddar cheese (for a sweet-salty combination) or with sliced bananas caramelized with brown sugar (for extra sweetness and banana flavor).

AFRICA

ANGOLA
COCADA AMARELA

MEDIUM · COOK TIME: 30 MINUTES · ACTIVE PREP TIME: 5 MINUTES

Cocada amarela is Portuguese for "yellow coconut," a name that comes from the large number of egg yolks that give this custard its yellow color. While first made in Angola, cocada amarela is reminiscent of the custard dishes of Portugal, its former colonizer, such as pastéis de nata (page 76). But the coconut in this custard makes it distinctly sub-Saharan African.

3 c. water
1 c. white sugar
2 whole cloves
1 stick cinnamon
2 c. unsweetened coconut, coarsely grated
6 egg yolks
¼ tsp. salt

Combine water, sugar, cloves, and cinnamon stick in a medium saucepan. Bring to a boil over High heat. Continue to cook until temperature reaches 235 degrees (use a candy thermometer to monitor temperature), stirring frequently.

Reduce heat to Medium-Low and remove cloves and cinnamon stick. Stir in coconut and simmer for 10 minutes longer, stirring frequently. Remove from heat and set aside.

Using an electric mixer, beat egg yolks and salt together on High speed until slightly pale. Stir a large spoonful of coconut mixture into egg yolks to temper. Stir egg yolk mixture into coconut mixture, a little at a time, beating on Low speed until completely incorporated.

Heat custard over Medium-Low heat, mixing constantly with a wire whisk, for 5 minutes or until smooth and thickened. Divide warm custard between 4 bowls and serve.

MAKES 4 SERVINGS

Per serving: 410 calories, 20 g fat, 14 g saturated fat, 168 mg sodium, 57 g carbohydrates, 6 g protein.

SERVING SUGGESTION: Top with cinnamon or a dollop of whipped cream and serve either warm or chilled. For a nice presentation, serve cocada amarela in coconut shells.

VARIATIONS: Add a small amount of lemon or vanilla extract for additional flavor.

TIP: If using fresh coconut, you will need the meat of ½ medium-sized coconut.

BENIN
YOVO DOKÔ

EASY · COOK TIME: 15 MINUTES · ACTIVE PREP TIME: 5 MINUTES · INACTIVE PREP TIME: 20 MINUTES

Benin's national dessert is a popular street food that are much like American "donut holes." In the Fon language, yovo dokô means "European pastry," and they are similar to deep-fried French pâte à choux. Brown and crisp on the outside and soft and white on the inside, yovo dokô present a contrast in textures that makes them a simple (and rather addictive) delight.

4 c. whole wheat flour
½ tsp. ground nutmeg
¼ tsp. salt
¾ c. white sugar
1 Tbsp. plus 1 tsp. active dry yeast
1-¾ c. water
½ tsp. vanilla extract

Peanut oil, for frying

Sift together flour, nutmeg, and salt and add to the bowl of a stand mixer with a dough hook attachment. Add sugar, followed by yeast. Slowly add water and vanilla extract and mix on Low speed to form a sticky, moist dough (add more water if necessary). Cover and let stand for 20 minutes or until doubled in size.

Heat about 2 inches of oil in a heavy skillet to a temperature of 350 degrees. Use a spoon to scoop balls of dough (about 1-2 Tbsp. each) and drop into hot oil until pan is filled. Fry each batch of yovo dokô for 2-3 minutes, turning frequently with a slotted metal spoon, until they are dark golden brown on all sides. Remove from pan and set on paper towels to drain.

MAKES ABOUT 30 PASTRIES

Per pastry: 143 calories, 7 g fat, 1 g saturated fat, 20 mg sodium, 18 g carbohydrates, 2 g protein.

SERVING SUGGESTIONS: Yovo dokô are best served warm. While usually eaten plain, they can be served sprinkled with powdered sugar or cinnamon sugar.

VARIATIONS: For chocolate- or hazelnut-filled yovo dokô, use a piping bag to make a hole in center of dough and squeeze with filling. Jam or preserves may also be used.

BOTSWANA
VETKOEKE WITH STONE FRUIT JAM

MEDIUM · COOK TIME: 1 HOUR, 15 MINUTES · ACTIVE PREP TIME: 20 MINUTES

Whether it's an elaborate braai with dozens of guests or a quick lunch from a street cart, it's rare to encounter a meal in Botswana that does not include vetkoeke (singular: vetkoek). These fried bread rolls, whose name means "fat cakes" in Afrikaans, are normally stuffed with savory fillings like ground beef, bologna, cheese, or pickled vegetables. But vetkoeke make an excellent sweet treat when rolled in cinnamon sugar and stuffed with jam.

4 c. cake flour
2 Tbsp. white sugar
1 Tbsp. plus 1 tsp. baking powder
1 tsp. salt
2 c. whole milk, lukewarm
4 eggs
Vegetable oil, for frying
Cinnamon sugar, for dusting
1-½ c. stone fruit jam (see recipe below)

Sift together flour, sugar, baking powder, and salt in a large bowl. In a smaller bowl, whisk together milk and eggs. Add dry ingredients to the bowl of a stand mixer with a dough hook attachment and slowly add wet ingredients, mixing together on Low speed to form a sticky, moist dough.

Heat about 2 inches of oil in a heavy skillet to a temperature of 350 degrees. Use a spoon to scoop balls of dough (about 1-2 Tbsp. each) and drop into hot oil until pan is filled. Fry each batch of vetkoeke for 2-3 minutes, turning frequently with a slotted metal spoon, until they are dark golden brown on all sides. Remove from pan and set on paper towels to drain. Roll vetkoeke in cinnamon sugar to coat while they are still warm.

Fill a large piping bag with stone fruit jam. One vetkoeke are cool, use a knife to make an incision in the center of each vetkoek and use the piping bag to fill with jam.

For stone fruit jam:
12 plums, pitted and quartered
10 nectarines, pitted and quartered
¾ c. brown sugar
Juice and zest of 1 lemon
¼ c. honey

Preheat oven to 350 degrees. Place fruit on a large, nonstick rimmed baking sheet and sprinkle evenly with brown sugar, lemon juice, and lemon zest. Bake for

45 minutes or until fruit is soft.

Preheat broiler to High. Drizzle honey over fruit and broil for 5 minutes. Allow fruit to cool slightly, and then mash with a potato masher or the back of a large spoon. Pour into sterile containers and refrigerate until ready to serve.

MAKES 20 VETKOEKE

Per vetkoek: 248 calories, 13 g fat, 3 g saturated fat, 140 mg sodium, 29 g carbohydrates, 5 g protein.

SERVING SUGGESTION: Serve with a cup of hot tea.

VARIATIONS: Any type of jam can be used to fill vetkoeke; they can also be filled with cream cheese or served without filling.

TIP: If you do not have a piping bag, simply cut the vetkoeke in half and spread cut sides with jam (this is common in Botswana).

BURKINA FASO
BANFORA WELSH CAKES

EASY · COOK TIME: 30 MINUTES · ACTIVE PREP TIME: 10 MINUTES · INACTIVE PREP TIME: 30 MINUTES

As their name suggests, Welsh cakes are native to Wales. How did these flapjack-like griddle cakes become associated with Burkina Faso, a former French colony in West Africa? Banfora Welsh cakes, named for the country's fourth-largest city and the center of its sugarcane industry, actually developed independently from their British counterpart and took on their name much later. This not-too-sweet Burkinabé dessert makes a tasty snack or breakfast as well.

2 c. all-purpose flour, plus more for flouring surface
1/3 c. white sugar

1 tsp. baking powder
¼ tsp. salt
¼ c. rendered lard
¼ c. butter, at room temperature
½ c. dried pineapple
1 egg
3 Tbsp. whole milk
Cooking spray, for coating pan
Powdered sugar, for dusting

Sift together flour, sugar, baking powder, and salt. Add to the bowl of a stand mixer with a paddle attachment and add lard and butter. Mix on Low speed just until dough is coarse and crumbly, and then add pineapple, egg, and milk until dough is soft but not sticky. Cover and refrigerate for at least 30 minutes.

On a floured surface, roll out dough to a ¼-inch thickness. Use a 3-inch round cookie cutter to cut circles from the dough.

Heat a heavy skillet, preferably cast iron, over Medium heat and coat with cooking spray. Fry cakes in batches for about 3-4 minutes on each side until light brown, flipping occasionally. Place cakes on a wire rack to cool. Dust with powdered sugar before serving.

MAKES 15 CAKES

Per serving: 144 calories, 7 g fat, 4 g saturated fat, 67 mg sodium, 18 g carbohydrates, 2 g protein.

SERVING SUGGESTION: Serve warm with butter and hot hibiscus or ginger tea.

VARIATIONS: Dried mango, papaya, or sweet potato can be used in place of or in addition to pineapple. Shredded coconut may also be added.

BURUNDI
BANANA PINEAPPLE SQUARES

EASY · COOK TIME: 30 MINUTES · ACTIVE PREP TIME: 10 MINUTES

Desserts aren't a regular part of the average diet in Burundi, a small Central African nation sandwiched between Rwanda and Tanzania. But since 80 percent of its total land is used for agriculture, local food definitely is. Bananas and pineapple are a few of the crops that thrive in its tropical highland climate.

4 c. all-purpose flour, plus more for flouring pan
1 c. plus 2 tsp. white sugar, divided
1 tsp. baking powder
¼ tsp. salt
1 c. plus 2 Tbsp. butter, divided, plus more for greasing pan
3 eggs
4 bananas, thinly sliced
1-½ c. fresh pineapple, thinly sliced and drained

Sift together flour, 1 c. sugar, baking powder, and salt and add to the bowl of a stand mixer with a paddle attachment. Add 1 c. butter and mix on Medium speed, slowly adding eggs one at a time. Continue to mix until a smooth and thick batter is formed.

Preheat oven to 350 degrees. Grease and flour an 8 x 8-inch square baking dish. Pour half of the batter into the dish and spread into an even layer. Top with bananas and pineapple, each in an even layer, followed by remaining batter. Spread the top of the cake so that it is smooth.

Slice remaining 2 Tbsp. butter into thin pats and dot surface of cake. Sprinkle with remaining 2 tsp. sugar. Bake for 30 minutes or until golden brown on top. Allow cake to cool, then cut into squares to serve.

MAKES 9 SERVINGS

Per serving: 408 calories, 17 g fat, 10 g saturated fat, 177 mg sodium, 60 g carbohydrates, 6 g protein.

SERVING SUGGESTION: Serve warm or at room temperature with coffee.

VARIATIONS: Chopped dates, coconut, or raisins may be used in place of pineapple. Nuts such as walnuts or almonds may also be added to the center layer.

CAMEROON
LEFOMBO

EASY · COOK TIME: 15 MINUTES · ACTIVE PREP TIME: 15 MINUTES · INACTIVE PREP TIME: 2 HOURS, 20 MINUTES

Much like yovo dokô (page 141) in nearby Benin, lefombo are remnants of a colonial culture. Sometimes called "African beignets," these fluffy donuts are very similar to the French choux pastries that one could expect to find in a Parisian boulangerie. But they are so well-loved in Cameroon that they have found a permanent place in the coastal West African nation's culinary world.

4 c. cake flour, divided, plus more for flouring surface
½ c. lukewarm water
1 Tbsp. active dry yeast
¼ c. white sugar, plus more for dusting
1 tsp. salt
½ tsp. ground nutmeg
¾ c. whole milk
2 eggs
¼ c. butter, at room temperature, plus more for greasing baking sheet
1 tsp. vanilla extract
Oil, for frying

Whisk together ¾ c. flour, water, and yeast in a small bowl. Cover with plastic wrap and allow to stand for 20 minutes.

Sift together remaining 3-¼ c. flour, sugar, salt, and nutmeg and add to the bowl of a stand mixer with a dough hook attachment. Add yeast mixture, milk, and eggs and mix on Medium speed to form a moist dough. Gradually mix in butter and vanilla extract and continue to mix for 5 minutes or until dough is smooth and elastic. Cover and allow to stand at room temperature for 1-½ hours or until doubled in size.

Turn dough onto a floured surface and knead until pliable. Roll dough to a thickness of about ½-inch and use a 3-inch cookie cutter to cut circles from dough. Place dough circles on a greased baking sheet, cover with plastic wrap, and allow to stand for 30 minutes longer.

Heat about 2 inches of oil in a heavy skillet to a temperature of 350 degrees. Fry 3-4 lefombo at a time for 3 minutes, turning once, until they are golden brown on both sides. Remove from pan and set on paper towels to drain. Dust lefombo liberally with sugar while still warm.

MAKES ABOUT 10-12 PASTRIES

Per pastry: 386 calories, 23 g fat, 5 g saturated fat, 239 mg sodium, 37 g carbohydrates, 6 g protein.

VARIATIONS: Lefombo can be cut into different shapes if desired. For jam- or hazelnut-filled lefombo, use a piping bag to make a hole in center of dough and squeeze with filling.

CAPE VERDE GUFONG

EASY · COOK TIME: 15 MINUTES · ACTIVE PREP TIME: 20 MINUTES

Corn and its many varieties, such as hominy, are of great importance to the people of Cape Verde, a chain of islands that were uninhabited before they were colonized by Portugal. Bananas are another dietary staple. Cornmeal and bananas marry beautifully in these simple fried pastries, which can be enjoyed at the end of a meal or during the meal itself.

¾ c. white sugar
½ c. water
1 dash salt
½ c. fine cornmeal
2 very ripe bananas, mashed
1 c. all-purpose flour
1-½ tsp. baking powder
¼ tsp. salt
Vegetable oil, for frying

Combine sugar, water, and salt in a small saucepan. Bring to a boil over high heat and continue to boil until sugar is completely dissolved. Set aside.

Add cornmeal to the bowl of a stand mixer with a dough hook attachment and slowly pour syrup into bowl while mixing on Low speed, followed by bananas. Sift together flour, baking powder, and salt and add (a spoonful at a time) to form a firm dough.

Heat about 1 inch of oil in a heavy skillet to a temperature of 350 degrees. Form dough into finger-sized logs. Fry each batch of gufong for 2-3 minutes, turning frequently with a slotted metal spoon, until they are dark golden brown on all sides. Remove from pan and set on paper towels to drain.

MAKES ABOUT 30 PIECES

Per piece: 113 calories, 7 g fat, 2 g saturated fat, 21 mg sodium, 12 g carbohydrates, 1 g protein.

SERVING SUGGESTIONS: Drizzle with chocolate syrup or dust with powdered sugar, if desired, and serve warm with coffee or rum.

VARIATION: Gufong can be made without bananas. If not using bananas, increase sugar and water each to 1 c.

CENTRAL AFRICAN REPUBLIC BENNE WAFERS

EASY · COOK TIME: 15 MINUTES · ACTIVE PREP TIME: 15 MINUTES · INACTIVE PREP TIME: 5 MINUTES

The word *benne* is Bantu for "sesame," and sesame seeds were first brought to the United States by enslaved people from central Africa. Benne wafers are also popular in the United States (particularly in South Carolina and Georgia) and in parts of the Caribbean. Sesame seeds were a symbol of good luck for the Bantu people, and Black Americans who celebrate Kwanzaa often include benne wafers in their holiday festivities.

2 c. sesame seeds, toasted
2 c. dark brown sugar
½ c. butter, at room temperature, plus more for greasing baking sheet
2 eggs
1 tsp. vanilla extract
Juice of 1 small lemon
1 c. all-purpose flour
1 tsp. baking powder
½ tsp. salt

Combine brown sugar and butter in the bowl of a stand mixer with a paddle attachment and mix on Medium speed. Add eggs, followed by vanilla extract and lemon juice. Sift together flour, baking powder, and salt and add to wet ingredients a little at a time. Once mixture is smooth and creamy, slowly add sesame seeds.

Preheat oven to 325 degrees. Grease two large baking sheets. Place rounded 1-Tbsp. spoonfuls of batter on baking sheets about 2 inches apart. Bake for 15 minutes or until brown and crisp at the edges.

Allow wafers to cool on baking sheet for 5 minutes after removing from oven, then transfer to wire racks to finish cooling.

MAKES ABOUT 24 WAFERS

Per wafer: 174 calories, 10 g fat, 3 g saturated fat, 88 mg sodium, 19 g carbohydrates, 3 g protein.

VARIATION: This recipe makes sweet wafers. For wafers that are more biscuit-like and savory, omit sugar, vanilla extract, and lemon juice. Use shortening or lard in place of butter along with ¼ c. plus 2 Tbsp. whole milk. Increase flour to 2 c. and reduce sesame seeds to 1 c.

TIP: To toast sesame seeds, place them in a heavy skillet that has been preheated over Medium heat. Stir constantly until they are golden brown in color (watch carefully, or they will burn).

CHAD
OUADDAÏ

EASY · COOK TIME: 10 MINUTES · ACTIVE PREP TIME: 15 MINUTES

Grains form the backbone of the regular diet of the people of Chad, a country where meat and fresh produce are sometimes scarce but millet, sorghum, rice, and fonio are in great supply. Millet is one of the first crops cultivated by humankind, and it was probably first grown in Africa. Much higher in protein and fiber than most other grains, millet is used by Chadian cooks to make bread, porridge, and these sweet snacks, which are named for the Ouaddaï region of eastern Chad.

2 c. fine millet flour (freshly ground if possible)
1 c. all-purpose flour, plus more for flouring surface
½ c. white sugar
1 c. vegetable oil, plus more for frying
1 egg
Juice and zest of 1 small orange
1 tsp. vanilla extract
Water, as needed

Sift together millet, flour, and sugar and add to the bowl of a stand mixer with a dough hook attachment. Slowly add the oil in a steady stream while mixing on Low speed, followed by egg, orange juice, orange zest, and vanilla extract, and continue to mix for 5 minutes. Dough should have the consistency of moist sand; add a small amount of water while mixing if it is too dry.

Roll out dough onto a floured surface to a width of ¼-inch. Use a sharp knife to cut dough into strips 1 inch wide and 3-4 inches long.

Heat about 1 inch of oil in a heavy skillet to a temperature of 300 degrees. Fry each batch of ouaddaï for 2-3 minutes, turning frequently with a slotted metal spoon, until they are dark golden brown on all sides. Remove from pan and set on paper towels to drain.

MAKES ABOUT 40 PIECES

Per piece: 97 calories, 6 g fat, 1 g saturated fat, 2 mg sodium, 10 g carbohydrates, 1 g protein.

SERVING SUGGESTION: Drizzle with honey, if desired, and serve with tea.

VARIATION: Cinnamon may be used in place of orange zest and juice in this recipe.

COMOROS
LADU

EASY · COOK TIME: 5 MINUTES · ACTIVE PREP TIME: 15 MINUTES

In the nineteenth century, the island nation of Comoros was used as a trading post by its French colonizers. Ships making the passage to and from India often carried coconuts, cashew nuts, and spices such as cardamom through Comoros. Trade with India helped form the islands' cultural identity; ladu, a simple no-bake Indian treat that is very popular in Comoros, is one example of this exchange.

1 c. shredded coconut
1 c. cashews
½ c. red rice
1 c. brown sugar
¼ c. water
1 tsp. ground cardamom

Heat a small skillet over Medium heat. Sauté coconut just until toasted, about 1 minute. Repeat with the cashews and rice, making sure that none of the ingredients are toasted long enough to burn.

Place coconut in a blender or food processor and pulse until very fine. Repeat with cashews and rice. When processing cashews, be careful not to grind them more than a few seconds (they will become pasty and oily if ground too finely).

In a small saucepan, combine brown sugar and water and heat over Medium-High heat just until melted. Remove from heat and allow to cool before mixture turns to a thick syrup. Stir in cardamom.

Combine coconut, cashews, and rice with brown sugar mixture and stir until completely combined. Roll mixture into 1-inch balls.

MAKES ABOUT 15-20 LADU

Per ladu: 99 calories, 5 g fat, 2 g saturated fat, 4 mg sodium, 14 g carbohydrates, 2 g protein.

SERVING SUGGESTION: Serve at room temperature or chilled with chai tea.

VARIATION: Finely chopped dried fruit, such as raisins, may be added with brown sugar and cardamom.

TIP: The cashews in this recipe should contain enough oil to bind the ingredients; however, if the mixture is loose you may add a few tsp. of ghee to help them stick together.

CONGO
CAAKIRI

EASY · COOK TIME: 5 MINUTES · ACTIVE PREP TIME: 10 MINUTES

One of the more distinctly African desserts, caakiri is similar to rice pudding but uses semolina couscous in place of rice. This makes it far easier and quicker to make, as couscous takes only minutes to cook. Sweet and tangy flavors marry perfectly in this simple dessert, thanks to the combination of sugar and sweetened condensed milk with yogurt and sour cream.

1 c. dry couscous
2 c. water
½ c. sweetened condensed milk
½ c. plain yogurt
¼ c. sour cream
2 Tbsp. white sugar
1-½ tsp. vanilla extract
½ tsp. ground nutmeg, plus more for serving

Bring water to a boil over High heat. Remove from heat and stir in couscous. Allow to stand for 5 minutes or until water is completely absorbed. Set aside and allow to cool completely.

In a large bowl, stir together condensed milk, yogurt, sour cream, sugar, vanilla extract, and nutmeg. Fold couscous into milk mixture and refrigerate until chilled.

Divide between four serving bowls, sprinkle with additional nutmeg, and serve.

MAKES 4 SERVINGS

Per serving: 363 calories, 7 g fat, 4 g saturated fat, 86 mg sodium, 63 g carbohydrates, 11 g protein.

SERVING SUGGESTIONS: Serve topped with raisins, toasted pumpkin seeds, sliced grapes, or crushed pineapple.

VARIATION: Serve caakiri in a large bowl, such as a glass trifle bowl, alternating layers of pudding with grapes, pumpkin seeds, or other fruits and nuts.

DJIBOUTI BANANA FRITTERS

EASY · COOK TIME: 10 MINUTES · ACTIVE PREP TIME: 5 MINUTES

Banana fritters are a popular snack or dessert throughout Africa, but methods of making them vary by region. In the Horn of Africa, where the small nation of Djibouti is located, they are fried in a skillet with a minimal amount of oil, like pancakes. In Djibouti they're usually enjoyed at afternoon tea, but Americans may not be able to resist cooking up a batch for breakfast.

3 very ripe bananas, mashed
¼ c. all-purpose flour
1 Tbsp. white sugar

¼ tsp. baking powder
¼ tsp. ground nutmeg
1 dash baking soda
1 dash salt
Oil, for frying

Sift together flour, sugar, baking powder, nutmeg, baking soda, and salt. Use a wooden spoon to fold together flour mixture and bananas in a medium bowl.

Heat about ¼-inch of oil in a heavy skillet over Medium-High heat. Drop batter into pan in 2 Tbsp. increments and smooth with the side of a small spatula or spoon to form silver dollar shapes. Fritters should be at least 1 inch apart in skillet. Cook for 1 minute on each side until fritters are brown around edges. Remove fritters from skillet and set on a wire rack to cool. Repeat with remaining batter.

MAKES 12 FRITTERS

Per fritter: 200 calories, 18 g fat, 2 g saturated fat, 26 mg sodium, 10 g carbohydrates, 1 g protein.

SERVING SUGGESTION: Serve warm with sliced bananas, or with powdered sugar or cane syrup.

VARIATIONS: While not traditional, chopped nuts, chocolate chips, cocoa powder, vanilla extract, or dried fruit may be added to batter if desired.

EQUATORIAL GUINEA
NKATE CAKE

MEDIUM · COOK TIME: 20 MINUTES · ACTIVE PREP TIME: 10 MINUTES

More of a candy than an American-style cake, nkate cake is an example of an African sweet that has a recognizable American equivalent: peanut brittle. The main difference is that it is not quite as tough to bite into; you don't have to worry about breaking a tooth from eating nkate cake. Its name means "peanut" in the Twi language, but nkate cake can be made using any types of nuts. This recipe includes both peanuts and cashews.

3 c. peanuts, roasted and coarsely chopped
1 c. cashews, roasted and coarsely chopped
2 c. white sugar
¼ c. water
2 Tbsp. vegetable oil
Juice and zest of 1 lemon
1 tsp. ground cinnamon

Combine sugar, water, and oil in a medium saucepan. Cook over Medium heat until syrup is light brown in color and temperature reaches 320 degrees (use a candy thermometer to monitor temperature), stirring constantly. Reduce heat to Low and stir in lemon juice and cinnamon. Add nuts and cook for about 3 minutes longer.

Set an 8-inch cake ring on top of a sheet of parchment paper. Press the nut mixture into the ring so that the entire ring is filled and the surface of the cake is as even as possible. Use a sharp knife to score the surface to form eight wedges. (It is important to complete this step as quickly as possible, as the mixture will not be pliable once it hardens.) Wait for the nkate cake to cool, and then cut the cake into eight pieces along the scored lines and serve.

MAKES 8 SERVINGS

Per serving: 627 calories, 38 g fat, 6 g saturated fat, 13 mg sodium, 65 g carbohydrates, 17 g protein.

VARIATIONS: Nkate cake can be made with only peanuts, only cashews, or a combination in any proportions. Extracts such as coconut or vanilla may be added for additional flavoring.

TIP: To roast your own nuts, preheat oven to 325 degrees. Spread nuts in a single layer on a rimmed baking sheet and roast for 10 minutes, stirring halfway through roasting time.

ERITREA
HIMBASHA

MEDIUM · COOK TIME: 30 MINUTES · ACTIVE PREP TIME: 15 MINUTES · INACTIVE PREP TIME: 2 HOURS, 25 MINUTES

Most often eaten by Coptic Christians for breakfast following Sunday Mass, himbasha has also become an important part of Christmas and other celebrations in Eritrea. One tradition is to break a loaf of himbasha over a child's back on his first birthday, a ritual that is said to give him strength. Himbasha is typical of eastern African sweet breads–sweet enough for a dessert but savory enough for a light snack.

2 c. all-purpose flour
½ c. warm water
¼ c. white sugar
1 tsp. active dry yeast
1 tsp. black sesame seeds
½ tsp. salt
½ tsp. ground cardamom
¼ c. Zante currants
2 Tbsp. olive oil, plus more for greasing pan and brushing

Combine water, sugar, and yeast in a small bowl and stir together to dissolve. Allow mixture to stand for 15 minutes.

Sift together flour, sesame seeds, salt, and cardamom and add to the bowl of a stand mixer with a dough hook attachment. Add Zante currants and oil while mixing on Low speed. Gradually pour yeast mixture into dry ingredients and knead for about 10 minutes to form a soft dough. Cover dough with plastic wrap and allow to stand at room temperature for 1-½ hours.

Grease a 9-inch round cake pan with high sides. Punch the dough slightly, then transfer dough to pan and spread evenly so that it touches the edge of the pan on all sides. Cover pan with plastic wrap and allow to stand for 30 minutes longer.

Preheat oven to 350 degrees. Use a knife to make patterns in the dough's surface. (To make the traditional Eritrean "spoked wheel" pattern, score lines to divide the dough into eight 45-degree wedges, and then create a pattern of concentric circles on top of those lines.) Brush lightly with olive oil and bake for 30 minutes or until golden.

Remove from oven and allow to cool in pan for 10 minutes. Transfer from pan to wire rack to finish cooling.

MAKES 8 SERVINGS

Per serving: 187 calories, 4 g fat, 1 g saturated fat, 149 mg sodium, 34 g carbohydrates, 4 g protein.

SERVING SUGGESTION: Serve warm or at room temperature with coffee or hot tea.

VARIATIONS: Himbasha can be made without currants and sesame seeds. Raisins or candied ginger may be included as well.

ESWATINI MELKTERT

MEDIUM · COOK TIME: 35 MINUTES · ACTIVE PREP TIME: 25 MINUTES · INACTIVE PREP TIME: 1 HOUR, 15 MINUTES

Melktert ("milk tart") is an Afrikaner custard pie that originated with the first Dutch settlers in the Cape region–making it nearly four centuries old. It is similar to other custard pies, such as the Portuguese pastéis de nata (page 76), but with a higher proportion of milk to eggs. As a result, melktert is lighter and fluffier in texture and has a heavier milk flavor than most custard desserts.

2 c. all-purpose flour
1 dash salt

½ c. cold butter, cut into cubes
3 Tbsp. cold water
2 c. whole milk, divided
1 stick cinnamon
1 vanilla bean, split open
½ c. plus 2 Tbsp. cake flour
½ c. white sugar
3 Tbsp. cornstarch
2 eggs, separated
Ground cinnamon, for dusting

Sift together all-purpose flour and salt in a large bowl. Add butter and mix with two knives until butter pieces are mostly chopped and mixture is crumbly. Add water and mix to form a firm dough. Knead dough until smooth, then wrap in plastic wrap and refrigerate for 15 minutes.

Turn dough onto a floured surface and roll into a 12-inch circle of even thickness. Press the dough circle into a 9-inch pie pan and prick several times with the tines of a fork. Cover with aluminum foil and place in freezer for 15 minutes longer.

Preheat oven to 375 degrees. Pull back foil, fill the pie shell with pie weights (or dry beans), replace foil, and bake for 20 minutes. Remove weights and foil and bake for 15 more minutes. Set aside to cool.

In a medium saucepan, heat 1-½ c. milk over Medium heat until it reaches a temperature of 180 degrees (use a candy thermometer to monitor temperature), stirring constantly to avoid scalding. Add cinnamon stick and vanilla bean and remove from heat. Cover and allow to sit for 45 minutes or until milk is infused with flavors; remove cinnamon stick and vanilla bean.

Combine remaining ½ c. milk, cake flour, sugar, cornstarch, and egg yolks and whisk vigorously until smooth, about 5 minutes. Add egg mixture to infused milk. Warm custard over Medium heat, whisking constantly, until thickened. (Do not allow the custard to become hot enough to cook the egg yolks.) Remove from heat and set aside.

Using an electric mixer, beat egg whites on High speed until stiff peaks form. Fold egg white mixture into custard. Pour custard into pie shell and refrigerate until set. Dust with cinnamon before serving.

MAKES 8-10 SERVINGS

Per serving: 315 calories, 13 g fat, 8 g saturated fat, 125 mg sodium, 43 g carbohydrates, 7 g protein.

VARIATIONS: Countless variations on the traditional melktert can be made by adding spices, extracts, or other ingredients to the custard. A few include lemon juice and zest, cardamom, almond extract, and cocoa powder. Top with almonds or shredded coconut instead of dusting with cinnamon.

TIP: To reduce preparation time, a prepared pie shell may be used.

ETHIOPIA
DESTAYE

HARD · COOK TIME: 35 MINUTES · ACTIVE PREP TIME: 30 MINUTES · INACTIVE PREP TIME: 15 MINUTES

The name of these popular Ethiopian street snacks means "my happiness." While Ethiopian cuisine does not typically include desserts or sweet snacks, these dumplings are nonetheless the perfect happy ending to a traditional Ethiopian meal. Ethiopians aren't afraid of using lots of spices, and this recipe is no exception.

1-½ c. buckwheat flour
1 c. all-purpose flour, plus more for flouring surface
¼ c. white sugar
½ tsp. salt
2 eggs, divided
½ c. plain yogurt
¼ c. butter, at room temperature, divided

½ c. unsweetened coconut, coarsely grated and toasted
¼ c. pistachios, coarsely chopped and toasted
¼ c. almonds, coarsely chopped and toasted
¼ c. golden raisins, coarsely chopped
1 Tbsp. brown sugar
1 tsp. ground cardamom
1 tsp. ground cinnamon
Water, for boiling

Sift together flours, sugar, and salt and add to the bowl of a stand mixer with a dough hook attachment. Whisk together 1 egg and yogurt and slowly add to dry ingredients while mixing on Low speed. Once dough is moist, turn onto a floured surface and knead until pliable. Return to bowl, cover with plastic wrap, and allow to stand for 15 minutes.

Combine coconut, pistachios, almonds, and raisins in a blender or food processor and pulse until combined but not finely ground.

Melt 3 Tbsp. butter in a medium skillet over Medium-Low heat. Add brown sugar, cardamom, and cinnamon and cook for about 1 minute or until brown sugar is melted but not caramelized, stirring constantly. Add coconut mixture and stir to coat.

Roll dough to a thickness of ⅛-inch on a floured surface. Use a large, round cookie cutter to cut circles from dough. Place a spoonful of coconut filling on each circle, fold in half, and press edges to seal.

Bring a large stockpot of water to a boil over Medium-High heat. Carefully lower destaye into water with a slotted spoon and boil for 2-3 minutes or until they begin to float on the water's surface. Lift out and set aside.

Once all destaye are cooked, heat remaining 1 Tbsp. butter in a large skillet over Medium-High heat. Add destaye and fry until brown on both sides, about 2 minutes per side.

MAKES ABOUT 24 DESTAYE

Per destaye: 91 calories, 4 g fat, 2 g saturated fat, 77 mg sodium, 12 g carbohydrates, 2 g protein.

SERVING SUGGESTIONS: Top with powdered sugar and whipped cream and serve

with a strong cup of coffee. If desired, add a scoop of ice cream with chocolate syrup.

VARIATION: To deep-fry destaye, heat about 2 inches of vegetable oil in a heavy skillet to a temperature of 350 degrees. Cook destaye (without boiling first) for 3 minutes or until golden brown. Drain on paper towels before serving.

GABON
FRIED BANANAS

EASY · COOK TIME: 10 MINUTES · ACTIVE PREP TIME: 10 MINUTES

With a name as simple as "fried bananas," this Gabonese dessert may seem very basic–but it's not. A number of sweet, sour, tangy, and bitter flavors are married in its combination of ingredients like orange juice, sour cream, coconut, and brown sugar. A blend of frying and baking creates a soft banana center with a crispy breaded shell.

4 bananas, peeled and cut lengthwise and crosswise into quarters
1 egg
Juice and zest of 1 small orange
¼ c. fresh breadcrumbs
2 Tbsp. finely grated coconut
2 Tbsp. finely ground peanuts
Oil, for frying
Cooking spray, for coating baking sheet
½ c. sour cream
¼ c. brown sugar

Whisk together egg, orange juice, and orange zest. In a separate bowl, combine breadcrumbs, coconut, and peanuts. Dip each banana slice in egg mixture, and then dredge in breadcrumb mixture.

Preheat oven to 350 degrees. Coat a large baking sheet with cooking spray. Heat about ¼-inch of oil in a heavy skillet over Medium-High heat. Fry bananas for about 5 minutes, turning once, until brown. Place bananas on baking sheet and bake for 5 minutes.

Divide bananas between 4 plates. Drizzle each serving with 2 Tbsp. sour cream, dust with 1 Tbsp. brown sugar, and serve.

MAKES 4 SERVINGS

Per serving: 389 calories, 24 g fat, 6 g saturated fat, 85 mg sodium, 43 g carbohydrates, 6 g protein.

VARIATIONS: While not traditional, whipped cream, chocolate syrup, or hazelnut spread may be used in place of sour cream.

THE GAMBIA
NAAN MBURU

HARD · COOK TIME: 20 MINUTES · ACTIVE PREP TIME: 20 MINUTES · INACTIVE PREP TIME: 50 MINUTES

Easter season in the Gambia is never complete without naan mburu, a fruity bread pudding with a soup-like consistency whose name means "drinking bread" and that is not widely eaten anywhere outside the tiny coastal country. Its signature flavor comes from the fruit of the baobab, a massive and unusual tree that is a symbol of Gambia and that can live to be over one thousand years old. Fresh baobab fruit is nearly impossible to find in the United States, but fortunately this recipe uses the powdered version, which has recently grown in popularity as a highly nutritious "superfood."

2 c. rice flour
1 qt. plus 1 c. warm water, divided
1 c. baobab powder

1 c. white sugar
1 tsp. vanilla extract
1 tsp. coconut extract
½ tsp. ground nutmeg

Combine rice flour and 1 c. water in a large microwave-safe bowl. Using your fingers, stir together water and rice flour until pebble-sized balls are formed. Cover with a damp paper towel and microwave on High for 5 minutes. Remove from microwave, stir, and repeat twice. The rice flour should form pebble-sized balls.

Cover rice balls with 1-½ c. water. Use your fingers to break up any clumps. Allow to stand for 30 minutes.

Place baobab powder in a large bowl and cover with 2 c. water. Stir until baobab powder is dissolved, and then allow to stand for 20 minutes. Use a fine sieve to strain any remaining large pieces from mixture and set aside.

Combine sugar and ½ c. water in a small saucepan. Cook over Medium heat until sugar is completely dissolved. Set aside to cool.

Stir rice ball mixture with a wooden spoon (it should have a milky appearance and consistency). Slowly stir in baobab mixture and syrup, followed by vanilla and coconut extracts and nutmeg. Refrigerate until ready to serve.

MAKES 4-6 SERVINGS

Per serving: 499 calories, 1 g fat, 0 g saturated fat, 0 mg sodium, 119 g carbohydrates, 4 g protein.

SERVING SUGGESTION: Serve chilled. Chopped bananas, apples, or other fruits may be added.

TIP: Pre-made rice balls, available in some African food stores, can be used in place of rice flour. They will need to be microwaved until completely soft (this can take an hour or longer).

GHANA
KELEWELE

EASY · COOK TIME: 15 MINUTES · ACTIVE PREP TIME: 5 MINUTES · INACTIVE PREP TIME: 20 MINUTES

Definitely one of the savorier dishes in this cookbook, kelewele is most often served as a side dish, an appetizer, or a late-night street food–but rarely as a dessert. Nonetheless, plantains of just the right ripeness will caramelize when fried, resulting in a perfect crispness and delightful sweetness even though this recipe uses no additional sugar.

4 ripe but firm sweet plantains, peeled and sliced on the bias (about 6 slices each)
2 Tbsp. dark rum (optional)
1-½ tsp. fresh ginger, grated
1 tsp. chili powder
1 tsp. ground nutmeg
½ tsp. salt
Peanut oil, for frying

Combine rum (if using), ginger, chili powder, nutmeg, and salt in a nonreactive bowl. Add sliced plantains, toss to coat, and marinate for 20 minutes.

Heat about ½-inch of oil in a heavy skillet over Medium-High heat. Fry plantain slices in batches for about 5 minutes, turning once, until golden brown. Remove from pan and set on paper towels to drain.

MAKES 4-6 SERVINGS

Per serving: 288 calories, 12 g fat, 2 g saturated fat, 244 mg sodium, 46 g carbohydrates, 2 g protein.

SERVING SUGGESTIONS: Dust with powdered sugar or garnish with whipped cream.

VARIATIONS: Some varieties of kelewele are more savory than sweet. Chopped onion, garlic, or bouillon may all be added to the marinade before frying. Aniseed, cinnamon, and cloves may also be used in a sweet version. The only essential ingredients are chili powder and ginger.

TIP: Make sure that the plantains used are not too ripe or unripe. Too-ripe plantains will absorb too much oil and will be greasy; too-unripe plantains will not caramelize properly and will taste bitter.

GUINEA
MANGO SPICE CAKE

EASY · COOK TIME: 1 HOUR, 25 MINUTES · ACTIVE PREP TIME: 10 MINUTES · INACTIVE PREP TIME: 15 MINUTES

As is the case with many African countries, desserts are not a major part of Guinean cuisine. But when desserts are served, local produce such as mangoes, sweet potatoes, and ginger take center stage. This African-style spice cake includes a number of ingredients that are native to Guinea and that figure widely into its cuisine.

2 large sweet potatoes, peeled and cut into cubes
Water, for boiling
2-¾ c. all-purpose flour, plus more for flouring pan
1 Tbsp. ground cinnamon
1 tsp. baking soda
1 tsp. salt
2 c. white sugar
1 c. canola oil, plus more for greasing pan
1 large ripe mango, peeled and mashed
4 eggs

1 Tbsp. fresh ginger, finely grated
1 tsp. vanilla extract
Powdered sugar, for serving

Bring a large saucepan of water to a boil. Add sweet potatoes and cook for 20 minutes or until soft. Drain and mash potatoes to form a puree. Set aside.

Sift together flour, cinnamon, baking soda, and salt. Using an electric mixer, beat sugar and oil together on Medium speed until combined. Add sweet potato puree, mango, eggs, ginger, and vanilla. Fold wet ingredients into dry ingredients and stir with a wooden spoon until a thick batter is formed.

Preheat oven to 325 degrees. Grease and flour a 10-inch springform pan. Pour batter into pan and bake for 1 hour or until cake is golden on top and a toothpick inserted in center of cake comes out clean. Remove cake from oven and allow to cool in pan for at least 15 minutes, then loosen wall belt and set on a wire rack until cooled completely. Dust with powdered sugar before slicing.

MAKES 10-12 SERVINGS

Per serving: 537 calories, 22 g fat, 2 g saturated fat, 359 mg sodium, 82 g carbohydrates, 6 g protein.

SERVING SUGGESTION: Serve with ginger or hibiscus tea.

VARIATIONS: Other tropical fruits, such as pineapple or papaya, may be used in place of mango. You will need about 1 c. of mashed fruit.

GUINEA-BISSAU
BOLO À MODA DA GUINÉ

EASY · COOK TIME: 1 HOUR, 30 MINUTES · ACTIVE PREP TIME: 10 MINUTES · INACTIVE PREP TIME: 20 MINUTES

This cake's Portuguese name means "Guinea-style cake." In the former Portuguese colony of Guinea-Bissau, it is by far the most popular dessert. Nearly every family has their own recipe for the bolo à moda. The one given here is at its most basic, but you will find that it is buttery, sweet, and delicious all on its own.

4 c. all-purpose flour, plus more for flouring pan
2 c. white sugar
2 c. butter, at room temperature, plus more for greasing pan
10 eggs
½ c. whole milk
1 Tbsp. baking powder
1 tsp. salt

Place the butter in the bowl of a stand mixer with a whisk attachment and beat on High speed until smooth. Add sugar and beat for 2 minutes longer or until pale and foamy. Reduce speed to Low and add eggs, one at a time, followed by milk. Pause to scrape down sides of bowl.

Sift together flour, baking powder, and salt. With stand mixer on Low speed, add flour mixture to bowl one spoonful at a time. Raise speed to Medium and continue to mix until a smooth batter is formed.

Preheat oven to 350 degrees. Grease and flour a 12-cup Bundt pan. Pour batter into pan and smooth the surface with a spatula. Bake for 1-½ hours or until a wooden skewer inserted in center of cake comes out mostly clean. Remove cake from oven and allow to cool in pan for at least 20 minutes, then invert from pan and set on a wire rack until cooled completely.

MAKES 16 SERVINGS

Per serving: 456 calories, 26 g fat, 16 g saturated fat, 354 mg sodium, 50 g carbohydrates, 7 g protein.

SERVING SUGGESTIONS: Top with whipped cream and berries or with chocolate or caramel syrup.

VARIATIONS: Add 1 Tbsp. vanilla extract and ½ tsp. ground nutmeg for additional flavor. Other spices and extracts may also be used.

TIP: This recipe makes a very large cake. For a smaller one, half all ingredients and reduce cooking time to 50 minutes.

IVORY COAST
GÂTEAU MOELLEUX À L'ANANAS

EASY · COOK TIME: 35 MINUTES · ACTIVE PREP TIME: 10 MINUTES · INACTIVE PREP TIME: 10 MINUTES

A gâteau moelleux ("soft cake") is a French one-layer sponge cake that is ideally very moist, fluffy, and, of course, soft. In France, a typical gâteau moelleux is made with chocolate and often has a fudgy liquid center. But in the former French colony of the Ivory Coast, this cake is more often made à l'ananas (with pineapple), of which it is a leading producer. Fans of pineapple upside-down cake, a Hawaiian invention, will enjoy its African counterpart.

1 fresh pineapple, peeled, cored, and cut into rings (about 1-¼ lb.)
¾ c. butter, divided, plus more for greasing pan
¾ c. dark brown sugar
¼ c. fresh pineapple juice
4 eggs

½ c. white sugar
1 tsp. vanilla extract
1-¼ c. all-purpose flour
1 tsp. baking soda

Grease the bottom and sides of a 9-inch round cake pan. Combine ¼ c. butter, dark brown sugar, and pineapple juice in a small saucepan. Heat over Medium-High heat until caramelized. Pour syrup in pan and swirl so that bottom is coated. Add pineapple rings in a single layer in bottom of pan over syrup.

Combine eggs, sugar, and vanilla extract in the bowl of a stand mixer with a whisk attachment and beat on Medium speed until pale and foamy. Sift together flour and baking soda and add to bowl a little at a time, mixing only until a moist batter is formed.

Preheat oven to 350 degrees. Pour batter in pan on top of pineapple and syrup layers and smooth the top with a spatula. Bake for 30 minutes or until cake is golden on top and a toothpick inserted in center of cake comes out clean. Allow cake to cool in pan for at least 10 minutes, then invert onto a serving dish so that pineapple side is facing upwards. Cut cake into slices and serve.

MAKES 8-10 SERVINGS

Per serving: 316 calories, 18 g fat, 10 g saturated fat, 280 mg sodium, 37 g carbohydrates, 4 g protein.

SERVING SUGGESTION: Top with whipped cream.

VARIATIONS: Pecans or other nuts may be added in pineapple layer. Add a small amount of rum to the syrup before pouring in pan. In the Ivory Coast cherries are not typically used in gâteau moelleux à l'ananas, as they are in American pineapple upside-down cake, but they may be included if desired.

TIP: One 20-oz. can of sliced pineapple rings may be used in place of fresh pineapple. Reserve the juice for making syrup.

KENYA
BISKUTI YA NAZI'

EASY · COOK TIME: 20 MINUTES · ACTIVE PREP TIME: 15 MINUTES

Biskuti ya nazi' (Swahili for "coconut biscuits") are very similar in appearance to macaroons, a type of cookie made from ground coconut or almonds that originated in medieval Europe. But they have many differences, most notably the lack of condensed milk as a sweetener and binder. Instead, oily ground cashews hold the ingredients together in these sticky treats.

2-½ c. finely shredded coconut
3 egg whites
1 c. white sugar
1 tsp. vanilla extract
1 c. cashew nuts, finely chopped
Butter, for greasing baking sheets

Add egg whites to the bowl of a stand mixer with a whisk attachment and beat on High speed until soft peaks form. Gradually add sugar and vanilla extract and continue to mix until glossy. Reduce speed to Low and slowly fold in coconut and cashews.

Preheat oven to 350 degrees. Grease two large baking sheets with butter. Use your hands to roll coconut mixture into 1-inch balls and place on baking sheets. Bake for 20 minutes or until golden brown. Remove cookies from oven and transfer to a wire rack to cool.

MAKES ABOUT 36 COOKIES

Per cookie: 60 calories, 3 g fat, 2 g saturated fat, 4 mg sodium, 8 g carbohydrates, 1 g protein.

SERVING SUGGESTION: Serve with coffee.

VARIATIONS: For chocolate-coated biskuti ya nazi', dip the cookies in melted chocolate and set on waxed paper to harden. Add ground ginger and cinnamon along with coconut and cashews for a different flavor. Substitute vanilla extract with almond extract if desired.

TIP: Biskuti ya nazi' can be stored for up to two days in a sealed container; they will not keep for longer.

LESOTHO
MAKOENVA

EASY · COOK TIME: 15 MINUTES · ACTIVE PREP TIME: 10 MINUTES · INACTIVE PREP TIME: 1 HOUR, 15 MINUTES

Makoenva is one of many African desserts based on fried dough, but it is uniquely reminiscent of the European cinnamon roll. This recipe may have originated with the Cape Malays, an ethnic group of Indonesian heritage who form a large community in Lesotho. Cinnamon and other spices have a significant place in Cape Malay cuisine.

2 c. all-purpose flour
1 c. lukewarm water
½ c. plus 1 Tbsp. white sugar, divided
2 tsp. active dry yeast
2 tsp. vegetable oil, plus more for frying
1 tsp. salt
¼ c. raisins
2 Tbsp. ground cinnamon

Combine water, 1 Tbsp. sugar, and yeast and whisk together. Cover and let stand for 15 minutes.

Sift together flour and salt and add to the bowl of a stand mixer with a dough hook attachment. Add yeast mixture and oil and mix on Low speed to form a crumbly dough. Cover bowl with plastic wrap and allow to stand for 1 hour or until dough is doubled in size. Add raisins and knead with your hands until fully incorporated.

Heat about 1 inch of oil in a heavy skillet to a temperature of 350 degrees. Pull dough into medium-sized pieces (they do not need to have any sort of regular shape or size; it is a matter of preference). Fry dough pieces in small batches for 2-3 minutes, turning them over halfway through. Remove from pan and set on paper towels to drain.

Mix together ½ c. sugar and cinnamon. While makoenva are still warm, roll them in cinnamon sugar to coat.

MAKES ABOUT 24 MAKOENVA

Per makoenva: 141 calories, 9 g fat, 2 g saturated fat, 98 mg sodium, 14 g carbohydrates, 1 g protein.

SERVING SUGGESTIONS: Serve with hot tea.

VARIATIONS: Ground ginger, cardamom, or nutmeg may be added to the dough if desired, as well as lemon, orange, or banana extracts.

LIBERIA
PAPAYA PIE

MEDIUM · COOK TIME: 55 MINUTES · ACTIVE PREP TIME: 15 MINUTES · INACTIVE PREP TIME: 30 MINUTES

While many African countries adopted European ingredients and cooking methods, Liberia might be the only one whose cuisine shows a significant American influence. Liberia was established in 1822 as a place where formerly enslaved people could resettle, and its first citizens brought their culinary knowledge to their new home.

This includes a baking tradition that is found nowhere else in West Africa.

1-½ c. all-purpose flour
1-¼ tsp. plus 1 dash salt
½ c. cold butter, cut into cubes
¼ c. cold water
2 c. half-and-half
1 c. white sugar, divided
¼ c. cornstarch
3 eggs, separated
1 c. mashed ripe papaya

Sift together flour and 1-¼ tsp. salt in a large bowl. Add butter and mix with two knives until butter pieces are mostly chopped and mixture is crumbly. Add water and stir to form a firm dough. Knead dough until smooth, then wrap in plastic wrap and refrigerate for 15 minutes.

Turn dough onto a floured surface and roll into a 12-inch circle of even thickness. Press dough circle into a 9-inch pie pan and prick several times with the tines of a fork. Cover with aluminum foil and place in freezer for 15 minutes longer.

Preheat oven to 375 degrees. Pull back foil, fill the pie shell with pie weights (or dry beans), replace foil, and bake for 20 minutes. Remove weights and foil and bake for 15 more minutes. Set aside to cool.

While pie shell is cooling, prepare filling. Pour half-and-half into a large pot and slowly bring to a boil over Medium heat; reduce heat to Low. In a separate bowl, combine egg yolks and ¾ c. sugar. Using an electric mixer, beat on Medium speed until pale and foamy, gradually adding cornstarch. Slowly add egg yolk mixture to milk and cook over Medium heat, stirring constantly, until a thick custard is formed. Pour custard into pie shell and smooth surface with a spatula.

Preheat oven to 350 degrees. Using an electric mixer, beat egg whites on High speed until opaque. Add ¼ c. sugar, one spoonful at a time, while continuing to beat egg whites until meringue is very stiff and glossy. Spread meringue on top of custard and cook for 10 minutes or until top of meringue is light brown. Allow to cool before slicing.

MAKES 8-10 SERVINGS

Per serving: 340 calories, 18 g fat, 11 g saturated fat, 378 mg sodium, 41 g carbohydrates, 5 g protein.

SERVING SUGGESTION: Serve at room temperature or chilled.

VARIATIONS: To top the pie, 1 c. chopped pecans can be used in place of meringue. Use a combination of mashed papaya and banana instead of papaya alone.

TIP: To reduce preparation time, a prepared pie shell may be used.

MADAGASCAR
KOBA AKONDRO

MEDIUM · COOK TIME: 35 MINUTES · ACTIVE PREP TIME: 20 MINUTES

Koba, a word meaning "dough" in the Malagasy language, is so popular in Madagascar that many of the island's residents eat it every day. It can be bought nearly everywhere, from gas stations to street carts. Koba akondro (banana dough) is one of many varieties of koba; others are made with sweet potato, cassava, or coconut. Vanilla, however, is not optional; it is by far Madagascar's most important natural resource, as it is the world's largest producer of this precious spice.

3 very ripe bananas, peeled and mashed
1 large banana leaf, for steaming
Water, for boiling and steaming
¾ c. brown sugar
1 c. peanuts, roasted and chopped, divided
1 Tbsp. vanilla extract
2 tsp. honey
1 c. glutinous rice flour

Cut banana leaf into four equal-sized, roughly square-shaped pieces. Bring a large pot of water to a boil. Place the banana leaf pieces in the water and boil for 5 minutes or until soft. (This step will make the banana leaf less brittle and easier to fold.) Pat leaves dry with paper towels and set aside.

Place ¾ c. of peanuts in a blender or food processor and pulse until finely ground. Using a wooden spoon, stir together ground peanuts, bananas, vanilla extract, honey, and brown sugar. Gradually fold in rice flour and stir until dough is moist and smooth.

Divide dough into four portions. Spread half of one portion of dough in the center of each banana leaf piece. Top with 1 Tbsp. peanuts, followed by other half of dough portion. Fold each banana leaf to encase the dough and tie with twine or raffia.

Boil a large pot of water and set a large steamer basket over the pot. Place banana leaf packets in steamer. Cover and steam for 30 minutes. Remove packets from steamer and allow to cool slightly before opening.

MAKES 4 SERVINGS

Per serving: 551 calories, 19 g fat, 3 g saturated fat, 15 mg sodium, 89 g carbohydrates, 13 g protein.

VARIATION: Replace mashed banana with 1 c. of cooked, mashed sweet potato.

TIP: While banana leaves are highly recommended (they add flavor as well as authenticity to this dessert), wax paper can be used instead.

MALAWI MBATATA

EASY · COOK TIME: 50 MINUTES · ACTIVE PREP TIME: 15 MINUTES · INACTIVE PREP TIME: 1 HOUR, 10 MINUTES

The sweet potato, which made its way to eastern Africa from southeast Asia in the sixteenth century, has since become a staple food in Malawi. In a country where meat is often scarce and where nutrient-low crops such as maize and millet form a large part of the typical diet, sweet potatoes are a valuable source of vitamins, minerals, and fiber. Mbatata have less sugar than other types of cookies, but they get a punch of sweetness from raisins as well as sweet potatoes.

2 medium sweet potatoes, peeled and chopped
Water, for boiling
½ c. brown sugar
¼ c. whole milk
1 egg
¼ c. butter, melted, plus more for greasing baking sheets
1-¼ c. all-purpose flour, plus more for flouring surface
2 tsp. baking powder
½ tsp. salt
1 tsp. ground cinnamon, plus more for sprinkling
½ c. raisins

Bring a large saucepan of water to a boil. Add sweet potatoes and cook for 20 minutes or until soft. Drain and mash potatoes. Set aside.

Combine sweet potatoes, brown sugar, milk, and butter in the bowl of a stand mixer with a paddle attachment and mix on Medium speed until smooth. Sift together flour, baking powder, and salt. Add egg to sweet potato mixture, followed by flour mixture (one spoonful at a time), cinnamon, and raisins. Cover with plastic wrap and refrigerate for 1 hour.

Preheat oven to 375 degrees. Grease two large baking sheets. On a floured surface, knead dough until smooth and flexible. Roll out the dough to a ½-inch thickness. Use cookie cutters to cut out shapes from the dough. Place cookies on baking sheets and bake for 15 minutes. Sprinkle with cinnamon and allow to cool on baking sheets for 5 minutes before transferring to wire racks to finish cooling.

MAKES ABOUT 40 COOKIES

Per cookie: 46 calories, 2 g fat, 1 g saturated fat, 43 mg sodium, 8 g carbohydrates, 1 g protein.

SERVING SUGGESTION: Serve with a glass of cold milk.

TIP: Sweet potatoes that are very ripe and slightly soft will yield cookies that are sweeter and have a deeper sweet potato flavor.

MALI
MENI-MENIYONG

MEDIUM · COOK TIME: 25 MINUTES · ACTIVE PREP TIME: 5 MINUTES · INACTIVE PREP TIME: 30 MINUTES

While after-dinner desserts are nearly unheard of in Mali, these crunchy and extremely sweet sesame seed snacks are found almost everywhere and eaten throughout the day. In Mali, the daily tea ceremony is an important social event that is taken very seriously (even if it's being held on the front steps or sidewalk outside the host's home). Meni-meniyong is an excellent accompaniment for Chinese green tea, most Malians' drink of choice.

1 c. sesame seeds
1 c. honey
¼ c. butter, plus more for greasing pan

¼ tsp. salt

Preheat oven to 450 degrees. Spread sesame seeds in an even layer on a nonstick baking sheet. Toast in the oven for 10 minutes, shaking baking sheet halfway through, or until seeds are light brown. Set aside.

Combine honey and butter in a medium saucepan and bring to a boil over Medium heat. Reduce heat to Low and cook for 10-15 minutes or until syrup is a deep brown color and its temperature reaches 235 degrees (use a candy thermometer to monitor temperature). Remove from heat and fold in sesame seeds and salt.

Grease an 8 x 8-inch baking pan. Pour sesame seed mixture into pan and spread in an even layer. Use a small spatula to smooth the surface. Use a sharp knife to score the surface, dividing the mixture into 1-inch by 3-inch strips. (It is important to complete this step as quickly as possible, as the mixture will not be pliable once it hardens, and it will be difficult to break the meni-meniyong into pieces.)

Once the meni-meniyong has hardened beyond toffee stage, which should take about 30 minutes, remove it from the pan by inverting the pan. Break the candy along the score lines to serve.

MAKES ABOUT 20 PIECES

Per piece: 113 calories, 6 g fat, 2 g saturated fat, 49 mg sodium, 16 g carbohydrates, 1 g protein.

SERVING SUGGESTION: Serve with sweetened, mint-flavored hot green tea.

VARIATIONS: Sugar can be used in place of honey (this is frequently done in Mali when making less expensive meni-meniyong). For a softer candy, reduce cooking time for caramel syrup by half. Meni-meniyong can also be poured into small candy molds to harden.

TIP: To test the doneness of the caramel syrup without using a candy thermometer, place a small drop of the syrup on a cold saucer. When it cools, the drop should be hard enough to keep its shape when squeezed between the fingers but soft enough to chew easily.

MAURITANIA
LAKH

EASY · COOK TIME: 35 MINUTES · ACTIVE PREP TIME: 10 MINUTES

With Morocco to the north and Senegal to the south, Mauritania represents a bridge between the cultures of North and West Africa. Millet is a common cereal grain in West African cuisine, while the yogurt dressing used in lakh is a North African contribution. Sweet enough to eat as a dessert, lakh is also a popular breakfast food in Mauritania, especially during the Eid al-Fitr holiday.

3 c. plain yogurt
½ c. pineapple juice
¼ c. plus 2 Tbsp. evaporated milk
½ tsp. vanilla extract
¼ tsp. ground nutmeg
¼ c. plus 2 Tbsp. white sugar, divided
2 c. millet
2 qt. water
¼ tsp. salt
¼ c. butter, at room temperature
¾ c. raisins

Whisk together yogurt and pineapple juice in a medium bowl until smooth. Add evaporated milk, vanilla extract, and nutmeg. Gradually whisk in ¼ c. sugar, one spoonful at a time. Cover with plastic wrap and refrigerate until ready to use.

Bring water and salt to a boil in a large saucepan. Add millet and reduce heat to Medium-Low. Cover with lid ajar and simmer for 35 minutes or until most of the liquid is evaporated and porridge is thick and creamy. Add butter and stir until completely melted.

Divide porridge between 6 serving bowls. Top each serving with 2 Tbsp. raisins and 1 tsp. sugar, followed by an equal amount of yogurt mixture.

MAKES 6 SERVINGS

Per serving: 540 calories, 13 g fat, 7 g saturated fat, 260 mg sodium, 88 g carbohydrates, 16 g protein.

SERVING SUGGESTION: Serve with sliced bananas and apples or dried fruit.

VARIATION: A popular protein-rich variation of lakh is made from peanut butter and baobab juice. Place 1 c. baobab powder in a large bowl and cover with 2 c. water. Stir until baobab is dissolved, and then allow to stand for 20 minutes. Use a fine sieve to strain mixture. Whisk together juice and 1 c. creamy peanut butter, and use in place of yogurt and pineapple juice in recipe. This variation is typically eaten as a main course rather than as a dessert.

MAURITIUS NAPOLITAINES

MEDIUM · COOK TIME: 20 MINUTES · ACTIVE PREP TIME: 25 MINUTES · INACTIVE PREP TIME: 30 MINUTES

By 1721, the year that the French first invaded Mauritius, sugar had already been introduced to the islands from Indonesia by the Dutch colonizers that came before them. At some point after that, the first napolitanas (or "French pastries," as some call them) were made. No one is certain how these jam-filled shortbread cookies originated, how they became associated with Mauritius, or why they are named after the Italian city of Naples. Today they are handed out to Mauritian schoolchildren every year on Independence Day (March 21) but can be purchased from roadside stands and street vendors year-round.

2 c. all-purpose flour, plus more for flouring surface
¾ c. butter, at room temperature

2 Tbsp. light rum
½ c. raspberry jam
2 c. powdered sugar
¼ c. whole milk, at room temperature
2 tsp. vanilla extract
Red or pink food coloring, as needed

Use a pastry blender to cut butter into flour. Sprinkle rum over mixture and knead together with your hands until a crumbly dough is formed. Cover with plastic wrap and refrigerate for 30 minutes.

Preheat oven to 350 degrees. Grease two large baking sheets. Roll out dough on a floured surface to a ¼-inch thickness. Using a 2-inch round cookie cutter, cut out circles from dough and place on baking sheets. Bake for 20 minutes or until fully cooked but not brown (firmly pressing the cookies should not leave an indentation). Remove from oven and allow to cool on a wire rack.

Once the cookies are completely cooled, spread 1 tsp. of jam over the surface of one cookie. Top with a second cookie and press together to form a sandwich. Repeat with remaining cookies. Set napolitaines on a wire rack with at least 1-2 inches between them and with a rimmed tray underneath.

To make icing, whisk together powdered sugar, milk, and vanilla extract until smooth and slightly runny (you may need to add more or less milk to achieve the correct consistency). Add a few drops of food coloring until the desired shade of pink is reached (Mauritian napolitaines are typically a very bright pink). Pour one large spoonful of icing on top of each napolitaine, allowing it to drip over the top and to cover the sides. Spread gently to completely cover the napolitaine's top and sides. Allow to stand until the icing is completely hardened before serving.

MAKES ABOUT 15 NAPOLITAINES

Per napolitaine: 239 calories, 10 g fat, 6 g saturated fat, 68 mg sodium, 36 g carbohydrates, 2 g protein.

SERVING SUGGESTION: Top with sprinkles or other decorations before icing hardens if desired, and serve with hot vanilla tea.

VARIATIONS: Other flavors of jam, such as strawberry, may be used instead of raspberry. While Mauritian napolitaines are almost always round, they can be made in other shapes; heart-shaped napolitaines are great for Valentine's Day.

MOZAMBIQUE
BOLO POLANA

EASY · COOK TIME: 1 HOUR, 20 MINUTES · ACTIVE PREP TIME: 10 MINUTES · INACTIVE PREP TIME: 15 MINUTES

Maputo, the capital city of Mozambique, is a jewel that is still off the radar for most tourists. The upscale neighborhood of Polana is one of Maputo's most exciting areas, with elegant hotels, boutiques, and restaurants and Modernist architecture galore. It lends its name to the bolo Polana, a Portuguese-style potato cake that includes typical Mozambican ingredients such as cashews and vanilla.

1 large potato, peeled and cut into large pieces
Water, for boiling
¾ c. butter, at room temperature, plus more for greasing pan
½ c. plus 2 Tbsp. white sugar
4 eggs, separated
1 c. finely ground cashews
¼ c. whole milk
Juice and zest of 1 lemon
2 tsp. vanilla extract
½ tsp. salt
1-½ c. all-purpose flour, plus more for flouring pan
Powdered sugar, for dusting

Bring a medium saucepan of water to a boil over High heat. Add potato pieces, reduce heat to Medium-Low, and simmer for 20 minutes or until potato is soft. Drain and mash potato and set aside.

Add butter and sugar to the bowl of a stand mixer with whisk attachment and beat on Medium speed until pale and foamy. Gradually add egg yolks, cashews, milk, lemon juice, lemon zest, vanilla extract, and salt and continue to mix until smooth. Transfer batter to a large bowl and use a wooden spoon to fold in flour and potato.

Add egg whites to the bowl of the stand mixer and mix on Medium speed until foamy. Gently fold egg whites into batter with a wooden spoon.

Preheat oven to 350 degrees. Grease and flour an 8-inch round springform pan. Pour batter into pan and bake for 1 hour or until golden brown on top and a toothpick inserted in center of cake comes out clean. Allow cake to cool in pan for 15 minutes, then dust the top of the cake with powdered sugar, loosen wall belt, and transfer to a wire rack to finish cooling.

MAKES 8-10 SERVINGS

Per serving: 370 calories, 25 g fat, 12 g saturated fat, 272 mg sodium, 31 g carbohydrates, 7 g protein.

SERVING SUGGESTION: Serve with coffee or dark rum.

VARIATION: Orange or lime juice and zest may be used in place of lemon juice and zest for a different flavor.

NAMIBIA
KOEKSISTERS

MEDIUM · COOK TIME: 25 MINUTES · ACTIVE PREP TIME: 35 MINUTES · INACTIVE PREP TIME: 30 MINUTES

Upon first inspection, it's easy to mistake a koeksister for an American pastry such as a glazed cruller or "tiger tail." But these fried Afrikaner confections pack a spicy flavor punch unlike any donuts you'll find in the United States. Dunking the fried pastry in cold syrup while still hot locks in its crisp and crunchy crust while keeping its inside soft. Interestingly, the word koeksister comes from the Dutch words for "cake sizzle," a reference to the sound made when the pastries are fried in hot oil.

2-½ c. cake flour
2 c. plus 2 Tbsp. white sugar, divided
2-½ tsp. baking powder
1 tsp. salt, divided
½ c. whole milk
1 egg
2 Tbsp. butter, melted
1 c. water
1 Tbsp. fresh ginger, grated
1-½ tsp. cream of tartar
Juice of 1 small lemon
1 stick cinnamon
3 cardamom pods, crushed
Vegetable oil, for frying

Sift together flour, 2 Tbsp. sugar, baking powder, and ¾ tsp. salt. Place in the bowl of a stand mixer with a dough hook attachment. Add milk, egg, and butter while mixing on Low and continue to mix until combined. Cover with plastic wrap and allow to stand for 30 minutes.

Combine 2 c. sugar, water, ginger, cream of tartar, ¼ tsp. salt, lemon juice, cinnamon stick, and cardamom pods in a medium saucepan. Bring to a boil, reduce heat to Low, and simmer for 10 minutes. Remove syrup from heat and refrigerate until ready to use.

On a floured surface, roll out dough to a ½-inch thickness. Use a pizza cutter or a sharp knife to cut the dough lengthwise into 1-inch strips (there should be about 12-15 strips of equal length). Cut each strip into thirds. Pinch the three small strips together at one end and braid together, alternately overlapping the left and right strands with the center strand. The end result should be a tightly braided loaf about 5 to 6 inches long. Repeat with the remaining dough.

Heat about 2 inches of oil in a heavy skillet to a temperature of 350 degrees. Fry koeksisters in small batches of 2 or 3 at a time for 3-4 minutes, turning them over halfway through. When each batch is finished frying, remove each koeksister with a slotted spoon and submerge in cold syrup, turning to make sure the entire surface is coated, and allow to soak in syrup for at least 2 minutes. Set koeksisters on a wire rack to cool before serving.

MAKES 12-15 KOEKSISTERS

Per koeksister: 314 calories, 17 g fat, 4 g saturated fat, 175 mg sodium, 41 g carbohydrates, 2 g protein.

SERVING SUGGESTION: Serve with coffee or tea. If desired, sprinkle with coconut flakes or cinnamon sugar after soaking in syrup.

VARIATIONS: Drizzle koeksisters in honey instead of syrup after frying. Aniseed or allspice may be used in place of ginger in syrup.

NIGER
SHUKU SHUKU

EASY · COOK TIME: 15 MINUTES · ACTIVE PREP TIME: 15 MINUTES

In West Africa, fresh coconut milk is a culinary staple. After the milk is harvested from the fruit, a large amount of "chaff" is left behind. This dry coconut pulp never goes to waste and is often used in place of flour in baked goods. The macaroon-like shuku shuku is one of the many Nigerien dishes that can be made from repurposed coconut chaff.

4 c. unsweetened coconut, finely grated
Butter, for greasing baking sheet
8 egg yolks

½ c. powdered sugar
2 tsp. vanilla extract
¾ c. self-rising flour

Whisk together egg yolks, powdered sugar, and vanilla extract. Fold into coconut and stir until moist.

Preheat oven to 350 degrees. Grease a large baking sheet. Form coconut mixture into balls, each about 2 Tbsp. Roll balls in flour to coat and set on baking sheet. Bake for 15 minutes or until light brown. Set on a wire rack and allow to cool slightly before serving.

MAKES ABOUT 30 SHUKU SHUKU

Per shuku shuku: 72 calories, 5 g fat, 4 g saturated fat, 4 mg sodium, 6 g carbohydrates, 1 g protein.

SERVING SUGGESTION: Serve warm, at room temperature, or chilled.

VARIATION: Nutmeg, cinnamon, or other spices can be added to shuku shuku.

NIGERIA
NIGERIAN WEDDING CAKE

MEDIUM · COOK TIME: 45 MINUTES · ACTIVE PREP TIME: 30 MINUTES · INACTIVE PREP TIME: 15 MINUTES

Those who are accustomed to seeing towering multi-layered white cakes at American weddings may find the Nigerian wedding cake a bit out of place. Even though many Nigerian couples choose festive Western-style cakes for their wedding celebrations today, this fruity wedding cake is traditionally served with no icing at all. But its rich texture and complex flavors make it suitable for even the most special events, and no Nigerian wedding reception is complete without a long line of guests waiting for a decadent slice.

4 c. all-purpose flour, plus more for flouring pans
1 Tbsp. baking powder
½ tsp. salt
½ tsp. ground nutmeg
1 c. raisins
3-½ c. white sugar
2 c. butter, at room temperature, plus more for greasing pans
10 eggs
¼ c. brandy
¼ c. burnt sugar syrup (see Tip)
2 Tbsp. dark molasses
1 tsp. vanilla extract
1 tsp. butterscotch extract
Buttercream frosting (optional; see recipe below)

Sift together flour, baking powder, salt, and nutmeg. Fold raisins into flour mixture and set aside.

Combine sugar and butter in the bowl of a stand mixer with a paddle attachment and mix at Medium speed for 5 minutes or until mixture is pale and fluffy. Add the eggs one at a time. Increase speed to High and mix for 2 minutes longer. Decrease speed to Low and gradually add brandy, burnt sugar syrup, molasses, and vanilla and butterscotch extracts. With mixer still on Low speed, add the flour mixture one spoonful at a time and mix only until smooth.

Preheat oven to 350 degrees. Grease and flour two 9-inch cake pans. Pour batter into pans and bake for 45 minutes or until cakes are golden on top and a toothpick inserted in center of cake comes out clean. Allow cakes to cool in pans for 15 minutes before inverting onto a wire rack to continue cooling.

If you are icing the cake, wait until the cakes are completely cooled to apply frosting. Spread frosting in an even layer on top of one cake, top with the second cake, and spread more frosting to cover sides and top.

For buttercream frosting:
1 c. butter, at room temperature
4 c. powdered sugar
¼ c. whole milk
1 tsp. vanilla extract
½ tsp. meringue powder
Food coloring, as needed (optional)

Using an electric mixer, whip butter on Medium speed until smooth and airy. Add powdered sugar 1 c. at a time, followed by milk, vanilla extract, meringue powder, and food coloring (if using).

Once all ingredients have been combined, increase speed to High and mix for about 1 minute longer. Refrigerate frosting until ready to use.

MAKES 10-12 SERVINGS

Per serving: 1124 calories, 55 g fat, 33 g saturated fat, 526 mg sodium, 150 g carbohydrates, 11 g protein.

SERVING SUGGESTION: Cake can be further decorated with marzipan or fondant if desired. If not using frosting, dust with powdered sugar before serving.

VARIATIONS: For a heavier brandy flavor, poke holes in surface of cake and brush with brandy while cake is cooling. Other dried fruits such as cherries can be used in place of or in addition to raisins. For a lighter-colored cake, replace burnt sugar syrup and molasses with light corn syrup.

TIP: Burnt sugar syrup, also called browning, can be difficult to find in prepared form. To make your own, heat 1 c. brown sugar in a small saucepan over Medium-High heat until completely melted, stirring constantly. Remove from heat, stir in 1 c. boiling water, and set aside until cooled. Syrup will thicken upon standing.

RWANDA
CHOCOLATE MANDAZI

MEDIUM · COOK TIME: 15 MINUTES · ACTIVE PREP TIME: 15 MINUTES · INACTIVE PREP TIME: 30 MINUTES

Originating on the Swahili Coast of eastern Africa, mandazi have spread throughout the African continent to become one of its most popular dishes, eaten in many forms. They are similar to American doughnuts, but not quite as sweet, usually not glazed, and with a wider range of spices and other seasonings. The variations on these tasty treats are endless; the version included here is made with cocoa powder.

3 c. all-purpose flour, plus more for flouring surface
¼ c. unsweetened cocoa powder
1 Tbsp. plus 1-½ tsp. baking powder
1 tsp. ground cinnamon
1 tsp. ground allspice
¾ tsp. salt
½ tsp. ground cardamom
¼ tsp. ground nutmeg
½ c. brown sugar
¼ c. butter, at room temperature
1 c. buttermilk
1 tsp. vanilla extract
Oil, for frying

Sift together flour, cocoa powder, baking powder, cinnamon, allspice, salt, cardamom, and nutmeg. Add brown sugar and butter and use a pastry blender to combine until a crumbly dough is formed. Add buttermilk and vanilla extract and knead with your hands until smooth and firm. Cover dough with plastic wrap and allow to rest for 30 minutes.

Roll out dough on a floured surface to a ¼-inch thickness. Use a sharp knife to cut dough into triangles (about 2-3 inches on each side).

Heat about 2 inches of oil in a heavy skillet to a temperature of 350 degrees. Fry mandazi in batches for 3-4 minutes, turning once, until crisp. Remove from pan and set on paper towels to drain.

MAKES ABOUT 18 PASTRIES

Per pastry: 231 calories, 15 g fat, 4 g saturated fat, 131 mg sodium, 21 g carbohydrates, 3 g protein.

SERVING SUGGESTION: Dust with powdered sugar and serve with tea.

VARIATIONS: For a different flavor, replace cocoa powder with an equal amount of ground peanuts or almonds, or replace buttermilk with full-fat coconut milk.

SÃO TOME AND PRINCIPE SONHOS DE BANANA

MEDIUM · COOK TIME: 20 MINUTES · ACTIVE PREP TIME: 10 MINUTES

The name of this dessert is Portuguese for "banana dreams," a name that most people who have tried it can understand. These banana-filled fritters, which are also popular in Brazil, have their origin in the smallest Portuguese-speaking country in the world, São Tome and Principe, where mashed bananas form a major component of both sweet and savory dishes.

4 ripe bananas, peeled and coarsely mashed
1-½ c. all-purpose flour
2 Tbsp. white sugar
1 tsp. ground cinnamon
½ c. whole milk

1 egg
½ tsp. vanilla extract
Oil, for frying

Fold together bananas, flour, sugar, and cinnamon. Whisk together milk, egg, and vanilla extract and stir into banana mixture.

Heat about 2 inches of oil in a heavy skillet to a temperature of 350 degrees. Carefully drop large spoonfuls of banana mixture into oil and fry for about 5 minutes, turning once, until fritters are crisp and golden brown. (Batter will settle at bottom of oil at first, but will rise to the surface as it cooks.) Lift from pan with a slotted spoon and set on paper towels to drain. Repeat with remaining batter. Allow to cool before serving.

MAKES 6-8 SERVINGS

Per serving: 380 calories, 29 g fat, 6 g saturated fat, 15 mg sodium, 29 g carbohydrates, 3 g protein.

SERVING SUGGESTIONS: Dust with powdered sugar, coat with cinnamon sugar, or drizzle with honey to serve.

VARIATIONS: Dip fritters in chocolate or hazelnut spread after frying. Add the zest and juice of 1 small orange to batter.

SENEGAL
CINQ CENTIMES

EASY · COOK TIME: 10 MINUTES · ACTIVE PREP TIME: 15 MINUTES · INACTIVE PREP TIME: 2 HOURS

It's not known for certain whether these Senegalese cookies got their name ("five cents" in French) from their original price or from their shape and size, which resemble a small coin. More than any other West African country, Senegal played a huge role in the global peanut industry while still under French colonial control. While that role has diminished considerably, these peanut butter sugar cookies are still as common as street vendors in Senegal.

3-¼ c. all-purpose flour, plus more for flouring surface
½ tsp. salt
½ tsp. ground cinnamon
¼ tsp. ground nutmeg
1 c. butter, at room temperature, plus more for greasing baking sheets
1 c. white sugar
2 eggs
1-½ c. smooth peanut butter
Chopped peanuts, for garnish

Sift together flour, salt, cinnamon, and nutmeg. Combine butter and sugar in the bowl of a stand mixer with a whisk attachment and mix at Medium speed until pale and fluffy. Add eggs one at a time. Gradually add flour mixture and continue to mix just until combined.

Roll dough onto a lightly floured surface to make a log about 12 inches in length. Wrap dough log in plastic wrap and refrigerate for 2 hours.

Preheat oven to 325 degrees. Grease two large baking sheets. Using a sharp knife, cut dough log into ½-inch thick slices and place slices in rows on baking sheets. Bake for 10 minutes or until light brown on top. Allow cookies to cool on wire racks.

Once cookies are completely cooled, spread 1 Tbsp. peanut butter on top of each cookie. Sprinkle with chopped peanuts and serve.

MAKES ABOUT 24 COOKIES

Per cookie: 225 calories, 14 g fat, 6 g saturated fat, 112 mg sodium, 23 g carbohydrates, 5 g protein.

VARIATIONS: Replace some of the butter with sour cream. Add 2 tsp. vanilla extract in place of cinnamon and nutmeg.

SEYCHELLES
NOUGA KOKO FANNEN

MEDIUM · COOK TIME: 15 MINUTES · ACTIVE PREP TIME: 20 MINUTES

One of the world's most ancient and popular types of candy, nougat comes in many forms. Most nougat is made using egg white and is lightweight and chewy, but nougat without egg white is denser and crunchier. One example of this type is nouga koko fannen (coconut nougat), which is considerably different from the Western conception of nougat. Like all nougats, nouga koko fannen incorporates nuts (or coconut, rather) and lots of sugar. Using different colors of food coloring to make these candies can result in a striking presentation.

4 c. fresh coconut, coarsely grated (see Tip)
2 c. white sugar
¾ c. water
Juice and zest of 1 orange
¼ tsp. vanilla extract
1 dash nutmeg
Food coloring, as needed (optional)

Combine sugar, water, and orange juice in a large saucepan and bring to a boil. Reduce heat to Medium and add coconut. Continue to cook for 15 minutes or until all liquid has evaporated. Remove from heat and stir in orange zest, vanilla extract, nutmeg, and food coloring (if using).

Use a 2-Tbsp. disher scoop to form small balls of coconut mixture. Place balls on a sheet of wax paper, working quickly so that the coconut mixture does not cool before you are finished (it will harden when cooled). Allow nougat to cool completely before serving.

MAKES 10 SERVINGS

Per serving: 264 calories, 11 g fat, 10 g saturated fat, 7 mg sodium, 45 g carbohydrates,

1 g protein.

VARIATIONS: Replace half of the coconut in this recipe with ripe mashed banana. Add banana to syrup and stir to combine before adding coconut.

TIP: To remove the flesh from a fresh coconut, use a hammer to crack the coconut's shell, rotating it as you strike, so that it breaks into pieces. To make this process easier, begin by drilling a hole in the coconut to drain the milk, then heat the whole coconut in a preheated oven at 475 degrees for 10 minutes to soften its shell. Carefully carve the white flesh from the shell in large pieces using a blunt knife, plunge the flesh into an ice water bath to stop the cooking process, and pat dry. Grate the coconut using the large holes of a box grater. For this recipe, you will need one large or 1-½ medium-sized coconuts.

SIERRA LEONE GINGER CAKE

EASY · COOK TIME: 45 MINUTES · ACTIVE PREP TIME: 10 MINUTES · INACTIVE PREP TIME: 10 MINUTES

Ginger is used profusely in Sierra Leonean cuisine, and it distinguishes it from that of other West African countries. After being interrupted by many years of civil war, the country's ginger trade aided in its economic and social recovery following that difficult era in its history. Ginger cake is not the only recipe using that ingredient that Sierra Leone is known for; ginger beer, a homemade non-alcoholic beverage, is found on the menu at nearly every meal.

1-½ c. all-purpose flour, plus more for flouring pan
1 tsp. baking powder
½ tsp. ground cinnamon
¼ tsp. salt

1 dash cayenne pepper

1 c. butter, at room temperature, plus more for greasing pan

1 c. brown sugar

2 Tbsp. fresh ginger, finely grated

2 eggs

½ c. whole milk

½ tsp. vanilla extract

Sift together flour, baking powder, cinnamon, salt, and cayenne pepper. Combine butter and brown sugar in the bowl of a stand mixer with a whisk attachment and mix on Medium speed until fluffy and lighter in color. Add eggs, fresh ginger, and vanilla extract. Gradually add flour mixture, one spoonful at a time, and mix just until a smooth batter is formed.

Preheat oven to 350 degrees. Grease and flour a standard-size loaf pan. Pour batter into pan and bake for 45 minutes or until a toothpick inserted in center of cake comes out clean. Let cool in pan for 10 minutes before transferring to a wire rack to finish cooling.

MAKES 6 SERVINGS

Per serving: 481 calories, 33 g fat, 20 g saturated fat, 352 mg sodium, 43 g carbohydrates, 5 g protein.

SERVING SUGGESTIONS: Dust with powdered sugar and sprinkle with chopped candied ginger to serve.

TIP: For a larger cake, double all ingredients and bake in a greased and floured 12-cup Bundt pan.

SOMALIA
DOOLSHO

EASY · COOK TIME: 35 MINUTES · ACTIVE PREP TIME: 15 MINUTES

Doolsho is a Somali sponge cake that closely resembles angel food cake, but with a touch of lemon and cardamom. While this light cake may seem simple and easy to make, in Somalia it is frequently baked over an open fire instead of in an oven, which makes for a rather unpredictable baking process. When prepared perfectly, doolsho has an airy texture that is unmatched by any African cake.

1 c. all-purpose flour, plus more for flouring pan
½ c. cornstarch
1 tsp. ground cardamom
¼ tsp. salt
¼ c. butter, melted
1 Tbsp. vanilla extract
Zest of 1 lemon
1 c. white sugar
6 eggs, separated and at room temperature

Sift together flour, cornstarch, cardamom, and salt. Combine butter, vanilla extract, and lemon zest and whisk to combine. Set aside.

Add egg whites and sugar to the bowl of a stand mixer with a whisk attachment and mix on Medium speed for 10 minutes or until very thick and foamy. Add egg yolks and beat 1 minute longer. Turn off stand mixer and use a spatula to gently fold in flour mixture, followed by butter mixture.

Preheat oven to 350 degrees. Grease and flour a 12-cup tube pan. Pour batter into pan (batter will not fill the pan; it will rise considerably while baking) and bake for 35 minutes or until a toothpick inserted in center of cake comes out clean. Allow cake to cool completely in pan before inverting onto a serving dish.

MAKES 10-12 SERVINGS

Per serving: 207 calories, 7 g fat, 3 g saturated fat, 118 mg sodium, 33 g carbohydrates, 4 g protein.

SERVING SUGGESTIONS: Serve with strawberries or other fresh fruit and whipped cream.

VARIATIONS: Use orange zest in place of lemon zest or add 2 Tbsp. of cocoa powder to batter.

SOUTH AFRICA
MALVAPOEDING

MEDIUM · COOK TIME: 45 MINUTES · ACTIVE PREP TIME: 10 MINUTES · INACTIVE PREP TIME: 15 MINUTES

Malvapoeding (malva pudding) is a rich, gooey, fluffy, spongy, and utterly decadent dessert that can be found throughout South Africa—and thanks to Oprah Winfrey, it has experienced a surge of popularity in the United States as well. The origin of its name has proven more elusive. It has been said that an Afrikaner woman named Malva invented it, while another story suggests that the geranium plant (malva in Afrikaans) was one of its original ingredients. Today, apricot jam, baking soda, and malt vinegar help to give it its unique flavor and texture.

1-¼ c. all-purpose flour
1-½ c. white sugar, divided
1 tsp. baking soda
½ c. whole milk
2 eggs
1 Tbsp. vanilla extract, divided

½ c. plus 1 Tbsp. butter, melted, divided, plus more for greasing baking dish
2 tsp. malt vinegar
¼ c. apricot jam
½ c. heavy cream
¼ c. warm water

Sift together flour, 1 c. sugar, and baking soda. In a separate bowl, whisk together milk, eggs, 2 tsp. vanilla extract, 1 Tbsp. butter, and vinegar. Combine wet and dry ingredients. Using an electric mixer, mix on Medium speed until smooth. Fold in apricot jam.

Preheat oven to 350 degrees. Grease an 8 x 8-inch baking dish. Pour batter into pan and bake for about 35 minutes or until a toothpick inserted in center of pudding comes out mostly clean (with a few crumbs).

While pudding is baking, prepare sauce. Combine ½ c. sugar and ½ c. butter in a medium saucepan and heat over Medium heat until sugar is melted. Add 1 tsp. vanilla extract and cream. Increase heat to Medium-High and bring to a boil, stirring constantly. Once sauce boils, remove from heat and stir in water. Cover and set aside until ready to use.

Remove pudding from oven and pour sauce on top. Let stand for 15 minutes or until sauce is completely absorbed into pudding.

MAKES 8 SERVINGS

Per serving: 332 calories, 16 g fat, 10 g saturated fat, 269 mg sodium, 45 g carbohydrates, 4 g protein.

SERVING SUGGESTION: Serve warm with vanilla ice cream or whipped cream.

VARIATIONS: For a chocolate malvapoeding, add 2 oz. semisweet baking chocolate to sauce with vanilla extract and cream. For a coconut version, add ½ c. finely grated coconut to batter with apricot jam. To make Cape brandy pudding, a popular variant, replace apricot jam with 1 c. chopped dates and add ½ c. brandy to sauce instead of water at end of cooking time. Another variant, Jan Ellis pudding, uses baking powder instead of baking soda and does not use vinegar.

TIP: If you wish to make your own apricot jam, see recipe on page 19.

SUDAN
BASEEMA

EASY · COOK TIME: 35 MINUTES · ACTIVE PREP TIME: 10 MINUTES

Sudan sits at a geographic crossroads between the Arab world, North Africa, and sub-Saharan Africa. Accordingly, its cuisine incorporates flavors from all of these places–and many more. Baseema, one of several sweet dishes popular in Sudan, is a lemon syrup-drenched coconut cake that in many ways resembles those of Egypt (page 108), Greece (page 44), and other Mediterranean countries.

1 c. powdered sugar

5 eggs

2 c. plain yogurt

¾ c. butter, melted, plus more for greasing baking dish

2 c. all-purpose flour

1 c. shredded coconut

2 tsp. baking powder

1-½ c. white sugar

1 c. water

1 Tbsp. lemon juice

Combine powdered sugar and eggs in a large bowl and beat with an electric mixer on Low speed until foamy. Add butter and yogurt and mix until combined. In a separate bowl, sift together flour, coconut, and baking powder and fold into egg mixture.

Preheat oven to 400 degrees. Grease a 9- x 13-inch baking dish. Spread batter into dish and smooth surface with a spatula. Bake for 30 minutes or until a toothpick inserted in center of cake comes out clean. Set cake aside and allow it to cool completely.

Combine sugar and water in a small saucepan. Cook over Medium-High heat for 5 minutes or until sugar is completely dissolved and syrup has thickened. Add lemon juice and stir.

Once the cake has cooled, use a skewer or other sharp object to poke holes in the surface of the cake, and then pour syrup over top of cake (while it is still hot). Cut into squares and serve.

MAKES 12 SERVINGS

Per serving: 359 calories, 16 g fat, 10 g saturated fat, 139 mg sodium, 47 g carbohydrates, 7 g protein.

SERVING SUGGESTION: Garnish with chopped pistachios and coconut or dust with powdered sugar.

TIP: When making syrup-drenched cake desserts, it is very important not to pour hot syrup onto a hot cake. Wait until the cake cools and pour the syrup while hot, or wait until the syrup cools and pour onto hot cake.

TANZANIA
N'DIZI NO KASTAD

MEDIUM · COOK TIME: 15 MINUTES · ACTIVE PREP TIME: 10 MINUTES · INACTIVE PREP TIME: 30 MINUTES

N'dizi no kastad (banana custard) is a specialty of Zanzibar, a small island off the eastern coast of Tanzania where Swahili, Arabic, and English are all official languages and the local food reflects Bantu, Portuguese, Indian, French, and Chinese influences. Tanzania is one of the world's greatest producer of bananas, and Zanzibar's position on the Indian Ocean has brought spices such as cinnamon, cloves, and nutmeg into its desserts.

3 bananas, sliced
3 c. whole milk
2 tsp. vanilla extract
1 tsp. butter
3 eggs
¾ c. plus 2 Tbsp. white sugar, divided
2 Tbsp. plus ½ tsp. cornstarch
¼ c. peanuts, finely chopped
1 tsp. ground cinnamon
½ tsp. ground cloves
¼ tsp. ground nutmeg

Combine milk, vanilla extract, and butter in a medium saucepan and bring to a near-boil over Medium heat. Reduce heat to Low.

Whisk together eggs, ¼ c. plus 2 Tbsp. sugar, and cornstarch in a small bowl. Add egg mixture to milk mixture and simmer, whisking constantly, for 5 to 10 minutes or until a thick custard is formed.

Add one-half of one banana to each of six serving dishes. Divide custard between the six dishes and refrigerate for 30 minutes or until custard is set.

Combine peanuts, cinnamon, cloves, and nutmeg and stir until peanuts are coated. Sprinkle an equal amount of peanut mixture on top of each custard.

MAKES 6 SERVINGS

Per serving: 307 calories, 10 g fat, 4 g saturated fat, 87 mg sodium, 48 g carbohydrates, 9 g protein.

VARIATION: Other fruits, such as pineapple, may be used in place of some or all of the bananas in this recipe.

TOGO
GÂTEAU À LA VANILLE

EASY · COOK TIME: 35 MINUTES · ACTIVE PREP TIME: 10 MINUTES

Togolese cuisine reflects the influence of France and Germany, both of which colonized the small West African nation. Gâteau à la vanille (vanilla cake), also known as kéké in Togo, is a simple version of the more elaborate cakes typical of French cuisine that is traditionally eaten without icing or other adornment.

1 c. plus 2 Tbsp. butter, at room temperature, plus more for greasing pan
1 c. white sugar
6 eggs
2 c. all-purpose flour, plus more for flouring pan
2 tsp. baking powder
½ c. brandy
1 Tbsp. vanilla extract

Combine butter and sugar in the bowl of a stand mixer with a whisk attachment and mix on High speed until light and fluffy. Add eggs and mix for 5 minutes longer. Fold in brandy and vanilla extract.

Sift together flour and baking powder. Fold flour mixture into wet ingredients, followed by brandy and vanilla extract.

Preheat oven to 300 degrees. Grease the bottom and sides of a 9-inch round cake pan. Pour batter into pan and bake for 30-35 minutes or until cake is golden on top and a toothpick inserted in center of cake comes out clean. Allow cake to cool in pan for at least 10 minutes, then invert onto a serving dish. Cut cake into slices and serve.

MAKES 8 SERVINGS

Per serving: 490 calories, 27 g fat, 16 g saturated fat, 212 mg sodium, 50 g carbohydrates, 8 g protein.

VARIATION: In Togo this cake would traditionally be served by itself, with no icing; however, a layer of buttercream icing or a dusting of powdered sugar may be added if desired.

UGANDA PLANTAIN CAKE

MEDIUM · COOK TIME: · ACTIVE PREP TIME: · INACTIVE PREP TIME:

Uganda's staple food is matoke, a type of banana that is starchy, low in sugar, and cannot be eaten raw. In this respect it is similar to the plantain, another common ingredient in Ugandan cuisine that is much easier to find in the United States. After-dinner desserts are not common in Uganda, so plantain cake would most likely be served as a side dish.

2 ripe plantains, sliced diagonally
3 Tbsp. olive oil, plus more for greasing baking dish
1 c. cottage cheese
1 Tbsp. white sugar
1 tsp. ground cinnamon
3 eggs, separated
1 Tbsp. breadcrumbs

Heat olive oil in a large skillet. Fry plantains for 1-2 minutes on each side or until brown. Remove from skillet and set aside to cool.

In a small bowl, combine cottage cheese, sugar, and cinnamon and stir until combined. Set aside.

In one bowl, beat egg yolks with an electric mixer on High speed until pale. Beat egg whites in a separate bowl until stiff peaks form. Gently fold egg yolks and whites together.

Preheat oven to 350 degrees. Grease an 8 x 8-inch baking dish with olive oil and sprinkle breadcrumbs across the bottom. Spread one-quarter of the egg mixture over the bottom of the pan and top with one-third of the fried plantain slices and one-third of cheese mixture. Repeat until all plantain slices and cheese mixture have been used, and finish with a layer of egg mixture. Bake for 40 minutes. Allow to cool slightly before serving.

MAKES 6 SERVINGS

Per serving: 211 calories, 10 g fat, 2 g saturated fat, 194 mg sodium, 24 g carbohydrates, 9 g protein.

SERVING SUGGESTION: While sweet enough to serve as a dessert, Ugandan plantain cake is typically served with meat and vegetables during the meal.

ZAMBIA
VITUMBUWA

EASY · COOK TIME: 10 MINUTES · ACTIVE PREP TIME: 5 MINUTES

Sometimes called "puff puff," these slightly sweet and very soft fried pastries are a popular street food in Zambia that have recently made their way to bakeries as well. They're far from being the only African treats based on fried dough, but vitumbuwa are distinguished by their use of baking powder instead of yeast.

2 c. all-purpose flour
½ c. white sugar
2 tsp. baking powder
1 c. whole milk, at room temperature
2 tsp. vanilla extract
Juice and zest of 1 small orange
Vegetable oil, for frying

Sift together flour, sugar, and baking powder in a medium bowl. Form a well in the center and add milk. Stir to combine with a wooden spoon until a thick batter is formed. Fold in vanilla extract and orange juice and zest.

Heat about 2 inches of oil in a heavy skillet to a temperature of 350 degrees. Use a spoon to scoop balls of dough (about 1-2 Tbsp. each) and drop into hot oil until pan is filled. Fry each batch of vitumbuwa for 2-3 minutes, turning frequently with a slotted metal spoon, until they are dark golden brown on all sides. Remove from pan and set on paper towels to drain.

MAKES ABOUT 15-20 PASTRIES

Per pastry: 170 calories, 11 g fat, 2 g saturated fat, 6 mg sodium, 15 g carbohydrates, 2 g protein.

SERVING SUGGESTION: Dust with powdered sugar if desired, or drizzle with icing.

VARIATIONS: For coconut vitumbuwa, use coconut milk in place of whole milk and add a few Tbsp. of coconut flakes. Spices such as cardamom and nutmeg may be used in place of vanilla extract and orange juice and zest for a different flavor.

ZIMBABWE PUMPKIN PUDDING

EASY · COOK TIME: 20 MINUTES · ACTIVE PREP TIME: 10 MINUTES

As in many African nations, desserts are not a huge part of the Zimbabwean people's diets. But as a former British colony, Zimbabwe's cuisine has adopted many English standards, including pudding. Pumpkin pudding could better be described as a porridge, often consumed as the first meal of the day. But this version is definitely sweet enough to end a meal on a satisfying note.

One 3- to 4-lb. pie pumpkin or butternut squash, peeled, seeded, and cubed

Water, for steaming
²/₃ c. white sugar
1 c. whole milk
½ c. plain yogurt
2 tsp. ground cardamom
1 tsp. ground ginger

Bring a pot of water to a boil. Place the pumpkin in a steamer basket and place basket over boiling water. Steam for about 10 minutes or until pumpkin is soft.

Mash pumpkin with a potato masher. While pumpkin is still warm, add sugar and stir until sugar has melted. Place pumpkin mixture in a medium saucepan and add milk, yogurt, cardamom, and ginger. Bring to a boil, reduce heat to Low, and simmer for 10 minutes or until a pudding-like consistency is reached.

MAKES 6-8 SERVINGS

Per serving: 145 calories, 2 g fat, 1 g saturated fat, 32 mg sodium, 31 g carbohydrates, 3 g protein.

SERVING SUGGESTION: Sprinkle with cinnamon and top with a pat of butter.

VARIATIONS: Coconut milk can be used in place of whole milk. Other spices such as cinnamon, nutmeg, and cloves may be added. In Zimbabwe, a popular variation includes 1 Tbsp. of smooth peanut butter.

TIP: While not recommended, two 14-oz. cans of pumpkin puree may be used in place of fresh pumpkin.

CENTRAL ASIA

AFGHANISTAN
GOSH-E-FEEL

EASY · COOK TIME: 20 MINUTES · ACTIVE PREP TIME: 20 MINUTES · INACTIVE PREP TIME: 2 HOURS

The name of these Afghan pastries, which are also popular in Iran, is Farsi for "elephant's ear." Their wide, flat shape is similar to the elephant ears that are sold at fairs in the United States. But instead of cinnamon sugar, gosh-e-feel are dusted with a generous layer of cardamom and crushed pistachios.

2 c. all-purpose flour, plus more for flouring surface
2 eggs
1 Tbsp. white sugar
¼ tsp. salt
½ c. whole milk
¼ c. butter, melted
Oil, for frying
1 c. powdered sugar
1 Tbsp. ground cardamom
½ c. finely crushed pistachios

Combine eggs, white sugar, and salt in a medium bowl and mix with an electric mixer on Medium speed until pale and foamy. Mix in milk and butter until fully incorporated. Using a wooden spoon, stir in flour one heaping spoonful at a time to form a thick dough.

Turn dough onto a floured surface and knead for about 10 minutes until pliable and slightly sticky. Return dough to bowl, cover with plastic wrap, and allow to stand for 2 hours.

Divide dough into about 30 small balls. Roll each ball into an oval shape about 4 inches in length. Pinch the long end of each oval to form a teardrop shape.

Heat about 2 inches of oil in a heavy skillet to a temperature of 350 degrees.

Carefully drop gosh-e-feel into oil and fry in batches until golden brown, turning once. Remove from pan and set on paper towels to drain.

Sift together powdered sugar and cardamom. Once gosh-e-feel have cooled, sprinkle evenly with powdered sugar mixture, followed by crushed pistachios.

MAKES ABOUT 30 PASTRIES

Per pastry: 145 calories, 10 g fat, 2 g saturated fat, 45 mg sodium, 12 g carbohydrates, 2 g protein.

SERVING SUGGESTION: Serve with hot tea.

VARIATION: Gosh-e-feel with cardamom and pistachios is most popular in Afghanistan; in Iran, flavorings such as vanilla, saffron, walnuts, rosewater, and rose petals are used.

ARMENIA
GATA

MEDIUM · COOK TIME: 45 MINUTES · ACTIVE PREP TIME: 15 MINUTES · INACTIVE PREP TIME: 4 HOURS

Gata is essentially a bread with a sweet, buttery filling, but throughout Armenia that basic description takes a different form, with each region having its own unique version (and decoration). Early Christians in Armenia associated gata with the Last Supper, in which Jesus Christ broke bread with his disciples. The first filled loaves were made after Christianity became the nation's state religion. It represents good fortune as well, and a gata is traditionally given to travelers before a departure. It is also served at weddings, where the loaf is broken over couple's heads for luck.

2-¼ c. all-purpose flour, divided
½ c. plain Greek yogurt

½ c. white sugar
$^1/_3$ c. vegetable oil
1 Tbsp. vanilla extract
½ tsp. baking powder
¼ tsp. active dry yeast
2 eggs, divided
¼ c. butter, at room temperature
½ c. powdered sugar
½ tsp. ground cinnamon
¼ tsp. ground nutmeg
¼ tsp. ground cardamom

Whisk together yogurt, sugar, oil, vanilla extract, baking powder, and yeast in a medium-sized bowl. In a separate bowl, use an electric mixer to beat 1 egg on High speed until pale and foamy. Fold beaten egg into yogurt mixture. Stir in 2 c. flour, a little at a time, and knead to form a smooth dough. Cover dough with plastic wrap and refrigerate for at least 4 hours.

Heat butter in a small saucepan. Stir in powdered sugar, cinnamon, nutmeg, and cardamom until melted. Slowly add remaining ¼ c. flour.

Punch the center of the dough to create a recess in the center. Fill with the butter mixture and pull the edges together to seal, forming a ball. Flatten the ball to form a round cake about 1-2" high.

Preheat oven to 350 degrees. Beat the remaining egg. Place the gata on a large parchment paper-covered baking sheet and brush with beaten egg. Prick the surface of the gata a few times with a fork; if desired, use a knife or spoon to make designs on the top of the gata.

Bake the gata for 35 minutes or until golden brown, rotating pan halfway through cooking. Transfer to a wire rack and allow to cool completely before slicing.

MAKES 6-8 SERVINGS

Per serving: 483 calories, 20 g fat, 8 g saturated fat, 123 mg sodium, 56 g carbohydrates, 19 g protein.

SERVING SUGGESTION: Serve with coffee.

VARIATIONS: If desired, add 1-2 Tbsp. of brandy or rum or ¼ c. of chopped nuts to the filling. Walnuts are traditional, though pecans, pistachios, or almonds may be used. Honey may be used in place of white sugar in dough.

AZERBAIJAN YAYMA

EASY · COOK TIME: 55 MINUTES · ACTIVE PREP TIME: 5 MINUTES · INACTIVE PREP TIME: 20 MINUTES

Worth more than its weight in gold, saffron is by far the most valuable spice in the world. It's also very important in Azeri cooking. In the past, Azeri people grew crocus flowers in their backyards or at their summer houses to produce the spice, which is made from the stamens of these flowers. It gives a bright yellow color and distinctive flavor to dishes such as yayma, a sweet rice pudding.

1 c. short-grain white rice, washed and rinsed
1 qt. whole milk
1 c. hot water, divided
3-4 threads saffron
1 dash salt
¾ c. white sugar
Ground cinnamon, for serving
Butter, for serving

Place saffron threads in about ¼ c. hot water and allow to stand for at least 5 minutes or up to 20 minutes. The water should be a deep yellow-orange color when fully infused.

Add rice and remaining ¾ c. water to a large saucepan and bring to a boil. Reduce heat to Medium, add salt, and continue to cook until water has fully evaporated (rice will not be fully cooked).

Add milk, infused water, and sugar to the pan and return to a boil. Reduce heat to Medium-Low, cover (leave lid partially open), and simmer for about 45 minutes or until the rice is very soft and most of the liquid has evaporated, stirring frequently.

Divide yayma between four bowls. Dust each serving with cinnamon and place a pat of butter on top.

MAKES 4 SERVINGS

Per serving: 472 calories, 12 g fat, 8 g saturated fat, 211 mg sodium, 83 g carbohydrates, 9 g protein.

SERVING SUGGESTION: If desired, serve drizzled with honey or topped with almonds as well as cinnamon and butter.

VARIATION: When saffron is unavailable, Azeri cooks often use turmeric in its place. Bear in mind that it will greatly change the yayma's flavor.

BANGLADESH
RASGULLA

HARD · COOK TIME: 50 MINUTES · ACTIVE PREP TIME: 25 MINUTES · INACTIVE PREP TIME: 1 HOUR

At some point in the eleventh century, a priest from a temple in the Bengali city of Odisha visited a village where cows outnumbered people. He was appalled to see the villagers discarding excess milk and decided to teach them the art of milk curdling. He also taught them how to make a sweet dish which to that point had only been made at his temple as an offering to the goddess Mahalakshmi . . . and that was how rasgulla was introduced to the world. Or was it? There are as many stories about rasgulla's origins as there are varieties, and possibly even more cities and regions that claim its origins. Whatever the truth is, rasgulla is a uniquely tasty treat and is worth the time and effort it takes to prepare.

2 qt. whole milk
2 Tbsp. freshly-squeezed lemon juice
1 qt. plus 1 c. water
1 c. white sugar
3 green cardamom pods, crushed

Bring milk to a boil in a large saucepan. Once the milk begins to boil, add lemon juice and reduce heat just low enough that the pot does not boil over. Continue to cook until the milk separates into liquid and curd.

Line a colander with a fine cheesecloth or jelly bag. Pour milk mixture into the colander and strain until all of the liquid has been drained away and only curd remains.

Squeeze the cloth to remove any excess liquid. Rinse the outside of the cloth with water, and then squeeze again. Do not squeeze enough to remove all moisture (this will result in dry rasgulla). Hang the curd (in the cloth) over a bowl and allow it to drain for 1 hour longer.

Remove the curd from the cloth and break it into pieces in a bowl. Use your hands to gently mash the curd for about 5-10 minutes or until it is has the consistency of smooth clay (do not knead it as you would bread dough). Roll the curd into about 15-20 balls, each about 1 inch in diameter. Set balls aside.

In a stockpot or Dutch oven, combine water, sugar, and cardamom pods. Stir until sugar is completely dissolved, and then bring to a boil. Boil the syrup until it reaches a temperature of 235 degrees Fahrenheit (use a candy thermometer to monitor temperature), and then reduce heat to Medium.

Use a slotted spoon to drop rasgulla into the syrup one at a time. Cover the pot and cook for 20 minutes or until the rasgulla are doubled in size.

As the rasgulla are cooking, prepare an ice water bath. Remove the rasgulla from the syrup and drop them in the ice water bath to stop the cooking process, reserving the syrup. (If the rasgulla are fully cooked, they should drop to the bottom of the ice water.)

When ready to serve, place rasgulla in a serving bowl and ladle syrup on top.

MAKES 4-6 SERVINGS

Per serving: 502 calories, 10 g fat, 6 g saturated fat, 208 mg sodium, 91 g carbohydrates, 13 g protein.

SERVING SUGGESTION: Serve chilled or at room temperature.

VARIATIONS: For orange rasgulla (komola bhog), replace 1 c. water with orange juice. For rose rasgulla, add 1 Tbsp. rosewater and 3-4 drops of pink food coloring to syrup after it has cooled slightly, and garnish with dried rose petals. For chocolate rasgulla, add 2 tsp. cocoa powder to curd while mashing it and drizzle with chocolate syrup before serving.

TIP: Rasgulla can be stored in the refrigerator (in their syrup) for up to one week.

GEORGIA
PELAMUSHI

EASY · COOK TIME: 20 MINUTES · ACTIVE PREP TIME: 5 MINUTES · INACTIVE PREP TIME: 4 HOURS

The people of the South Caucasus have been making wine for over 8,000 years—making Georgia a contender for its possible birthplace. The grape harvest occurs in the fall months, and a small amount of grape juice is usually reserved to make pelamushi, a thick and fruity pudding that uses cornflour as a thickener.

4 c. red grape juice (preferably freshly-squeezed)
¼ c. all-purpose flour
¼ c. finely ground white cornmeal
1 dash salt

Place grape juice in a large saucepan. Sift together flour, cornmeal, and salt and add to grape juice. Stir until all flour and cornmeal is dissolved.

Bring the grape juice mixture to a boil over High heat. Reduce heat to Medium-Low and continue to cook, stirring constantly, until mixture has reached the consistency of pudding.

Spoon pelamushi into 6 medium-sized ramekins. Chill for 4 hours (or overnight) before serving.

MAKES 6 SERVINGS

Per serving: 240 calories, 0 g fat, 0 g saturated fat, 52 mg sodium, 33 g carbohydrates, 2 g protein.

SERVING SUGGESTION: Garnish with walnuts, almonds, or other tree nuts.

VARIATIONS: Pelamushi can be made with white grape juice. The pudding can also be poured into a pie crust before refrigerating to make a pelamushi tart. One variation on pelamushi, tatara, uses wheat flour instead of cornmeal.

TIP: If you have difficulty reaching the correct consistency, add more flour (just a small amount at a time) until the pelamushi thickens.

INDIA
GULAB JAMUN

MEDIUM · COOK TIME: 25 MINUTES · ACTIVE PREP TIME: 30 MINUTES · INACTIVE PREP TIME: 3 HOURS

Sometimes called "Indian doughnuts," gulab jamun originated in Persia during the Medieval era. As the legend goes, they made their way to India through the court of Mughal emperor Shah Jahan. Today they're enormously popular in India and throughout the Indian diaspora. The dish's name loosely translates to "rose plum," a reference to the rose-scented syrup in which they are soaked before serving, and to their size (about the same as a small plum).

3 c. white sugar
3 c. water
8 green cardamom pods, lightly crushed
1 Tbsp. rosewater
2 c. powdered milk
½ c. plus 2 Tbsp. all-purpose flour
¼ tsp. baking soda
¼ c. whole milk (more if needed)
2 tsp. lemon juice
Ghee, for greasing hands
Oil, for frying
Finely chopped pistachios, for garnish

Combine sugar, water, and cardamom pods in a stockpot and bring to a boil over High heat. Boil the syrup until it reaches a temperature of 235 degrees Fahrenheit (use a candy thermometer to monitor temperature). Remove from heat, add rosewater, cover, and set aside.

Sift together powdered milk, flour, and baking soda. In another bowl, combine milk and lemon juice. Stir milk mixture into powdered milk mixture to form a dough, adding more milk if necessary.

Use a small amount of ghee to grease your hands, and then apply gentle pressure to the dough until it is smooth with no cracks (do not knead the dough aggressively as you would when making bread dough). Once the dough is completely smooth, use a knife to cut the dough into 25-30 smaller portions. Roll each portion into a smooth ball.

Heat about 2 inches of oil in a heavy skillet to a temperature of 350 degrees. Drop the dough balls into the oil and cook for about 2 minutes, then reduce heat and continue to cook until balls are a deep brown color, stirring frequently so that they are evenly brown on all sides. Remove gulab jamun from oil and drain on paper towels.

Once the gulab jamun are fully drained, carefully drop them into the syrup. Allow them to stand in syrup for 3 hours. Garnish with pistachios and serve.

MAKES 6-8 SERVINGS

Per serving: 772 calories, 32 g fat, 4 g saturated fat, 249 mg sodium, 113 g carbohydrates, 15 g protein.

SERVING SUGGESTION: Serve either warm or at room temperature. Warm gulab jamun are sometimes served with a scoop of vanilla ice cream.

VARIATION: For coconut gulab jamun, add 2 Tbsp. of desiccated coconut to the dough and roll in coconut before serving.

TIPS: It is of great importance to start with smooth dough before frying gulab jamun. Any cracks that are present in the surface will widen after frying. It is also important not to add the gulab jamun to the syrup while both are still hot. Allow them to cool for a few minutes first. The syrup should be warm but not hot.

KASHMIR SHUFTA

EASY · COOK TIME: 15 MINUTES · ACTIVE PREP TIME: 5 MINUTES · INACTIVE PREP TIME: 30 MINUTES

In a region of northern India not exactly known for its sweet dishes, "shufta" is nearly synonymous with "dessert." A delicious and protein-rich mainstay at Kashmiri weddings and festivals, shufta is very simple to make. But its flavor is far from simple. Spicy, sweet, sour, bitter, and salty flavors compete for attention in this crunchy and sticky treat.

1 c. almonds
1 c. walnuts
1 c. cashews
1 c. golden raisins

½ c. dates, pitted and chopped

Warm water, for soaking

2 Tbsp. ghee

1 c. paneer, cut into cubes

½ c. fresh coconut, thinly sliced

1 c. white sugar

¼ c. water

1 tsp. freshly ground black pepper

1 tsp. ground ginger

1 tsp. ground cinnamon

1 tsp. ground cardamom

Place almonds, walnuts, cashews, raisins, and dates in a large bowl and cover with warm water. Soak nuts and dried fruits for 30 minutes, and then drain and pat dry with a paper towel.

Heat the ghee in a large skillet over Medium heat. Add paneer to skillet and fry for 5 minutes or until browned. Remove paneer from skillet and set aside.

Add coconut to skillet and fry for 3 minutes longer or until light brown. Remove from skillet and set aside.

Add soaked nuts and fruits to skillet and cook for 2 minutes or until just lightly toasted. Add sugar and ¼ c. water and continue to cook until sugar is melted and a syrup forms (add more water if necessary). Stir in pepper, ginger, cinnamon, and cardamom.

Just before serving, return paneer and coconut to pan and stir to combine before transferring to a serving dish.

MAKES 8-10 SERVINGS

Per serving: 456 calories, 25 g fat, 5 g saturated fat, 43 mg sodium, 54 g carbohydrates, 12 g protein.

SERVING SUGGESTION: Garnish with dried rose petals and serve with spiced green tea.

VARIATIONS: Add saffron (soaked in water) with other spices. Dried apricots, figs, pistachios, hazelnuts, or basically any other dried fruits and nuts can be used to make shufta.

TIP: If paneer is not available, ricotta, mozzarella, or feta cheese can be used in its place. If using ricotta, drain the cheese on paper towels to remove as much moisture as possible before slicing into cubes and frying.

KAZAKHSTAN
ÇÄKÇÄK

MEDIUM · COOK TIME: 20 MINUTES · ACTIVE PREP TIME: 20 MINUTES · INACTIVE PREP TIME: 2 HOURS, 30 MINUTES

Çäkçäk (or chak-chak) is a specialty of Tatarstan, which has been part of Russia since the sixteenth century. Much cultural diffusion occurred during the Soviet era, which included the spread of culinary traditions. As a result, the sticky syrup-drenched çäkçäk became a popular dish in several Soviet republics, particularly Kazakhstan, whose northern border lies near Tatarstan. Kazakh çäkçäk is characterized by the way the dough is cut into short, thin noodles before frying.

2 c. all-purpose flour, plus more for flouring surface
3 eggs
1 Tbsp. vodka (optional; inhibits gluten formation)
1 Tbsp. heavy cream
¼ tsp. baking powder
¼ tsp. salt
Oil, for frying
1 c. honey
½ c. white sugar
½ c. water

In a large bowl, use an electric mixer to beat the eggs on Low speed until they are slightly foamy. Stir in vodka (if using) and heavy cream. Sift together flour, baking powder, and salt. Add flour mixture a little at a time to form a soft dough. Turn the dough onto a floured surface and knead until pliable. Cover and allow to rest for 30 minutes.

Roll the dough to a thickness of ¼-inch. Use a dough cutter or kitchen shears to cut the dough into ¼-inch vertical strips. Cut these strips horizontally into 1-inch sections.

Heat about 2 inches of oil in a heavy skillet to a temperature of 350 degrees. Fry the dough sections in batches until golden brown (they will swell considerably when fried). Remove with a slotted spoon and set on paper towels to drain.

Combine honey, sugar, and water in a medium saucepan and bring to a boil. Remove from heat and stir.

Place çäkçäk in a large bowl and pour syrup over top. Stir so that the dough pieces are completely coated with syrup. Press mixture into a 9-inch springform pan, working quickly so that the syrup does not harden. Allow to stand for 2 hours.

Loosen wall belt and cut çäkçäk into slices to serve.

MAKES 8 SERVINGS

Per serving: 565 calories, 30 g fat, 5 g saturated fat, 100 mg sodium, 72 g carbohydrates, 6 g protein.

VARIATIONS: Instead of slicing the dough, it can be rolled into pea-sized balls before frying. Almonds, raisins, or other nuts or dried fruits can be mixed into the çäkçäk before pouring syrup.

TIP: Make sure that the çäkçäk is completely cooled before adding the hot syrup.

KYRGYZSTAN
BOORSOQ

EASY · COOK TIME: 15 MINUTES · ACTIVE PREP TIME: 15 MINUTES · INACTIVE PREP TIME: 4 HOURS

Desserts aren't a major part of Kyrgyz cuisine, but bread definitely is. The Kyrgyz people place great importance on bread, and breadmaking is a fine art for Kyrgyz bakers. Fried bread is ubiquitous in Central Asia, and its Kyrgyz rendition, boorsoq, is more than just a dietary staple. When a family member passes away, it is traditional in Kyrgyzstan to bake boorsoq every Thursday for one year after their death. As the boorsoq is eaten, it is believed that the deceased joins their family for the feast.

2 c. all-purpose flour, plus more for flouring surface
1 Tbsp. plus 2 tsp. active dry yeast
1 tsp. white sugar
½ tsp. salt
1-⅓ c. warm water
½ c. sunflower oil, plus more for frying

Sift together flour, yeast, sugar, and salt and add to the bowl of a stand mixer with a dough hook attachment. Add water and oil and mix on Medium speed until dough is moist. Cover dough with a damp towel and allow to stand for 4 hours.

Turn dough onto a floured surface and knead until smooth and pliable. Roll the dough to a thickness of ¼-inch. Use a sharp knife or dough cutter to cut the dough into 2-inch triangles.

Heat about 2 inches of oil in a heavy skillet to a temperature of 350 degrees. Fry boorsoq in batches until golden brown, turning once. Remove from oil and drain on paper towels before serving.

MAKES ABOUT 20 PASTRIES

Per pastry: 94 calories, 6 g fat, 1 g saturated fat, 59 mg sodium, 10 g carbohydrates,

1 g protein.

SERVING SUGGESTION: Serve with strawberry jam, honey, or cream cheese. While not traditional, boorsoq can also be served dusted with powdered sugar while warm.

MALDIVES
DHONKEYO KAJURU

EASY · COOK TIME: 15 MINUTES · ACTIVE PREP TIME: 10 MINUTES

The Maldives archipelago includes 185 inhabited islands—and coconuts are grown on all of them. Virtually every popular Maldivian dish incorporates coconut in some form, whether it be coconut milk, coconut oil, or (as this recipe does) grated coconut flesh. Like most places near the equator, the Maldives is also a major source of bananas. The islands are best known for a smaller, very sweet variety that is difficult to find in the United States.

2 large, very ripe bananas, mashed
½ c. white sugar
¾ c. all-purpose flour
½ tsp. baking powder
¼ c. freshly grated coconut
¼ tsp. vanilla extract
Oil (preferably coconut), for frying
Powdered sugar, for dusting

In a medium bowl, stir the sugar into the mashed banana. Sift together flour and baking powder and stir into banana mixture a little at a time until fully incorporated, followed by coconut and vanilla extract.

Heat about 2 inches of oil in a heavy skillet to a temperature of 350 degrees. Once oil is hot, drop the batter into the oil by the spoonful and fry in batches until brown, turning once. Remove from oil and drain on paper towels before serving.

Dust dhonkeyo kaju with powdered sugar before serving.

MAKES 4-6 SERVINGS

Per serving: 589 calories, 45 g fat, 39 g saturated fat, 2 mg sodium, 49 g carbohydrates, 3 g protein.

VARIATION: One popular variation uses rosewater in place of vanilla. (But don't use them both together!)

PAKISTAN
SOHAN HALWA

HARD · COOK TIME: 5 HOURS, 30 MINUTES · ACTIVE PREP TIME: 15 MINUTES

Sohan halwa is extremely popular in Pakistan, but it's usually commercially produced. Homemade sohan halwa is a rarity today, and after making this recipe you'll probably understand why. Originating in the Pakistani city of Multan, sohan halwa is made by boiling milk and sprouted wheat until the mixture becomes solid—and that takes a very long time. You will need an entire afternoon to spare when making this extremely time-consuming and labor-intensive confection.

3 qt. whole milk, divided
¾ c. sprouted wheat
½ c. all-purpose flour
1 c. plain yogurt
1 c. water
3 c. white sugar
½ c. ghee
1 c. pistachios
1 c. walnuts

Combine 2 c. milk, sprouted wheat, and flour and stir vigorously with a wooden spoon. In a separate bowl, whisk together yogurt and water.

In a large stockpot, bring remaining milk to a boil. Add sprouted wheat mixture followed by yogurt mixture and stir well. Cover and continue to boil for 15-20 minutes.

Remove lid and stir. At this point, milk should start to curdle. Reduce heat to Low, cover, and simmer for 4 hours, stirring once per hour.

Remove lid, add sugar, and stir until dissolved. Raise heat to Medium and continue to stir until remaining liquid is reduced by half. Add ghee and stir until completely melted. Continue stirring until all liquid has evaporated (mixture should still be moist and not dry).

Spoon mixture into a 10-inch round dish and spread into an even layer. Sprinkle with pistachios and walnuts and press nuts into surface. When the mixture has cooled, invert the dish to remove the sohan halwa and cut into pieces to serve.

MAKES 10-12 SERVINGS

Per serving: 677 calories, 26 g fat, 11 g saturated fat, 189 mg sodium, 101 g carbohydrates, 15 g protein.

VARIATIONS: Almonds, cashews, or sunflower seeds can be used in sohan halwa, as can dried fruits. Cardamom, saffron, or lemon zest can be added for additional flavor.

SRI LANKA
ALUWA

MEDIUM · COOK TIME: 15 MINUTES · ACTIVE PREP TIME: 10 MINUTES

The Sinhalese New Year (Aluth Avurruda) is celebrated each April on the night of the new moon. Today it is a national holiday in Sri Lanka that is observed not only by the Sinhalese people, but throughout the Sri Lankan diaspora. Like most New

Year celebrations, the Sinhalese New Year is associated with many time-honored traditions, including games, family gatherings, and special dishes. These almost always include aluwa, a treat originally made with only rice flour and coconut oil. This modern recipe includes a few additional ingredients.

2 c. rice flour, plus more for flouring surface
1 c. white sugar
¾ c. full-fat coconut milk
1-½ tsp. ground cardamom
¼ c. cashews

Heat a large skillet over Medium heat. Add rice flour and cook for about 7-8 minutes or until toasted. Remove from pan and set aside.

Add sugar and coconut milk to skillet. Cook over Medium heat until sugar is fully dissolved, stirring frequently. Stir in cardamom, followed by toasted rice flour (one spoonful at a time), reserving about ¼ c. of flour, and remove from heat.

Place cashews in a blender or food processor and grind to a coarse paste. Stir ground cashews into batter. The batter should be thick but still very moist.

Pour the batter onto a floured surface. Use a dough scraper to form the batter into a square shape. Dust the top and sides with reserved rice flour and cut into squares. Allow aluwa to cool completely before serving (they will become firm at room temperature).

MAKES 9 SERVINGS

Per serving: 274 calories, 6 g fat, 4 g saturated fat, 6 mg sodium, 52 g carbohydrates, 3 g protein.

SERVING SUGGESTION: Press whole cashew nuts into surface to decorate if desired.

TIP: To make your own rice flour, pulse 1 c. of dry long-grain white rice in a high-powered blender or food processor until coarsely ground, and then raise speed to High for 1 minute or until rice has the consistency of fine flour. Sift through a fine sieve to remove any large pieces that remain and repeat as necessary until desired quantity is reached.

TAJIKISTAN
HALVAITAR

EASY · COOK TIME: 20 MINUTES · ACTIVE PREP TIME: 5 MINUTES

Sometimes called "flour halva" or "liquid halva," halvaitar is definitely among the simpler Central Asian confections—and the more unusual. In Tajikistan, halvaitar is traditionally prepared using mutton fat instead of the butter and oil used in this recipe. Here, the halvaitar is cooked to the point that most liquid is evaporated, but in some regions it is served in a liquid form as a soup.

2 c. all-purpose flour
½ c. butter, at room temperature
½ c. vegetable oil
2 c. whole milk
1 Tbsp. vanilla extract
2 c. white sugar
Almonds and walnut halves, for garnish

Heat butter in a large saucepan over Medium-High heat. Add oil, and then slowly add flour, stirring after each addition. Mixture will be thick and somewhat crumbly after all flour is added.

Continue to stir until mixture has darkened to a medium-brown color. Once it reaches this point, stir in milk 1 c. at a time, followed by vanilla extract and sugar. Reduce heat to Medium-Low and continue to cook until all of the liquid has evaporated (mixture should still be moist).

Press the mixture into a gelatin mold. (To make individual servings, use smaller-sized molds.) Release from mold and decorate with almonds and walnut halves.

MAKES 6 SERVINGS

Per serving: 808 calories, 42 g fat, 15 g saturated fat, 143 mg sodium, 104 g carbohydrates, 9 g protein.

VARIATION: Nuts can also be mixed into halvaitar instead of used as a garnish.

TURKMENISTAN PISHME WITH BEKMES

MEDIUM · COOK TIME: 4 HOURS · ACTIVE PREP TIME: 20 MINUTES

Like many other Central Asian countries, Turkmenistan has a fried dough as one of its national dishes. Pishme are sweeter than most others, although they can also be made using savory ingredients. While pishme are often served with honey or jam, this rendition pairs them with bekmes, a sweet fruit syrup for which every Turkmen tribe has its own recipe.

For pishme:
2 c. all-purpose flour, plus more for flouring surface
1 tsp. baking powder
½ tsp. salt
1 egg
½ c. whole milk, warmed
¼ c. sweetened condensed milk
Oil, for frying

Sift together flour, baking powder, and salt. Add egg, warm milk, and condensed milk to the bowl of a stand mixer with a dough hook attachment. Slowly add flour mixture and mix on Medium speed for 3 minutes to form a smooth dough. Cover bowl with plastic wrap and allow to stand for 30 minutes.

Roll dough to a thickness of about ¼-inch. Use a dough cutter or sharp knife to cut the dough into 2-inch wide strips, then rotate dough 30 degrees and cut into strips again (diamond shapes should result).

Heat about 2 inches of oil in a heavy skillet to a temperature of 350 degrees.

Once oil is hot, drop the dough pieces into the oil and fry in batches until brown, turning once. Remove from oil and drain on paper towels before serving.

For bekmes:
3 qt. freshly-squeezed red grape juice
3 Tbsp. sifted wood ash

Place grape juice in a large stockpot and bring to a boil. Add wood ash and continue to boil for abut 5 minutes. Remove from heat and strain through a fine-weave jelly bag.

Return strained grape juice to pot and bring to a boil again. Reduce heat to Medium-Low and simmer uncovered for 3-4 hours or until juice is reduced to one-tenth of its original volume (it will have the consistency of maple syrup when ready). Serve with pishme.

MAKES ABOUT 50 PISHME AND 1-1/2 C. BEKMES

Per serving (2 pishme and 2 tsp. bekmes): 205 calories, 9 g fat, 2 g saturated fat, 61 mg sodium, 28 g carbohydrates, 3 g protein.

SERVING SUGGESTION: Serve with green tea.

TIP: Bekmes (or grape molasses, as it is also called) can be purchased in its prepared form by the jar. But it is so much more rewarding to make your own!

UZBEKISTAN
KHVOROST

MEDIUM · COOK TIME: 15 MINUTES · ACTIVE PREP TIME: 30 MINUTES

Sometimes called "Russian twigs," these little pastries are one of many dishes that made their way throughout the Soviet Union during the twentieth century. But khvorost originated in Uzbekistan, where they are most often described by locals as "addictive." While khvorost are a mainstay at special events, such as weddings and christenings, their simplicity makes them a popular everyday treat as well.

2 c. all-purpose flour, plus more for flouring surface
2 eggs
1 c. whole milk
2 Tbsp. vodka
½ c. plus 1 Tbsp. powdered sugar, divided
1 Tbsp. sour cream
1 tsp. salt
1 c. butter or lard
Oil, for frying
Zest of 1 lemon

Combine eggs, milk, vodka, 1 Tbsp. powdered sugar, sour cream, and salt in the bowl of a stand mixer with a dough hook attachment. Gradually add flour while mixing on Low speed for about 3 minutes.

Turn dough onto a floured surface and knead until smooth. Roll the dough to a thickness of ¼-inch. Use a dough cutter or sharp knife to cut dough into strips about 4-5 inches long and ½-inch wide (they do not have to be uniform in size).

To assemble each khvorost, take two or three strips of dough and twist or braid them together loosely. Pinch one end to secure. If desired, use a knife to "fray" the ends of the strips.

Melt butter or lard in a heavy skillet. Add oil to the skillet for a total depth of 1 inch and heat to a temperature of 350 degrees. Fry khvorost in small batches for about 2-3 minutes or until brown, turning once. Remove from oil and drain on paper towels.

Sift together ½ c. powdered sugar and lemon zest. Dust khvorost generously and serve.

MAKES ABOUT 12-18 KHVOROST

Per khvorost: 273 calories, 21 g fat, 9 g saturated fat, 258 mg sodium, 18 g carbohydrates, 3 g protein.

SERVING SUGGESTION: Serve with green tea (traditional in Uzbekistan) or black tea.

VARIATIONS: Cinnamon or vanilla can be used in place of lemon zest for a different flavor. Other liquors, such as brandy, may be used in place of vodka.

EAST ASIA

BHUTAN
SHRIKAND

MEDIUM · ACTIVE PREP TIME: 15 MINUTES · INACTIVE PREP TIME: 2 HOURS

Shrikand, a strained yogurt-based porridge, originated in the central Indian state of Maharashtra—far from the Himalayan kingdom of Bhutan. But the abundance of dairy products and spices such as cardamom in Bhutanese cuisine has made it one of its few popular desserts. In Bhutan, shrikand would most likely be made with yak milk.

6 c. full-fat plain yogurt
5-6 threads saffron
¼ c. hot milk or water
1 tsp. powdered cardamom
½ c. powdered sugar
½ c. finely chopped almonds, pistachios, or a combination

Line a large sieve with fine cheesecloth or a jelly bag. Pour yogurt into the sieve and allow it to stand until most of the liquid has drained off (about 45 minutes). Squeeze the cloth to remove any extra liquid.

Wrap the drained yogurt in a thick towel. Set the wrapped yogurt on a plate and lay a heavy weight on top (such as a cast-iron pan). Refrigerate yogurt for 1 hour longer.

Place saffron threads in hot milk or water and allow to stand for at least 15 minutes. Liquid will turn a deep yellow-orange color.

Combine yogurt, saffron mixture, powdered sugar, and cardamom in a large bowl and stir with a wooden spoon until completely smooth. Divide shrikand between four serving bowls and top with nuts.

MAKES 4 SERVINGS

Per serving: 352 calories, 18 g fat, 8 g saturated fat, 173 mg sodium, 34 g

carbohydrates, 15 g protein.

SERVING SUGGESTION: Served chilled.

VARIATIONS: Add pureed fruit such as mango or berries. (Fruits with high water content such as oranges usually do not do well in shrikand.) Other variations can be made using nutmeg or rosewater.

TIP: If time is a constraint, Greek yogurt can be used in place of regular yogurt and will not require straining. Use 3 c. instead of 6 c. if using Greek yogurt.

BRUNEI
BUBUR KETAN HITAM

EASY · COOK TIME: 1 HOUR · ACTIVE PREP TIME: 5 MINUTES · INACTIVE PREP TIME: 4 HOURS

Made using black glutinous rice, palm sugar, and coconut milk, bubur ketan hitam (black rice pudding) is not your typical rice pudding. Like many Bruneian dishes, it made its way to the tiny country from its larger neighbor, Indonesia. Bubur ketan hitam can be served as a dessert or as a sweet breakfast.

¾ c. black glutinous rice
1 qt. water, plus more for soaking
2 pandan leaves
½ tsp. salt
½ c. palm sugar
1 c. full-fat coconut milk

Wash the black rice and add enough water to cover. Soak rice for at least 4 hours or overnight. Drain and rinse rice.

Bring water and pandan leaves to a boil in a large saucepan. Add rice, reduce heat to Low, cover, and simmer for 45-50 minutes, stirring occasionally. Remove from heat and remove pandan leaves. Add sugar and stir until dissolved.

Heat coconut milk in a small saucepan over Medium-High heat until warm. Remove from heat.

Divide rice between four bowls. Top each serving with an equal amount of coconut milk.

MAKES 4 SERVINGS

Per serving: 358 calories, 15 g fat, 13 g saturated fat, 66 mg sodium, 56 g carbohydrates, 4 g protein.

SERVING SUGGESTION: Top with sesame seeds, almonds, cinnamon, or sliced bananas.

TIPS: Coconut sugar or brown sugar can be substituted for palm sugar. If pandan leaves are not available, add a small amount of vanilla extract to rice along with sugar

CAMBODIA
NUM CHAK KACHAN

HARD · COOK TIME: 1 HOUR, 30 MINUTES · ACTIVE PREP TIME: 15 MINUTES

An auspicious treat traditionally served at wedding ceremonies and on Buddhist holidays, num chak kachan is prepared in the same manner as more savory Cambodian dishes, by steaming. It includes a trinity of ingredients found in nearly all Cambodian sweet dishes: rice, tapioca, and coconut. When made correctly—which is not easy to do—num chak kachan makes a very impressive jewel-toned presentation. While any colors are suitable, red and green are the most common in Cambodia.

2-½ c. palm sugar
1-½ c. rice flour
1-½ c. tapioca flour
¼ tsp. salt
3-½ c. full-fat coconut milk
1 c. water, plus more for boiling
Food coloring, as needed

Sift together palm sugar, rice and tapioca flours, and salt. Heat coconut milk and water in a large saucepan (do not bring to a boil).

Add wet ingredients to dry ingredients a little at a time, whisking vigorously after each addition. Strain the mixture through a fine sieve to remove any remaining lumps from the batter. Divide batter into equal portions, the number depending on how many colors you wish to have, and add a small amount of food coloring to each portion.

Bring a large pot of water to a boil. Place a large steamer basket above the pot and place a 9 x 9-inch glass baking dish inside the steamer. Ladle a small amount of batter into the dish and spread so that it covers the bottom of the dish in a $1/8$- to ¼-inch thick layer. Cover the steamer and steam for 5 minutes.

Remove lid and add a second layer of batter (in a different color). Replace lid and steam for 5 minutes longer. Repeat the process, alternating batter colors, until all batter is used. Depending on how thick and even your layers are, you should have between 6 and 12 layers total. Once all batter is used, steam the entire cake for 40 minutes longer.

Remove cake from steamer and allow to cool completely before slicing into squares.

MAKES 9-12 SERVINGS

Per serving: 377 calories, 17 g fat, 15 g saturated fat, 155 mg sodium, 58 g carbohydrates, 3 g protein.

SERVING SUGGESTION: Garnish with shredded coconut before serving.

VARIATIONS: If desired, add 1-2 tsp. banana, orange, vanilla, or jasmine extract to

batter along with coconut milk.

TIP: If condensation from the inside of the lid dripping onto the num chak kachan becomes a problem, lay a dry towel over the steamer before placing the lid on top.

CHINA
SNOW CAKE

MEDIUM · COOK TIME: 10 MINUTES · ACTIVE PREP TIME: 15 MINUTES · INACTIVE PREP TIME: 4 HOURS

Ovens are not as common in China as they are in other places, so cakes and other desserts are rarely baked. Snow cake, named for its flaky white appearance and the temperature at which it is served, is one example. This Chinese dessert dates back to at least the sixteenth century, when a number of new and eclectic treats made their way to the Ming Dynasty's imperial court. The use of cornstarch as a thickener instead of gelatin gives snow cake a more solid foundation than similar sweet coconut-based dim sum dishes.

1 c. full-fat coconut milk
1 c. whole milk
½ c. cornstarch
¼ c. white sugar
1 c. desiccated coconut

Combine coconut milk and whole milk in a large saucepan and bring to a boil. Sift together cornstarch and sugar and whisk into milk mixture, a little at a time, until completely dissolved.

Heat over Medium heat until mixture begins to thicken, whisking constantly. Remove from heat and continue to stir until mixture develops a paste-like consistency.

Line a 9 x 9-inch square baking dish with parchment paper or plastic wrap. Pour mixture into pan and spread evenly. Refrigerate for at least 4 hours.

Invert cake onto a serving plate and remove paper or wrap. Slice cake into 12 pieces. Coat each piece with desiccated coconut on all sides.

MAKES 12 SERVINGS

Per serving: 219 calories, 18 g fat, 15 g saturated fat, 19 mg sodium, 16 g carbohydrates, 2 g protein.

SERVING SUGGESTION: Serve chilled.

VARIATIONS: For a fruit-flavored snow cake, add ¼ c. jam (any flavor) to mixture before cooking. Vanilla extract or cocoa powder can also be added.

HONG KONG STEAMED MILK PUDDING

MEDIUM · COOK TIME: 15 MINUTES · ACTIVE PREP TIME: 15 MINUTES

Before it was returned to China as a special administrative region, Hong Kong had been a British colony for over 150 years. Its modern culture combines Cantonese and British elements. Pudding is a mainstay of British cuisine, as is well known, but silky milk puddings have long been enjoyed in Guangdong as well—especially when lightly flavored with ginger. In Hong Kong, steamed milk pudding is eaten at breakfast as well as for dessert.

1 small hand ginger, peeled
4 egg whites
2 Tbsp. white sugar
1 dash salt
2 c. whole milk
Water, for boiling

Grate the ginger with a fine grater into a small bowl. Press the grated ginger against a fine sieve with the back of a spoon to collect the juice (you will need about 2 Tbsp. of juice). Set aside.

Combine egg whites, sugar, and salt in a medium bowl and stir vigorously with a whisk until sugar dissolves. Add milk a little at a time, whisking after each addition. Pour the mixture through a sieve into another bowl and whisk in ginger juice. Divide mixture between four 8-oz. ramekins and cover each tightly with plastic wrap.

Bring a large pot of water to a boil. Place a large steamer basket above the pot and place the ramekins inside the steamer. Cover the steamer and steam for 15 minutes. Remove plastic wrap and serve.

MAKES 4 SERVINGS

Per serving: 113 calories, 4 g fat, 2 g saturated fat, 121 mg sodium, 12 g carbohydrates, 8 g protein.

SERVING SUGGESTION: Serve warm or chilled. If serving chilled, do not refrigerate until puddings have reached room temperature.

VARIATIONS: Ginger juice may be omitted, or it may be replaced with lemon juice or other flavorings of choice.

TIP: When choosing ginger for this recipe, look for mature, ripe ginger. It will be easier to extract the juice from.

INDONESIA
KLEPON

MEDIUM · COOK TIME: 25 MINUTES · ACTIVE PREP TIME: 20 MINUTES

Klepon (Indonesian rice balls) originated in Java but have become popular throughout the Indonesian diaspora. They contain a number of quintessential southeast Asian ingredients, most notably glutinous rice flour, coconut milk, and shredded coconut. Pandan gives it its grassy vanilla-like flavor, while the sweet liquid center comes from solid palm sugar, a product made by boiling the sap of the palm tree.

3 c. glutinous rice flour
One 15-oz. can full-fat coconut milk
2 tsp. pandan extract
¼ tsp. salt
½ c. solid palm sugar, chopped into ½-inch cubes
Water, for boiling
1-½ c. desiccated coconut

Combine coconut milk, pandan extract, and salt in a small saucepan and heat over Medium heat just until warm. Remove from heat and pour into a large bowl. Sift glutinous rice flour and add to coconut milk mixture, one spoonful at a time, stirring after each addition to form a smooth dough. Knead the dough with your hands until pliable.

Divide dough into 20 portions and roll each portion into a ball. Make an indentation in each with your thumb and insert a cube of palm sugar, and then fold the dough over the sugar to enclose it in the center.

Bring a large pot of water to a boil over High heat. Carefully drop the klepon, one at a time, into the boiling water (this is best done in two or three batches). Once the klepon float on the water's surface, scoop them from the water with a slotted spoon.

While warm, roll the klepon in coconut until coated on all sides.

MAKES 20 KLEPON

Per klepon: 236 calories, 13 g fat, 12 g saturated fat, 50 mg sodium, 28 g carbohydrates, 3 g protein.

SERVING SUGGESTION: Klepon can be served at any temperature, as long as the palm sugar center is cooled (it may burn your mouth if it is not). In Indonesia, klepon are served wrapped in banana leaves.

VARIATION: For chocolate klepon, replace the palm sugar with cubed bar chocolate.

TIP: Coconut will stick to the klepon best if it is soft. Steaming the coconut for a few minutes in a steamer basket will soften it.

JAPAN
KASUTERA

MEDIUM · COOK TIME: 40 MINUTES · ACTIVE PREP TIME: 15 MINUTES

Portuguese merchants first visited Japan in the sixteenth century. The port of Nagasaki, founded as a joint venture led by a daimyo and a Jesuit missionary, became Japan's only port where Europeans were allowed to trade and remained so for three centuries. The Portuguese introduced the *pão de Castela* (bread from Castille) to Japan, and it became known as castella. Still a specialty of Nagasaki, it is now referred to by its japanized name and is served with all four sides trimmed. Unlike most pound cakes, kasutera contains no leavening agents, and therefore it takes a little trial and error to achieve the ideal airy texture.

3 large eggs, at room temperature
¾ c. bread flour
½ c. white sugar
3 Tbsp. honey, divided
1 Tbsp. plus 1 tsp. warm water, divided
Melted butter, for brushing pan

Add eggs to the bowl of a stand mixer with a whisk attachment. Whisk on High speed until beaten and add sugar a little at a time. Continue to whisk for 5 minutes or until mixture is very thick and pale.

Stir together 2 Tbsp. honey and 1 Tbsp. warm water. Reduce speed to Low and add honey mixture to egg mixture. Sift bread flour and add to egg mixture a little at a time, allowing mixer to whisk after each addition.

Preheat oven to 325 degrees. Brush the sides and bottom of a Pullman loaf pan with melted butter. Coat the sides and bottom of the pan with a single layer of parchment paper (cut to fit). Pour the batter into the pan and tap the bottom of the pan on a hard surface a few times to release any air bubbles that may be in the batter. Bake for 40 minutes or until a toothpick inserted in center comes out clean.

Combine remaining honey and water and brush the surface of the cake. Remove cake from pan and peel off parchment paper. Wrap cake in plastic wrap (while still warm) and refrigerate for 12 hours.

Remove cake from refrigerator and unwrap plastic. With a sharp knife, trim the sides of the cake so that only the top and bottom have a crust. Slice cake and serve.

MAKES 8 SERVINGS

Per serving: 140 calories, 2 g fat, 1 g saturated fat, 27 mg sodium, 28 g carbohydrates, 4 g protein.

SERVING SUGGESTION: Serve at room temperature with green tea.

VARIATIONS: For a green tea kasutera, omit honey and add 2 Tbsp. matcha powder. For a chocolate kasutera, add 2 Tbsp. cocoa powder (do not omit honey). For a brown sugar kasutera, replace honey and sugar with an equal amount of brown sugar.

KOREA
HOTTEOK

MEDIUM · COOK TIME: 30 MINUTES · ACTIVE PREP TIME: 20 MINUTES · INACTIVE PREP TIME: 2 HOURS, 10 MINUTES

The exact origins of hotteok have been debated, but it is certain that they were invented in Korea by Chinese immigrants. In the 1920s, the city of Incheon received an influx of Chinese migrant workers, who helped to popularize the handheld snack.

Today, hotteok is a common street food that is especially popular in the winter, as its crisp outside and gooey filling make it a warming cold weather treat.

4-½ c. bread flour
2 c. whole milk, slightly warmed
1 Tbsp. plus 2 tsp. white sugar
1-½ tsp. active dry yeast
1-½ tsp. salt
1 c. brown sugar
3 Tbsp. finely chopped peanuts
2 tsp. ground cinnamon
½ tsp. vanilla extract
Oil, for frying

Whisk together milk, sugar, and yeast in a medium bowl. Allow mixture to stand for about 10 minutes.

Sift together flour and salt and add to the bowl of a stand mixer with a dough hook attachment. Add milk mixture and mix on Low speed for 5 minutes. Cover with plastic wrap and allow to stand for 2 hours.

Combine brown sugar, peanuts, cinnamon, and vanilla in a small bowl. Set aside.

Divide dough into about 18 portions. Use your hands to roll each portion into a ball and then stretch the edges into a circle. Place 1 Tbsp. of brown sugar mixture in the center of each dough circle and fold the edges upwards to close. Flatten the ball slightly.

Heat about 1 inch of oil in a heavy skillet over Medium heat. In small batches, fry the hotteok seam side down for about 3 minutes. Flip the hotteok, flatten them with the back of a spatula, and cook 3 minutes longer or until golden brown. Remove from oil and drain on paper towels.

MAKES ABOUT 18 HOTTEOK

Per hotteok: 190 calories, 5 g fat, 1 g saturated fat, 142 mg sodium, 32 g carbohydrates, 4 g protein.

VARIATIONS: Less traditional hotteok fillings include hazelnut spread, mashed bananas, chocolate chips, sweetened bean paste, and peanut butter. Savory hotteok can be made with cheese, vegetable, or kimchi fillings and with glutinous rice flour instead of bread flour.

LAOS
MANGO STICKY RICE

EASY · COOK TIME: 45 MINUTES · ACTIVE PREP TIME: 20 MINUTES · INACTIVE PREP TIME: 12 HOURS, 20 MINUTES

The key staple of Lao cuisine is glutinous (sticky) rice, which Laotians prefer over other types (even though it is considered an inferior product elsewhere in southeast Asia). It forms the basis of virtually every sweet or savory dish. Mango sticky rice, which is enjoyed throughout the Mekong River Basin as well as in Laos, combines three pivotal ingredients of the region: glutinous rice, mangoes, and coconut milk.

4 ripe but firm mangoes
1-½ c. glutinous rice
Water, for soaking
One 15-oz. can full-fat coconut milk
½ c. granulated palm sugar
½ tsp. salt
Sweet basil leaves, for garnish

Place sticky rice in a medium bowl and cover with water to a depth of at least 3 inches. Allow rice to soak for at least 12 hours. Drain rice and spread onto a plate.

Boil a large pot of water and set a large steamer basket over the pot. Place rice on plate in steamer. Cover and steam for 30-45 minutes.

Combine coconut milk, palm sugar, and salt in a small saucepan and simmer over Medium heat until sugar is completely dissolved (it does not have to reach a boil). Remove from heat.

Add steamed rice and half of coconut milk mixture to a medium bowl and stir to combine. Cover with a cloth towel and allow to stand for 20 minutes.

Peel each mango and cut in half away from the pit. Slice the mango halves diagonally.

To serve, divide sticky rice and mango equally between 4 shallow bowls. Spoon remaining coconut milk mixture over rice. Garnish with basil leaves.

MAKES 4 SERVINGS

Per serving: 544 calories, 30 g fat, 26 g saturated fat, 313 mg sodium, 68 g carbohydrates, 7 g protein.

VARIATIONS: Black sticky rice, which actually has a more purple hue when cooked, may be used in place of plain glutinous rice. Peaches or papayas may be used in place of mangoes.

MACAU
BOLO MENINO

MEDIUM · COOK TIME: 1 HOUR, 5 MINUTES · ACTIVE PREP TIME: 20 MINUTES · INACTIVE PREP TIME: 1 HOUR

While bolo menino may have a Portuguese name (meaning "little boy's cake" or "Christ child cake"), this indulgent sponge cake is native to Macau and distinctly Asian. Taking its flavor from coconut, almonds, and pine nuts and its soft, airy texture from its ten egg yolks, bolo menino is frequently made for christenings and baby showers, and around Christmas.

2 c. panko breadcrumbs
1-¼ c. desiccated coconut
¼ c. finely ground almonds

2 Tbsp. finely ground pine nuts
5 eggs plus 5 egg yolks, separated
1-1/3 c. superfine white sugar
1-1/2 tsp. butter, at room temperature, plus more for brushing and greasing pan
1 tsp. baking powder
1/4 c. powdered sugar

Preheat the oven to 325 degrees. Combine breadcrumbs, coconut, and almonds on a rimmed baking sheet and toast for 30 minutes or until golden brown, turning at least twice. Remove from oven, transfer to a separate baking sheet, and allow to cool completely.

With an electric mixer, beat egg yolks and superfine sugar on High speed until pale and fluffy. Add butter and baking powder. Slowly fold in breadcrumb mixture.

In a separate bowl, beat egg whites on High speed until stiff and glossy. Fold egg whites into batter.

Grease the sides and bottom of an 8-inch tube pan with butter. Pour batter into pan and bake for 35 minutes or until a toothpick inserted in center comes out clean. Allow to cool slightly in pan before removing.

Brush the top and sides of the cake with melted butter and sprinkle with powdered sugar. Cut into slices to serve.

MAKES 8-10 SERVINGS

Per serving: 432 calories, 24 g fat, 17 g saturated fat, 87 mg sodium, 50 g carbohydrates, 10 g protein.

SERVING SUGGESTION: Serve with tea.

VARIATION: Substitute ½ c. of superfine sugar with brown sugar for a distinctly different result.

MALAYSIA
KUIH BAHULU

EASY · COOK TIME: 15 MINUTES · ACTIVE PREP TIME: 15 MINUTES

Often compared to the French madeleine, the Malaysian kuih bahulu is a tiny egg-heavy pastry with a crispy outside and soft inside traditionally baked in a star-shaped bahulu mold. While the cakes are probably of European origin, they are enjoyed across Malaysia on Muslim holidays and at Chinese New Year celebrations alike.

1 c. all-purpose flour
5 eggs, separated
¾ c. white sugar
½ tsp. vanilla extract
¼ tsp. baking powder
1 dash salt
Oil, for brushing pan

Preheat oven to 350 degrees. Place a bahulu mold or mini-muffin tin in the oven to heat.

Add egg whites to the bowl of a stand mixer with a whisk attachment. Mix on Medium speed until foamy. Add sugar and continue to mix until stiff, then add egg yolks and vanilla extract and mix for 2 minutes longer.

Sift together flour, baking powder, and salt. Fold dry ingredients into wet ingredients a little at a time.

Remove the bahulu mold or mini-muffin tin from the oven and brush the cups with oil. Pour about 1 Tbsp. of batter into each cup (using a pastry bag with a small tip will make this easier). Return to oven and bake for 15 minutes or until golden.

Gently remove bahulu from mold or tin and set on a wire rack to cool.

MAKES ABOUT 30 PASTRIES

Per pastry: 45 calories, 1 g fat, 0 g saturated fat, 14 mg sodium, 8 g carbohydrates, 1 g protein.

SERVING SUGGESTION: Serve with coffee.

VARIATIONS: For kuih cara manis, replace ½ c. white sugar with sweetened shredded coconut, 4 of the eggs with 1 c. full-fat coconut milk, and vanilla extract with pandan extract. While not traditionally Malaysian, 2 Tbsp. cocoa or matcha powder can be added for chocolate or green tea bahulu.

MONGOLIA
EEZGII

HARD · COOK TIME: 7 HOURS, 20 MINUTES · ACTIVE PREP TIME: 10 MINUTES

Before the rise of globalization, agriculture was nearly non-existent in Mongolia, and its people ate a diet that was almost entirely animal-based. So it should come as no surprise that eezgii, which Mongolians often enjoy at the end of meals, is perhaps the least sweet recipe in this cookbook. Made entirely from dairy products and containing no sugar or other added sweeteners, eezgii is naturally sweetened from prolonged roasting, which caramelizes its lactose.

4 qt. whole milk, preferably unpasteurized
1 c. kefir

Bring milk to a boil in a large stockpot over High heat. Add kefir and stir well. Cover and continue to boil for 15-20 minutes.

Remove lid and stir. Reduce heat to Low, cover, and simmer for up to 4 hours, stirring once every 30 minutes. At this point (or before), the milk should be mostly curdled. Strain the curds through a cheesecloth-lined colander.

Preheat oven to 300 degrees. Line a 9 x 13-inch baking dish with parchment paper. Place curds in dish and bake for 3 hours longer, stirring once every 30 minutes. Eezgii is ready when it is completely dry and rich brown in color.

MAKES 4-6 SERVINGS

Per serving: 501 calories, 27 g fat, 16 g saturated fat, 337 mg sodium, 38 g carbohydrates, 27 g protein.

TIP: Yogurt may be used in place of kefir, though the results may not be as reliable.

MYANMAR
SANWIN MAKIN

MEDIUM · COOK TIME: 50 MINUTES · ACTIVE PREP TIME: 15 MINUTES

Even though it originated in India, sanwin makin is today a very popular *mont* (snack food) offered by Myanmar's street vendors. The Burmese New Year is celebrated with a custom called Satuditha, in which slices of sanwin makin and other foods are offered to strangers as an act of good will, illustrating the importance of charity in Burmese culture.

One 15-oz. can full-fat coconut milk
2 c. water
1 c. fine semolina
1 c. white sugar
¼ c. ghee, plus more for greasing pan
½ tsp. ground cardamom
1 dash salt
3 eggs, separated
3 Tbsp. white poppyseeds

Combine coconut milk, water, and semolina in a large saucepan and stir with a whisk to remove lumps. Add sugar and bring to a boil over Medium-High heat. Reduce heat to Low and add ghee, a little at a time, and stir until mixture is very thick. Remove from heat and stir in cardamom and salt.

Beat egg yolks with a whisk and stir into semolina mixture with a wooden spoon. With an electric mixer, beat egg whites on High speed until stiff and glossy. Fold egg whites into batter.

Preheat oven to 325 degrees. Grease a 9 x 9-inch square pan with ghee. Pour batter into pan and use a spatula to spread into an even layer. Sprinkle poppyseeds over top. Bake for 40 minutes or until a toothpick inserted in center comes out mostly clean. Allow cake to cool in pan before slicing into squares.

MAKES ABOUT 12 SERVINGS

Per serving: 270 calories, 16 g fat, 12 g saturated fat, 34 mg sodium, 30 g carbohydrates, 5 g protein.

SERVING SUGGESTION: Serve warm, at room temperature, or chilled. If desired, garnish with slivered almonds and serve with vanilla ice cream.

VARIATIONS: Replace sugar with 1 ripe mashed banana or add ½ c. raisins to batter. Use potato flour in place of semolina. Sesame seeds or desiccated coconut may be used in place of white poppyseeds.

NEPAL
KHAJURI

EASY · COOK TIME: 30 MINUTES · ACTIVE PREP TIME: 10 MINUTES · INACTIVE PREP TIME: 20 MINUTES

The Hindu festival of Chhat Parva is celebrated in Nepal during the autumn months. On the second day of this three-day observance, lighted oil lamps are released from the river banks and the Sun deity Lord Surya is presented with offerings of fruits, nuts, and sweets. Khajuri are almost always included. At the end of the festival, the devotees break their fasts as the offerings are distributed.

2 c. all-purpose flour, plus more for flouring surface
¾ c. fine semolina
1 tsp. ground cardamom
1 dash salt
2 c. ghee, divided
¾ c. whole milk
1 c. powdered sugar

Sift together flour, semolina, cardamom, and salt and add to the bowl of a stand mixer with a dough hook attachment along with 1 c. ghee. Mix on Low speed until combined, and then slowly add milk followed by powdered sugar. Cover bowl with plastic wrap and allow to stand for 20 minutes.

Roll out dough onto a floured surface. Use a medium-sized cookie cutter to cut shapes from dough.

Heat remaining ghee in a heavy skillet to a temperature of 300 degrees. Carefully drop each cookie into the hot ghee and fry in batches for 2-3 minutes on each side or until they reach a golden brown color. Remove from pan and set on paper towels to drain.

MAKES ABOUT 40 COOKIES

Per cookie: 138 calories, 10 g fat, 7 g saturated fat, 6 mg sodium, 10 g carbohydrates, 1 g protein.

VARIATIONS: Some variations of khajuri include fennel seed or grated coconut. Others use wheat flour in place of semolina.

PHILIPPINES
HALO-HALO

MEDIUM · COOK TIME: 1 HOUR · ACTIVE PREP TIME: 20 MINUTES · INACTIVE PREP TIME: 2 HOURS

Anthony Bourdain once described halo-halo (or "mix-mix" in Tagalog) as "oddly beautiful." A typical American who is unfamiliar with it will probably agree that it's odd. But if you give it a try, you may be very surprised at how well incongruous ingredients like adzuki beans and corn go with ice cream and coconut jelly. The bright purple ube ice cream, which gets both its earthy flavor and vivid hue from the purple yam, has been popular in the Philippines since ice cream was first introduced there in the 1920s. Only recently has its popularity spread outside of the Philippines.

¼ c. white sugar, divided

3 egg yolks

½ c. sweetened condensed milk, divided

Two 12-oz. cans evaporated milk, divided

1 c. canned adzuki beans

8 c. ice cubes, crushed or shaved

1 c. coconut jelly cubes

1 c. canned sweet corn, drained

1 tsp. pandan extract (optional)

2 c. ube ice cream

¼ c. crushed cornflakes

Place 1 Tbsp. sugar in a small heat-proof glass dish. Place dish over a low flame on stove until sugar is melted and caramelized, stirring constantly. Remove from heat.

Preheat oven to 375 degrees. Whisk together egg yolks and 2 Tbsp. sweetened condensed milk. Add ¼ c. evaporated milk. Pour egg yolk mixture into glass dish. Set dish inside a larger glass baking dish and fill dish with hot (but not boiling) water.

Bake custard for about 1 hour or until a toothpick inserted in center comes out clean. Allow custard to cool completely, and then refrigerate until chilled.

Combine remaining sugar and adzuki beans and stir together until sugar is mostly dissolved. Divide sweetened adzuki beans between four tall sundae glasses, followed by one-third of crushed ice. Divide jelly cubes between glasses, followed by another one-third of crushed ice. Divide corn between glasses, followed by remaining crushed ice. Top with remaining sweetened condensed milk.

Cut chilled custard into cubes. Divide custard cubes among glasses.

Stir pandan extract (if using) into remaining evaporated milk. Divide evaporated milk mixture between glasses.

Top each glass with a scoop of ube ice cream and sprinkle with cornflakes.

MAKES 4 SERVINGS

Per serving: 688 calories, 25 g fat, 15 g saturated fat, 297 mg sodium, 99 g carbohydrates, 19 g protein.

VARIATIONS: This recipe is really just a suggestion. Possible ingredient combinations for halo-halo are basically endless; aside from those used here, they can include shredded coconut, bananas, mangos, jackfruit, coconut milk, sweet potatoes, sago or tapioca pearls, mung beans, chickpeas, rice, boiled taro, cantaloupe, and cheese. While ube ice cream is sometimes regarded as the only mandatory ingredient, it can be omitted or replaced with vanilla or mango ice cream.

SINGAPORE
PANDAN CHIFFON CAKE

MEDIUM · COOK TIME: 1 HOUR · ACTIVE PREP TIME: 15 MINUTES

The chiffon-style sponge cake, which uses vegetable oil instead of butter to achieve a texture that is both airy and moist, is actually an American invention popularized in

1948 by a Betty Crocker pamphlet. Yet at some point in Singapore (probably in the 1970s), the chiffon cake crossed paths with one of the most Southeast Asian of all ingredients, the pandan leaf. It provides this cake with a gentle green hue as well as a grassy, earthy flavor.

15 fresh pandan leaves, chopped
½ c. full-fat coconut milk, divided
2 Tbsp. water
5 eggs, divided
¼ c. plus 2 Tbsp. fine white sugar, divided
1/3 c. coconut oil, in liquid form, plus more for greasing pan
¾ c. cake flour
1 tsp. baking powder
½ tsp. white vinegar
½ tsp. salt

Combine pandan leaves, 2 Tbsp. coconut milk, and water in a blender or food processor. Pulse until leaves are finely ground. Strain pandan juice through a fine sieve and set aside.

Add egg yolks to the bowl of a stand mixer with a whisk attachment. Mix on Medium speed until very pale. Add 2 Tbsp. sugar and continue to mix until creamy. Add coconut oil, pandan juice, and remaining coconut milk. Sift together flour and baking powder and add to egg yolk mixture a little at a time.

With an electric mixer, beat egg whites on High until soft peaks form. Slowly add remaining sugar, a little at a time, until all sugar is dissolved and mixture is foamy. Add vinegar, followed by salt. Continue to beat just until stiff peaks form (do not overbeat).

Preheat oven to 300 degrees. Use a wooden spoon to slowly fold egg white mixture into batter. Grease the sides and bottom of an 8-inch tube pan with coconut oil. Pour batter into pan and bake for 1 hour or until a toothpick inserted in center comes out clean.

After removing from oven, turn the cake upside down and place on a wire rack. Allow the cake to cool completely before removing from pan.

MAKES 8-10 SERVINGS

Per serving: 195 calories, 14 g fat, 11 g saturated fat, 165 mg sodium, 15 g carbohydrates, 5 g protein.

SERVING SUGGESTION: Pandan chiffon cake is usually served plain and at room temperature, but it can be glazed or dusted with powdered sugar. To make a glaze for the cake, whisk together 2 c. powdered sugar and ¼ c. water, milk, or coconut milk and drizzle over cake after removing from pan.

TIP: The pandan juice will give the cake a light green color. For a stronger shade, add a small amount of green food coloring.

TAIWAN
MANGO BAOBING

EASY · ACTIVE PREP TIME: 20 MINUTES · INACTIVE PREP TIME: 4 HOURS

Shaved ice is taken very seriously in Taiwan. It is believed that the frozen dessert (called baobing in Chinese) was first enjoyed in China in the seventh century CE. In Taiwan, baobing is usually made with milk and flavored or topped with fruit—although like its cousin halo-halo (page 253), it can include a wide variety of flavors. Baobing is made in a different manner from American shaved ice and takes the form of thin sheets or ribbons rather than fine snow-like flakes.

3 fresh mangoes, peeled and cored
1 qt. whole milk
¼ c. sugar
1 c. sweetened condensed milk

Chop two of the mangoes. Place in a blender with milk and sugar and pulse to form a smooth puree. Pour the mango puree into ice trays or other small containers and freeze until solid.

Cut remaining mango into cubes. Set aside.

Grind the frozen mango puree in a shaved ice maker. (If your shaved ice maker has a setting that will shave the ice in a spiral or ribbon shape, it should be used.) Divide shaved mango ice between four bowls. Top with cubed mango and condensed milk and serve immediately.

MAKES 4-6 SERVINGS

Per serving: 472 calories, 12 g fat, 7 g saturated fat, 158 mg sodium, 82 g carbohydrates, 13 g protein.

SERVING SUGGESTION: Top baobing with other fruits, such as raspberries, lychees, or kiwi, or with tapioca pearls, mung beans, or peanuts.

VARIATIONS: For strawberry baobing, replace mangoes with 3 c. of fresh strawberries. For a vegan version, soy or other non-dairy milks can be used in place of whole milk.

TIP: If you do not have a shaved ice maker, a blender can be used to grind the ice instead (although the texture will not be as smooth).

THAILAND
KLUAI THOT WITH COCONUT ICE CREAM

MEDIUM · COOK TIME: 20 MINUTES · ACTIVE PREP TIME: 10 MINUTES · INACTIVE PREP TIME: 4 HOURS, 20 MINUTES

Kluai thot, or fried bananas, is a Thai street food that is so prevalent that for some it is difficult to avoid. Street vendors sell kluai thot not only from stalls but also at busy intersections in large cities, soliciting motorists who are stopped in traffic. Ice cream is another well-loved Thai snack, but in Thailand flavors such as coconut, ginger, green tea, gooseberry, mung bean, and sour plum are more popular than chocolate or vanilla.

For kluai thot:
3 large, firm bananas, peeled and quartered
¾ c. water
½ c. rice flour
½ c. unsweetened shredded coconut
3 Tbsp. sesame seeds
2 Tbsp. white sugar
1-½ tsp. baking soda
1-½ tsp. salt
Vegetable oil, for frying

Whisk together water, rice flour, coconut, sesame seeds, sugar, baking soda, and salt to form a thick batter.

Heat about 1 inch of oil in a heavy skillet to a temperature of 350 degrees. Dredge bananas in batter until they are heavily coated, and fry in small batches until brown on both sides, about 2-3 minutes. Remove from pan and set on paper towels to drain.

For coconut ice cream:
One 15-oz. can full-fat coconut milk
½ c. coconut palm sugar, chopped
¼ c. white sugar
1 dash salt
1-½ c. coconut water
2 Tbsp. vodka (optional; prevents overfreezing)
¼ c. shredded and toasted coconut, plus more for garnish

Combine coconut milk, palm sugar, white sugar, and salt in a large saucepan and heat over Medium heat until palm sugar is completely dissolved. Stir in coconut water. Chill mixture in refrigerator for at least 2 hours, and then stir in vodka (if using).

Churn mixture in a standard ice cream maker, following manufacturer's instructions for making sorbet. Add shredded coconut to ice cream maker shortly before cycle is completed. Pour ice cream into a freezer-safe container and freeze for 2 hours longer.

MAKES 6 SERVINGS

Per serving (2 kluai thot and ½ c. ice cream): 720 calories, 52 g fat, 30 g saturated fat, 725 mg sodium, 63 g carbohydrates, 6 g protein.

VARIATIONS: Spices such as ginger, cinnamon, or anise can be added to ice cream or to kluai thot batter if desired.

TIP: If you do not have an ice cream maker, place mixture in a freezer-safe container and place in freezer for at least 4-6 hours or until frozen, stirring with a fork every 30 minutes.

TIBET
THUE

EASY · ACTIVE PREP TIME: 10 MINUTES · INACTIVE PREP TIME: 4 HOURS

One of very few sweet dishes in Tibetan cuisine, thue is often eaten to celebrate Losar, the Tibetan New Year festival, and is sometimes decorated with butter shaped into the form of a crescent moon or swastika (a highly auspicious symbol in Tibetan Buddhism). In Tibet, the cheese and butter used in thue are made from dri, or yak's milk. Any hard, aged cheese can be used to make thue.

2-¾ c. grated dry cheese (such as dri, churpi, Parmesan, or Pecorino Romano)
¾ c. brown sugar
1-½ c. unsalted sweet cream butter, at room temperature

Use a pastry blender to sift together cheese and brown sugar until completely incorporated. Using your hands, fold in butter a little at a time and knead to form a moist dough.

Pack the dough into a 3-cup plastic or glass dish. Refrigerate for at least 4 hours.

When ready to serve, invert dish onto a plate to loosen thue and cut into slices with a sharp knife.

MAKES 4 SERVINGS

Per serving: 1072 calories, 104 g fat, 67 g saturated fat, 1372 mg sodium, 4 g carbohydrates, 37 g protein.

VARIATION: Jaggery, a type of sugar made from cane juice and date or palm sap, can be used in place of brown sugar for a much different flavor.

TIMOR-LESTE BIBINGKA

EASY · COOK TIME: 45 MINUTES · ACTIVE PREP TIME: 15 MINUTES

In Timor-Leste, like in the Philippines (where it originated), it is difficult to imagine celebrating Christmas without bibingka. For the nine days preceding Christmas, street vendors in the overwhelmingly Roman Catholic island nation gather outside churches to sell slices of the sweet rice cake to Mass goers. In Timor-Leste, bibingka is often wrapped in banana leaves and cooked over a charcoal grill. This version uses the oven instead.

1-¾ c. white sugar, divided
1 c. glutinous rice flour
1 c. all-purpose flour
1-½ tsp. baking powder
¼ tsp. salt
1 c. full-fat coconut milk

1 c. whole milk
2 eggs
½ c. unsalted butter, melted, divided
½ c. cream cheese, cubed

Sift together sugar, rice flour, all-purpose flour, baking powder, and salt. In a separate bowl, combine coconut milk, whole milk, and eggs and mix on Medium speed with an electric mixer. Gradually fold dry ingredients into wet ingredients, followed by ¼ c. melted butter.

Preheat oven to 350 degrees. Line a 9- x 13-inch baking dish with parchment paper. Pour batter into dish and drop cream cheese cubes into batter, spacing at even intervals.

Bake for 25 minutes. Remove from oven, brush with remaining butter, and sprinkle with remaining sugar. Return to oven and bake for 20 minutes longer or until golden brown. Allow cake to cool slightly before slicing.

MAKES 12 SERVINGS

Per serving: 319 calories, 18 g fat, 12 g saturated fat, 155 mg sodium, 38 g carbohydrates, 5 g protein.

SERVING SUGGESTION: Serve warm with coffee or milk.

VARIATIONS: Banana leaves are traditionally used to line the baking dish. If using banana leaves, spray them with cooking spray before pouring batter. For a savorier bibingka, reduce sugar to ½ c. and use Cheddar cheese in place of cream cheese.

VIETNAM
BANH CHUOI

MEDIUM · COOK TIME: 30 MINUTES · ACTIVE PREP TIME: 15 MINUTES

Its name literally means "banana bread," but banh chuoi is more like a banana pudding. While bananas, rice, cinnamon, and coconut are all ingredients native to Southeast Asia, puddings such as this one evolved in Vietnam as a result of French colonial influence. Banh chuoi can be either steamed, as it is here, or baked.

3 large bananas, peeled and sliced
¼ c. brown sugar
½ c. tapioca flour
¼ c. plus 1 Tbsp. rice flour
1 tsp. ground cinnamon
½ tsp. salt, divided
1 c. water, divided, plus more for boiling
One 15-oz. can full-fat coconut milk
1 Tbsp. white sugar
1 Tbsp. plus 2 tsp. cornstarch
Toasted sesame seeds, for garnish

Combine banana slices and brown sugar and toss to coat. Set aside.

Sift together tapioca and rice flours, cinnamon, and ¼ tsp. salt. Stir in ½ c. water and mix until a batter is formed. Fold the banana mixture into the flour mixture.

Bring a large pot of water to a boil. Place a large steamer basket above the pot and place an 8 x 8-inch glass baking dish inside the steamer. Ladle the batter into the dish and spread in an even layer. Cover the steamer and steam for 25 minutes or until a toothpick inserted in center comes out clean. Remove from steamer and set aside to cool.

While banh chuoi is cooling, prepare sauce. Heat coconut milk, ¼ c. water, sugar, and remaining salt in a small saucepan over Medium-High heat. Once mixture is warmed and sugar is dissolved, whisk together cornstarch and remaining water to form a slurry and add to the coconut milk mixture. Continue to cook until thickened, stirring constantly, and remove from heat.

To serve, slice the banh chuoi and divide between eight plates. Top each serving with an equal amount of sauce and garnish with sesame seeds.

MAKES 8 SERVINGS

Per serving: 252 calories, 15 g fat, 13 g saturated fat, 159 mg sodium, 32 g carbohydrates, 2 g protein.

VARIATION: Plantains may be used instead of bananas.

TIP: If condensation from the inside of the lid dripping onto the banh chuoi becomes a problem, lay a dry towel over the steamer before placing the lid on top.

OCEANIA

AUSTRALIA
LAMINGTONS

MEDIUM · COOK TIME: 25 MINUTES · ACTIVE PREP TIME: 30 MINUTES · INACTIVE PREP TIME: 1 HOUR

Australia's national cake was named for Charles Wallace Alexander Napier Cochrane-Baillie, second Baron of Lamington (1860-1940), who served as governor of Queensland from 1896 to 1901. As the story goes, the first lamingtons were made out of necessity when Lord Lamington's cook was forced to make a dish for unexpected guests and had to improvise using a stale sponge cake. He cut the cake into squares, dipped the squares in chocolate sauce, and rolled them in shredded coconut. While Lord Lamington was reportedly not a fan of the dessert named after him, referring to them as "those bloody poofy woolly biscuits," the first recipe for "lammos" appeared in an Australian newspaper only a few years later and became instantly popular.

1 c. white sugar
5 eggs
1 c. all-purpose flour
1 tsp. baking powder
¼ tsp. salt
¾ c. heavy cream
8 oz. milk chocolate, chopped
¼ c. butter, cubed
3 c. desiccated coconut

Add sugar and eggs to the bowl of a stand mixer with a whisk attachment. Mix on Medium speed until pale and foamy. Sift together flour, baking powder, and salt and slowly add to egg mixture.

Preheat oven to 350 degrees. Line an 8 x 8-inch square pan with parchment paper. Pour batter into pan and bake for 20 minutes or until a toothpick inserted in center of cake comes out clean. Allow cake to cool in pan for 10 minutes, then invert onto a wire rack, remove parchment paper, and allow to cool completely.

Heat heavy cream in a small saucepan until very warm (do not bring to a boil). Place chocolate in a bowl, cover with cream, and stir until chocolate is completely melted. Add butter and continue to stir to form a smooth chocolate sauce.

Use a sharp knife to cut the cake into 16 equal squares. Dip each square in chocolate sauce to cover all sides, and then roll in coconut to coat. Place lamingtons on a sheet of waxed paper to set.

MAKES 16 LAMINGTONS

Per lamington: 496 calories, 38 g fat, 31 g saturated fat, 104 mg sodium, 37 g carbohydrates, 7 g protein.

SERVING SUGGESTION: Serve at room temperature or chilled.

VARIATIONS: For filled lamingtons, slice in half crosswise, spread whipped cream or strawberry jam on one half, and top with other half. For a raspberry version, popular in New Zealand, replace chocolate sauce with raspberry sauce.

TIP: Freezing the sponge cake after slicing it will make the squares easier to coat in chocolate sauce without breaking. Allow cake to thaw completely before serving.

FIJI
PURINI

MEDIUM · COOK TIME: 1 HOUR · ACTIVE PREP TIME: 15 MINUTES

Like so many steamed puddings, purini probably developed as a result of British influence. But it is a genuinely Melanesian dish, with the native coconut providing its most dominant flavor. Like virtually all Fijian desserts, brown sugar figures widely in purini; plain white sugar is not easy to obtain on these islands.

2 c. brown sugar
One 15-oz. can full-fat coconut milk, divided
3 c. all-purpose flour
2 tsp. baking powder
1 tsp. baking soda
½ tsp. salt
¼ c. liquid coconut oil
1 tsp. vanilla extract
Water, for steaming

Heat brown sugar in a heavy skillet over Medium heat until completely melted, stirring constantly. Stir in half of coconut milk and continue to cook until sugar has crystallized, then add remaining milk. Remove from heat and allow to cool completely.

Sift together flour, baking powder, baking soda, and salt. Stir in brown sugar mixture and add coconut oil and vanilla extract. Mix well until a thick batter is formed and no lumps remain.

Bring a large pot of water to a boil. Place a large steamer basket above the pot. Line a 9-inch cake pan with parchment paper. Pour batter into pan and tap the bottom a few times to level and to remove air bubbles. Place the pan inside the steamer. Cover the steamer and steam for 45 minutes or until a toothpick inserted in center comes out clean. Remove from steamer and set aside to cool.

When ready to serve, invert purini onto a serving dish, remove parchment paper, and slice.

MAKES 8 SERVINGS

Per serving: 509 calories, 22 g fat, 19 g saturated fat, 328 mg sodium, 75 g carbohydrates, 6 g protein.

SERVING SUGGESTION: Dust with powdered sugar, garnish with fruit, and spread with butter.

VARIATIONS: Some Fijian cooks use butter in place of coconut oil or add cocoa powder, cinnamon, or nutmeg. Raisins or mashed ripe bananas may also be added.

TIP: If condensation from the inside of the lid dripping onto the purini becomes a problem, lay a dry towel over the steamer before placing the lid on top.

KIRIBATI
BUATORO

MEDIUM · COOK TIME: 1 HOUR, 30 MINUTES · ACTIVE PREP TIME: 20 MINUTES

The island nation of Kiribati covers approximately 1.4 million square miles, although just over three hundred of those are above water. Its rather tiny islands are spread far apart in the western Pacific Ocean, and accordingly its cuisine relies on a few native ingredients. Taro is chief among these, as are bananas and coconuts. Seafood, rice, and other dishes are typically prepared like this taro pudding—wrapped in banana leaves and baked in the oven.

2-½ lb. taro, peeled and cut into large pieces
1 large banana leaf, for steaming
1-½ c. brown sugar
One 15-oz. can full-fat coconut milk
Water, for boiling and steaming

Bring a large pot of water to a boil. Add taro, reduce heat to Low, and simmer for 40 minutes or until taro is fully cooked. Drain and set aside.

Cut banana leaf into four equal-sized, roughly square-shaped pieces. Bring a large pot of water to a boil. Place the banana leaf pieces in the water and boil for 5 minutes or until soft. (This step will make the banana leaf less brittle and easier to fold.) Pat leaves dry with paper towels and set aside.

Place cooked taro in a large bowl and mash with a potato masher until smooth. Add brown sugar and mix until combined. Stir in coconut milk until a thick batter is formed (you may not need to use it all).

Spread one-quarter of batter in the center of each piece of banana leaf. Fold each banana leaf to encase the batter and tie with twine or raffia.

Preheat oven to 350 degrees. Place banana leaf packets on a rimmed baking sheet and bake for 45 minutes. Remove packets from oven and allow to cool slightly before opening.

MAKES 4 SERVINGS

Per serving: 559 calories, 29 g fat, 25 g saturated fat, 42 mg sodium, 77 g carbohydrates, 5 g protein.

VARIATION: Sweet potato can be used in place of taro. It will not take as long to boil.

TIP: While banana leaves are highly recommended (they add flavor as well as authenticity to this dessert), parchment paper or nonstick aluminum foil can be used instead.

MARSHALL ISLANDS AMETAMA

MEDIUM · COOK TIME: 20 MINUTES · ACTIVE PREP TIME: 40 MINUTES

A specialty of the island of Jaluit, ametama is a Marshallese coconut candy traditionally made with jekaro, a sweet sap extracted from the coconut tree's flowering stalks that is sometimes fermented to make a liqueur. Jekaro is difficult to find in the United States, so this recipe substitutes melted coconut palm sugar.

2 large coconuts
2 c. coconut palm sugar

Use a screwdriver or other sharp object to poke three holes in each coconut. Drain the water from the coconuts and reserve for another use. Hit the side of each coconut with a mallet or heavy knife, rotate slightly, and hit again. Continue until you hear the coconut crack. Strike the coconut against a hard surface to break open.

Peel the brown outside layer from the pieces of coconut with a sharp knife and cut the white flesh into smaller pieces. Use a food processor or the small holes of a box grater to grate coconut flesh as finely as possible. Set aside.

Heat sugar in a skillet over Medium-Low heat until fully melted, stirring frequently. Add the grated coconut and continue to stir until the mixture is smooth and consistent (the sugar may crystallize after adding the coconut, but it will melt again).

Cover your working surface with a layer of wax paper. Working quickly, scoop the coconut mixture in 2 Tbsp. portions and lay on the wax paper. Once all of the mixture has been scooped and has cooled enough to touch with bare hands, shape each portion into a ball and wrap in plastic wrap.

MAKES ABOUT 30 CANDIES

Per candy: 189 calories, 13 g fat, 12 g saturated fat, 37 mg sodium, 19 g carbohydrates, 1 g protein.

TIP: Frozen coconut (unsweetened) can be used in place of fresh coconut. You will need about 4 c. of grated coconut for this recipe.

MICRONESIA
UTER

EASY · COOK TIME: 20 MINUTES · ACTIVE PREP TIME: 20 MINUTES · INACTIVE PREP TIME: 1 HOUR

The most popular traditional dessert in the Federated States of Micronesia, uter, is also one of the simplest. There are a few different ways to prepare these simple no-bake treats. Some cooks steam the taro, while others boil it; some cook the taro just long enough to make it tender but still firm, while others cook it longer for a softer product; some use white sugar, others use brown sugar, and still others leave the sugar out completely. The only constants are its two main ingredients, taro and coconut, both staples of Micronesian cuisine.

2 lb. taro, peeled and cut into large pieces
Water, for steaming
2 c. grated coconut, divided
¼ c. plus 2 Tbsp. white sugar

Bring a large pot of water to a boil. Place taro in a large steamer basket over pot and cover. Steam for 20 minutes or until taro is tender enough to pierce easily with a toothpick. Set aside to cool.

Once taro is cool enough to handle, mash with a fork or potato masher until smooth and without lumps. Gradually stir sugar into mashed taro until combined, followed by ½ c. coconut. Scoop the taro mixture in 2 Tbsp. portions and form into balls. Roll each taro ball in remaining coconut to coat. Refrigerate for 1 hour or until ready to serve.

MAKES ABOUT 35-40 UTER

Per uter: 35 calories, 2 g fat, 1 g saturated fat, 2 mg sodium, 5 g carbohydrates, 0 g protein.

VARIATIONS: Use sweet potato or unripe banana in place of taro.

NAURU
COCONUT MOUSSE

MEDIUM · COOK TIME: 5 MINUTES · ACTIVE PREP TIME: 15 MINUTES · INACTIVE PREP TIME: 2 HOURS, 35 MINUTES

The smallest nation in the world that is not a city-state, Nauru has a land mass of only eight square miles, much of which has been decimated by phosphate mining. Coconut farming remains an industry in Nauru, however, and most of its dishes incorporate coconut in some manner. Like a traditional mousse (page 40), this coconut version uses egg whites and yolks to create a dessert that is both light and rich.

4 eggs, separated
½ c. coconut sugar
One 15-oz. can full-fat coconut cream
½ c. coconut water
1 dash salt
¼ c. hot water
2 tsp. agar agar

Combine egg yolks and sugar in a medium bowl. Beat with an electric mixer on Medium speed for 3 minutes or until mixture is pale and sugar has dissolved.

Heat the coconut cream in a saucepan over Medium heat until warm (do not bring to a boil). Slowly add half of the coconut cream to the egg yolk mixture, whisking slowly. Add the remaining coconut cream while whisking at a faster speed. Return mixture to saucepan and heat over Medium-Low heat, stirring constantly, until thickened. Return mixture to bowl and refrigerate until completely cooled, about 30 minutes.

Combine egg whites and salt and beat on High speed until stiff peaks form. Dissolve agar agar in hot water and allow to stand for about 5 minutes.

Remove coconut cream mixture from refrigerator and add coconut water. Beat with an electric mixer on Medium speed until soft peaks form.

Gently fold egg whites into coconut cream mixture until combined, followed by agar agar mixture, taking care not to let the mousse lose its airiness. Spoon mousse into six 8-oz. ramekins. Chill for at least 2 hours before serving.

MAKES 6 SERVINGS

Per serving: 290 calories, 22 g fat, 18 g saturated fat, 103 mg sodium, 22 g carbohydrates, 6 g protein.

SERVING SUGGESTION: Serve with fresh fruit, such as sliced bananas or mango.

VARIATION: For a creamier mousse, use heavy cream in place of coconut water.

NEW ZEALAND PAVLOVA

HARD · COOK TIME: 1 HOUR, 30 MINUTES · ACTIVE PREP TIME: 1 HOUR · INACTIVE PREP TIME: 6 HOURS

It is known that New Zealand's national dessert was named for the legendary Russian prima ballerina Anna Pavlova (1881-1931), but the rest of the details are disputed. New Zealanders place its origins with a Wellington chef who created it in the ballerina's honor during her 1926 tour of the country; Australians, who also lay claim to "the Pav," tell a different story about how it was invented. Some food historians have argued that the dessert made its way down under from Austria or even from the United States. Wherever it was first made, in New Zealand today it is almost invariably served topped with sliced kiwifruit.

8 egg whites
2 c. caster sugar
1 Tbsp. cornstarch
2 tsp. white vinegar
1 c. heavy whipping cream, very cold
3 Tbsp. powdered sugar
2 tsp. vanilla extract
1-½ c. kiwifruit, peeled and sliced
1-½ c. strawberries, sliced

Place egg whites in the bowl of a stand mixer with a whisk attachment. Mix on

Medium speed until soft peaks form. Add the caster sugar one spoonful at a time, pausing frequently to scrape down the sides of the bowl. Continue to mix until mixture is thick and glossy and sugar is completely dissolved.

Combine cornstarch and vinegar to form a slurry. Add to egg white mixture and increase speed to High. Mix for 1 minute longer.

Preheat oven to 300 degrees. Cut a 9-inch circle from a piece of parchment paper and place in the center of a rimmed baking sheet. Use a rubber spatula to spoon the meringue in the center of the parchment paper circle and spread over the circle, reserving about ½-inch around the edge. With a smaller icing spatula, smooth the surface of the meringue so that it resembles a mound with a flat top.

Place meringue in the oven, reduce oven temperature to 225 degrees, and bake for 1 hour, 30 minutes. Turn off the oven and allow the meringue to stand in the closed oven for 6 hours. (Resist the urge to open the oven door!)

With an electric mixer, beat whipping cream, powdered sugar, and vanilla extract on Medium speed until stiff peaks form. Refrigerate Chantilly cream until ready to use.

To assemble the pavlova, spread the Chantilly cream over the flat surface. Top with kiwifruit and strawberry slices and serve immediately.

MAKES 12 SERVINGS

Per serving: 203 calories, 4 g fat, 2 g saturated fat, 27 mg sodium, 41 g carbohydrates, 3 g protein.

VARIATIONS: Other fruits such as berries, peaches, mango, or currants, or lemon curd, can be used to top pavlova. Add liqueur or cocoa powder to Chantilly cream for additional flavor.

TIP: Pavlova should be eaten on the day it is prepared. If necessary, the meringue can be made up to 24 hours in advance and stored at room temperature (never refrigerated) before adding Chantilly cream and fruit.

PALAU
PICHI-PICHI

MEDIUM · COOK TIME: 1 HOUR, 15 MINUTES · ACTIVE PREP TIME: 20 MINUTES

An archipelago of over 300 islands, Palau shares several staple foods with other Pacific island nations, such as taro and coconut. Cassava, from which tapioca is made, is one that is more unique to it and that reflects the influence of its closest neighbor, the Philippines. Palau also shares many dishes with the Philippines, among them pichi-pichi, which originated in the Philippine province of Quezon.

1 lb. cassava, peeled
2 c. water, plus more for steaming
¾ c. white sugar
1 tsp. lye water (see Tip)
1-½ c. grated coconut

Use a food processor or the small holes of a box grater to grate cassava as finely as possible. With a dish towel or cheesecloth, strain any excess liquid from the grated cassava. Combine cassava, water, sugar, and lye water and stir until smooth. Divide the batter between 24 silicone baking cups.

Bring a large pot of water to a boil. Place a large steamer basket above the pot. Set the baking cups inside the steamer basket (you will need to work in batches) and cover with lid. Steam each batch for 25 minutes or until the liquid batter firms up and becomes translucent. Remove from steamer and set aside to cool (refrigerate if necessary).

Remove each pichi-pichi from its baking cup and roll in shredded coconut to coat.

MAKES 24 PICHI-PICHI

Per pichi-pichi: 65 calories, 1 g fat, 1 g saturated fat, 4 mg sodium, 14 g carbohydrates, 0 g protein.

SERVING SUGGESTION: While not as common in Palau, in the Philippines pichi-pichi are sometimes served with shredded cheese.

VARIATION: Add food coloring to batter for colorful pichi-pichi. Pandan extract (green) and ube extract (purple) can be used to add both color and flavor.

TIP: Lye water is highly alkaline and should be handled with care. For a less caustic substitute, spread a layer of baking soda on an aluminum foil-lined baking sheet and bake at 250 degrees for 1 hour. Combine one part baked baking soda with four parts water.

PAPUA NEW GUINEA
SAKSAK

MEDIUM · COOK TIME: 45 MINUTES · ACTIVE PREP TIME: 30 MINUTES

Many of the desserts of the Pacific islands have been greatly influenced by European colonization. But not this one! Globalization has had very little impact on Papua New Guinea's cuisine, desserts included. Sago, a product that has yet to become popular in Western countries, is the chief staple of Papuan cooking. These sago and banana dumplings, which are steamed in banana leaves and then simmered in coconut milk, get their name from the Papuan word for this starchy product.

3 c. ground sago flour
3 very ripe bananas, peeled and mashed
1 large banana leaf, for steaming
Water, for boiling and steaming
Two 15-oz. cans light coconut milk

Cut banana leaf into four equal-sized, roughly square-shaped pieces. Bring a large pot of water to a boil. Place the banana leaf pieces in the water and boil for 5 minutes or until soft. (This step will make the banana leaf less brittle and easier to fold.) Pat leaves dry with paper towels and set aside.

Peel and mash bananas with a wooden spoon. Gradually fold in sago flour and stir until dough is moist and smooth.

Divide dough into four portions. In the center of each banana leaf, spread one portion of dough. Fold each banana leaf to encase the dough and tie with twine or raffia.

Boil a large pot of water and set a large steamer basket over the pot. Place banana leaf packets in steamer. Cover and steam for 20 minutes. Remove packets from steamer and allow to cool slightly before opening.

Bring coconut milk to a boil in a Dutch oven or large skillet. Reduce heat to Low, add unwrapped dumplings, and simmer for 20 minutes longer. Serve dumplings in shallow bowls and ladle warm coconut milk on top.

MAKES 4 SERVINGS

Per serving: 416 calories, 3 g fat, 2 g saturated fat, 20 mg sodium, 101 g carbohydrates, 1 g protein.

VARIATIONS: Cassava or tapioca flour can be used in place of sago flour. Sago in pearl form can also be used. While saksak are very sweet on their own, if more sweetness is desired add 2-3 Tbsp. of white or brown sugar to the dough.

TIP: While banana leaves are highly recommended (they add flavor as well as authenticity to this dessert), wax paper can be used instead.

SAMOA
PANIPOPO

MEDIUM · COOK TIME: 30 MINUTES · ACTIVE PREP TIME: 20 MINUTES · INACTIVE PREP TIME: 2 HOURS, 10 MINUTES

Samoan coconut buns, or panipopo, are almost as loved in Hawaii as they are in the islands where they originated. Although they are very sweet, panipopo are seldom eaten as desserts; most Samoans serve them along with a meal, much like regular dinner rolls in the United States, or at breakfast.

3-½ c. all-purpose flour, plus more for flouring surface
¾ c. warm water
2 tsp. active dry yeast
1-¼ c. white sugar, divided
¼ c. powdered milk
1-¼ tsp. salt, divided
2 eggs
¼ c. butter, at room temperature
Oil, for greasing bowl and dish
One 15-oz. can full-fat coconut milk
1 Tbsp. cornstarch

Mix together warm water and yeast and allow to stand for 5-10 minutes. Sift together flour, ¼ c. sugar, powdered milk, and 1 tsp. salt.

Combine yeast mixture and eggs, add to the bowl of a stand mixer with a dough hook attachment, and mix on Medium speed. Gradually add flour mixture and mix for 3-4 minutes. Gradually add butter while mixing for 3 minutes longer.

Grease a large bowl and a 9 x 13-inch baking dish. Transfer dough to bowl, cover with a towel, and allow to rise for 1 hour or until doubled in bulk. Turn dough onto a floured surface and knead until smooth.

Divide dough into 12 portions and form each portion into a ball. Place dough balls in rows in a deep-sided baking dish (they should not touch each other). Cover dish with a towel and allow to rise for 1 hour longer.

White dough is rising, heat coconut milk, cornstarch, and remaining sugar and salt in a saucepan over Medium-High heat until thickened. Pour half of the sauce on top of the dough balls in the baking dish, reserving the rest.

Preheat oven to 350 degrees. Bake panipopo for 25 minutes or until golden brown. Remove from oven and pour remaining sauce on top. Serve while hot.

MAKES 12 BUNS

Per bun: 327 calories, 15 g fat, 11 g saturated fat, 253 mg sodium, 45 g carbohydrates, 6 g protein.

VARIATION: Coconut oil and/or coconut flour may be used in place of butter and all-purpose flour.

TIP: To reduce the time and effort required, use frozen dinner rolls in place of scratch-made dough. Thaw rolls completely and follow package directions to allow for rising, then bake with sauce as directed in recipe. Hawaiian rolls work well when making panipopo this way.

SOLOMON ISLANDS CASSAVA PUDDING

EASY · COOK TIME: 45 MINUTES · ACTIVE PREP TIME: 20 MINUTES

It's difficult to leave the Solomon Islands without sampling cassava pudding, a dish that can be savory or sweet. Savory cassava pudding is often wrapped in banana leaves and grilled alongside fish in an umu (an above-ground oven lined with volcanic stones) and then eaten as a side dish. Sugar is added to the leftovers to make a sweet dessert version.

2 lb. cassava, peeled

3-½ c. brown sugar

One 15-oz. can full-fat coconut milk

1 tsp. ground cinnamon

1 tsp. baking powder

2 eggs, beaten

¼ c. plus 2 Tbsp. butter, melted, plus more for greasing pan

1 c. hot water

Use a food processor or the small holes of a box grater to grate cassava as finely as possible. With a dish towel or cheesecloth, strain any excess liquid from the grated cassava.

Combine grated cassava, brown sugar, coconut milk, cinnamon, and baking powder and stir with a wooden spoon. Add eggs and butter and stir until fully incorporated. Slowly add hot water, stirring constantly.

Preheat oven to 350 degrees. Grease a 9 x 9-inch glass baking pan. Pour batter into pan in an even layer. Bake for 45 minutes or until top is golden brown and a toothpick inserted in center of pudding comes out mostly clean. Allow pudding to cool slightly before serving.

MAKES 6 SERVINGS

Per serving: 860 calories, 36 g fat, 27 g saturated fat, 185 mg sodium, 134 g carbohydrates, 6 g protein.

SERVING SUGGESTION: Serve with sliced bananas or papaya.

VARIATION: Use a mixture of cassava and grated sweet potato instead of cassava alone.

TONGA
FAIKAKAI TOPAI

EASY · COOK TIME: 25 MINUTES · ACTIVE PREP TIME: 15 MINUTES

In Tonga, faikakai topai is a delicacy usually reserved for special occasions, even though it is relatively easy to prepare. After sampling this dish, it's easy to see why. While nearly all traditional Tongan dishes utilize coconut milk or cream in some manner, very few are as rich and indulgent as these dumplings, topped with a thick, luscious coconut caramel sauce.

1-½ c. dark brown or turbinado sugar
One 15-oz. can full-fat coconut cream, divided
3 c. all-purpose flour
1 Tbsp. baking powder
1 Tbsp. white sugar
½ tsp. salt
1 c. water, plus more for boiling
½ c. shredded coconut (optional)

Melt brown sugar over Medium heat in a heavy skillet until completely melted and bubbly. Add coconut cream, reserving about ¼ c., and stir until smooth. Set aside.

Sift together flour, baking powder, sugar, and salt. Add water and stir with a wooden spoon to form a batter. Stir remaining coconut cream and shredded coconut (if using) into batter.

Bring a large pot of water to a boil. Drop 2 Tbsp. scoops of batter into water using a slotted spoon and boil gently for 15-20 minutes. Remove dumplings from water, set on a wire rack to drain, and serve drizzled with coconut sauce.

MAKES 6 SERVINGS

Per serving: 537 calories, 22 g fat, 19 g saturated fat, 219 mg sodium, 80 g

carbohydrates, 9 g protein.

VARIATIONS: To make faikakai malimali, replace 1 c. flour with 2 ripe mashed bananas. Another variation uses mashed sweet potatoes, cassava, or taro in place of part of the flour. Some Tongan cooks roll the dumplings in toasted coconut before drizzling with coconut sauce.

TUVALU
COCONUT BANANA FRITTERS

EASY · COOK TIME: 20 MINUTES · ACTIVE PREP TIME: 10 MINUTES

As with most Pacific island nations, bananas and coconut products are essential to Tuvaluan dishes, both sweet and savory. Meals are a major social event in Tuvalu, especially the midday meal on Sunday, and neighbors often gather together to eat. This recipe for coconut banana fritters makes enough to feed a large crowd (but it can easily be reduced if less is needed).

4 ripe bananas, mashed
1 c. all-purpose flour
½ c. cornstarch
1 tsp. baking powder
¼ tsp. salt
1 c. desiccated coconut
¼ c. brown sugar
4 egg yolks, beaten
½ c. full-fat coconut milk
Oil, for frying

Sift together flour, cornstarch, baking powder, and salt. Fold flour mixture together with bananas, desiccated coconut, and brown sugar, followed by egg yolks and coconut milk.

Heat about 2 inches of oil in a heavy skillet to a temperature of 350 degrees. Carefully drop large spoonfuls of banana mixture into oil and fry for about 5 minutes, turning once, until fritters are crisp and golden brown. (Batter will settle at bottom of oil at first but will rise to the surface as it cooks.) Lift from pan with a slotted spoon and set on paper towels to drain. Repeat with remaining batter. Allow to cool before serving.

MAKES ABOUT 30 FRITTERS

Per fritter: 173 calories, 14 g fat, 6 g saturated fat, 25 mg sodium, 12 g carbohydrates, 2 g protein.

SERVING SUGGESTION: Dust with powdered sugar and serve warm with a glass of coconut milk.

VANUATU COCONUT CAKE

EASY · COOK TIME: 25 MINUTES · ACTIVE PREP TIME: 10 MINUTES

Vanuatuan coconut cake is much different from the towering frosted multi-layer coconut cakes popular in the United States. Rather, it's arguably as simple as a coconut cake can get. Containing just a few basic ingredients, it's light and delicate and is best enjoyed straight from the oven while still warm.

1 c. desiccated coconut
¼ c. water
½ c. all-purpose flour
1 tsp. baking powder
¼ tsp. salt
½ c. white sugar

¼ c. butter, at room temperature, plus more for greasing pan

2 eggs

Stir together coconut and water and set aside. In another bowl, sift together flour, baking powder, and salt and set aside.

With an electric mixer, mix sugar and butter on Medium speed until light and fluffy. Add eggs one at a time, followed by flour mixture and then coconut mixture.

Preheat oven to 350 degrees. Grease an 8-inch round cake pan. Pour batter into pan and bake for 25 minutes or until cake is golden on top and a toothpick inserted in center of cake comes out clean.

MAKES 8 SERVINGS

Per serving: 329 calories, 25 g fat, 20 g saturated fat, 141 mg sodium, 26 g carbohydrates, 4 g protein.

SERVING SUGGESTION: Serve with a scoop of vanilla ice cream or mango sorbet.

VARIATIONS: Add vanilla or lemon extract for additional flavor. In Vanuatu, this cake is usually made using fresh coconut.

THE AMERICAS

ANTIGUA AND BARBUDA
ANTIGUAN BREAD PUDDING

EASY · COOK TIME: 55 MINUTES · ACTIVE PREP TIME: 10 MINUTES

The people of Antigua and Barbuda love freshly-baked bread. The island nation is known for its bakeries and especially for its "Sunday bread," which is made with lard or shortening instead of butter for an extra-rich loaf. But bread that is baked but not finished on Sunday doesn't go to waste. Bread pudding is a fine art here, and it makes a perfect platform for local ingredients like raisins, spices, and rum.

One small loaf day-old white bread (about 10 slices)
1 c. golden raisins
1 c. aged rum
1-¾ c. whole milk
1-¾ c. brown sugar, divided
½ c. butter, at room temperature, divided, plus more for greasing baking dish
5 eggs
1-½ c. heavy cream, divided
1 Tbsp. vanilla extract, divided
1 tsp. ground cinnamon
½ tsp. ground nutmeg

Preheat oven to 375 degrees. Place bread slices on a baking sheet and toast until golden brown. Meanwhile, place raisins in a small bowl rum and allow to soak.

Heat milk, ¾ c. brown sugar, and ¼ c. butter in a medium saucepan over Medium-High heat until sugar is melted. Set aside.

Whisk together eggs, ½ c. heavy cream, 2 tsp. vanilla extract, cinnamon, and nutmeg. Set aside.

Grease a 9 x 13-inch glass baking dish with butter. Strain raisins, reserving rum. Fold raisins and milk mixture into egg mixture and pour about one-quarter of the batter into the bottom of the dish. Tear the slices of bread into pieces, arrange in an even layer, and pour remainder of the batter on top. Bake for 45 minutes or until a toothpick inserted in center of pudding comes out mostly clean.

While pudding is cooking, prepare sauce. Cook remaining butter and brown sugar on Low heat in a heavy skillet until sugar is completely melted and mixture begins to darken (be careful not to let it burn). Remove from heat and stir in reserved rum and remaining heavy cream and vanilla extract. Continue to simmer over Low heat until mixture is thickened. Serve pudding with sauce.

MAKES 8 SERVINGS

Per serving: 488 calories, 22 g fat, 12 g saturated fat, 358 mg sodium, 51 g carbohydrates, 8 g protein.

VARIATIONS: Use chopped pineapple in place of raisins. For a coconut bread pudding, replace whole milk with full-fat coconut milk and add ½ c. shredded coconut to batter.

ARGENTINA CHOCOTORTA

EASY · ACTIVE PREP TIME: 20 MINUTES · INACTIVE PREP TIME: 4 HOURS

In 1982, advertising executive Marité Mabragaña came up with what would be a very successful marketing idea: an ad campaign featuring the products of two of her agency's clients and a recipe made using both of them. Mabragaña's original chocotorta was made with Mendicrim cream cheese and Chocolinas chocolate cookies, and it was introduced to the world with a catchy jingle and thirty-second commercial.

2 c. cream cheese, at room temperature
One 13-oz. can dulce de leche
Five 6-oz. boxes chocolate wafer cookies

1-½ c. whole milk, at room temperature
Cocoa powder, for garnish

With an electric mixer, mix together cream cheese and dulce de leche on Low speed until combined. Set aside.

Line an 8 x 8-inch baking dish with parchment paper. Begin by soaking chocolate wafer cookies in milk for just a few seconds (do not allow them to become soggy and oversaturated). Lay the cookies in a single layer at the bottom of the dish and top with about one-sixth of the cream cheese mixture. Repeat, alternating cookie and cream cheese layers, ending with a cream cheese layer. Use a flat knife to smooth the surface of the chocotorta and refrigerate for at least 4 hours.

Dust the top of the chocotorta with a thick, even layer of cocoa powder and serve.

MAKES 12 SERVINGS

Per serving: 551 calories, 29 g fat, 14 g saturated fat, 544 mg sodium, 68 g carbohydrates, 8 g protein.

SERVING SUGGESTION: Serve with milk or coffee.

VARIATIONS: In an interview, Mabragaña revealed that in her original chocotorta recipe the cookies were soaked in sweet port wine instead of milk. Espresso or strong coffee can be used as well.

TIP: To make your own dulce de leche, bring 2 c. whole milk, 1 c. white sugar, and ¼ tsp. baking soda to a boil in a heavy saucepan. Reduce heat and simmer, stirring frequently, for 1-½ hours or until mixture is very thick and has darkened in color. Transfer to a separate bowl and allow to cool before using.

BAHAMAS
GUAVA DUFF

MEDIUM · COOK TIME: 1 HOUR, 30 MINUTES · ACTIVE PREP TIME: 25 MINUTES

The guava is one of the few fruits known to be native to the Bahamas, having grown there before Christopher Columbus's arrival in 1492. The term "duff" is English slang for "pudding," particularly a steamed one containing fruit, but today it is most commonly used to refer to this tropical version of the traditional English plum pudding. While the spongy roulade is excellent on its own, Bahamians will argue that the rum sauce served with guava duff is a mandatory element.

1 lb. guava fruits, peeled and halved
Water, for boiling and steaming
2-½ c. white sugar, divided
1 tsp. ground cinnamon
1 tsp. ground allspice
4 c. all-purpose flour, plus more for flouring surface
1 Tbsp. baking powder
1 tsp. salt
¾ c. vegetable shortening
¾ c. whole milk
1 egg, beaten
¼ c. butter
2 Tbsp. rum

Place guava fruits in a large saucepan and add enough water to cover. Bring to a boil over High heat. Reduce heat to Medium and simmer for 15 minutes. Drain guavas, allow to cool slightly, and remove seeds with a spoon.

Place guavas, 1-½ c. sugar, and a small amount of cooking water in a food processor and pulse until smooth. Reserve about ¼ c. of the pureed guava mixture. Transfer to a saucepan and simmer over Low heat until jam is thickened and most of the water has evaporated. Set aside.

Sift together flour, baking powder, and salt. Add shortening, milk, and egg to the bowl of a stand mixer with a dough hook attachment. Gradually add flour mixture while mixing on Low speed for about 5 minutes to form a thick dough.

Turn dough onto a floured surface and roll out into a rectangle about 12 inches wide and ¼-inch thick. Spread guava jam in an even layer over the dough, stopping 1 inch from the edge. Starting at the closest end, roll the dough in a spiral and seal the ends to close. Wrap the sealed dough roll in parchment paper, followed by a layer of aluminum foil. (A muslin cloth may also be used.)

Boil a large pot of water and set a large steamer basket over the pot. Place the wrapped dough in the steamer. Cover and steam for at least 1 hour.

While dough is steaming, prepare sauce. Mix together remaining sugar, butter, and reserved guava puree in a small bowl using an electric mixer on Medium speed. Set bowl over a small saucepan of boiling water and stir until warm and slightly thickened. Stir in rum.

Carefully unwrap guava duff and slice with a sharp knife or a piece of thread. Top each slice with sauce to serve.

MAKES 8 SERVINGS

Per serving: 697 calories, 27 g fat, 10 g saturated fat, 352 mg sodium, 106 g carbohydrates, 9 g protein.

VARIATIONS: Other fruits like mango, papaya, and pineapple may be used in place of guava fruit. Raisins or coconut may be added as well. Brandy can be substituted for rum in sauce.

TIP: Canned guava or prepared guava jam can be used in place of fresh guava fruit.

BARBADOS PLAIN CAKE

EASY · COOK TIME: 1 HOUR, 15 MINUTES · ACTIVE PREP TIME: 15 MINUTES

The name of this cake really couldn't be more descriptive. While many American cooks add sour cream, cream cheese, or buttermilk to their pound cakes to make them moister and spices or extracts to enhance their flavor, the Bajan plain cake sticks with four traditional ingredients: butter, sugar, flour, and eggs (with just a little vanilla extract and milk). As simple as this basic version is, each Bajan family has its own recipe for plain cake, and in Barbados no Christmas is celebrated without it.

1 c. unsalted butter, at room temperature, plus more for greasing pan
2 c. white sugar
4 eggs
2 tsp. vanilla extract
2-¾ c. all-purpose flour, plus more for flouring pan
½ tsp. baking powder
½ tsp. baking soda
½ tsp. salt
1 c. whole milk

Place the butter in the bowl of a stand mixer with a whisk attachment and beat on High speed until smooth. Add sugar and beat for 2 minutes longer or until pale and creamy. Reduce speed to Low and add eggs, one at a time, followed by vanilla extract. Pause to scrape down sides of bowl.

Sift together flour, baking powder, baking soda, and salt. With stand mixer on Low speed, gradually add flour mixture and milk, alternating between the two. Raise speed to Medium and continue to mix until a smooth batter is formed.

Preheat oven to 325 degrees. Grease and flour a 12-cup Bundt pan. Pour batter into pan and bake for 1 hour, 15 minutes or until a toothpick inserted in center of cake comes out clean. Allow cake to cool in pan for 5 minutes before inverting onto a plate to serve.

MAKES 12 SERVINGS

Per serving: 372 calories, 18 g fat, 11 g saturated fat, 287 mg sodium, 51 g carbohydrates, 5 g protein.

SERVING SUGGESTION: To make a glaze for the plain cake, whisk together 1 c. powdered sugar with 2 Tbsp. whole milk and drizzle over cake before serving.

VARIATIONS: For a fruit-flavored plain cake, fold ½ c. chopped maraschino cherries or raisins into batter before baking. For a coconut-flavored plain cake, fold in ½ c. sweetened shredded coconut.

BELIZE
POWDER BUNS

EASY · COOK TIME: 35 MINUTES · ACTIVE PREP TIME: 15 MINUTES

Powder (pow-da) buns are one of many Belizean dishes associated with the Kriols, a diverse ethnic group that makes up about one-quarter of the small country's population. These dense, sweet pastries resemble British scones and get their name from one of their ingredients, baking powder. Powder buns are frequently seen at breakfast and tea and can be made with raisins and evaporated milk (as here) or with shredded coconut and coconut milk.

4 c. all-purpose flour
¼ c. baking powder
½ tsp. salt
1-½ c. white sugar
1 tsp. ground cinnamon
1 tsp. ground nutmeg

½ c. butter, at room temperature, plus more for greasing baking sheets
One 12-oz. can evaporated milk
1 tsp. vanilla extract
1 c. raisins
Brown sugar, for dusting (optional)

Sift together flour, baking powder, and salt. Add to a large bowl and stir in sugar, cinnamon, and nutmeg, followed by butter. Use your hands or a pastry blender to blend the butter into the dry ingredients. Add evaporated milk, a little at a time and mixing after each addition, followed by vanilla extract. Fold in raisins and knead to form a smooth dough.

Preheat oven to 350 degrees. Grease two large baking sheets. Divide the dough into 20 portions. Roll each portion into a ball, flatten slightly, and set on baking sheet. Dust with brown sugar (if using). Bake for 30-35 minutes or until golden brown.

MAKES ABOUT 20 BUNS

Per serving: 243 calories, 7 g fat, 5 g saturated fat, 209 mg sodium, 40 g carbohydrates, 5 g protein.

SERVING SUGGESTION: Serve with coffee or tea. Powder buns can be eaten plain or with butter or jam.

VARIATION: For coconut powder buns, replace evaporated milk with full-fat coconut milk and replace some or all of the raisins with shredded coconut.

BOLIVIA
HELADO DE CANELA

MEDIUM · COOK TIME: 15 MINUTES · ACTIVE PREP TIME: 15 MINUTES · INACTIVE PREP TIME: 4 HOURS, 20 MINUTES

To Bolivians, to whom ice cream stands and parlors (or "heladerias") are as beloved as they are to Americans, nothing says summer like helado de canela. Its name means "cinnamon ice cream," which is a bit of a misnomer because it more resembles a sorbet that is made without milk. It makes a sweet, spicy, and refreshing treat for when the weather is hot.

1 c. white sugar
1 Tbsp. ground cinnamon
2 tsp. cornstarch
1 dash salt
1 qt. water
2 sticks cinnamon
3 egg whites, at room temperature

Stir together sugar, ground cinnamon, cornstarch, and salt. Add to a large saucepan with water and cinnamon sticks and heat over Medium heat until sugar is melted (do not bring to a boil). Remove from heat and refrigerate until cold (at least 2 hours).

Use an electric mixer to beat egg whites on Medium speed until soft peaks form. Strain syrup through a fine sieve. Carefully fold together egg whites and syrup.

Churn mixture in a standard ice cream maker, following manufacturer's instructions for making sorbet. Pour sorbet into a freezer-safe container and freeze for 2 hours longer.

MAKES 1 QUART

Per one-half cup: 105 calories, 0 g fat, 0 g saturated fat, 32 mg sodium, 26 g

carbohydrates, 1 g protein.

VARIATION: In Bolivia, red food coloring is frequently added to helado de canela to give it a bright red color.

TIP: If you do not have an ice cream maker, place mixture in a freezer-safe container and place in freezer for at least 4-6 hours or until frozen, stirring with a fork every 30 minutes.

BRAZIL
QUINDIM

MEDIUM · COOK TIME: 35 MINUTES · ACTIVE PREP TIME: 20 MINUTES · INACTIVE PREP TIME: 1 HOUR

Like every country in the Portuguese diaspora, Brazil has its own take on the pastéis de nata (page 76). But this version more resembles the Spanish flan (page 92) in the manner in which it is prepared, and its name most likely originates from the Bantu language. Historians generally agree that the dessert itself has its origins in the seventeenth-century sugar plantations of eastern Brazil, and that its inventors were probably enslaved people.

2 eggs, separated, plus 10 egg yolks
Hot water, for water bath
1-½ c. white sugar
2 Tbsp. butter, at room temperature, plus more for greasing pan
1 dash salt
2 c. shredded coconut (preferably fresh)

Grease the cups of a 12-cup muffin pan. Place the pan inside a deep glass baking dish and fill dish with hot (but not boiling) water. Set aside to allow water to warm muffin pan while quindim is being prepared.

Whisk egg yolks until smooth. In a separate bowl, use an electric mixer to mix together sugar, butter, and salt on Low speed. Fold in coconut. Gradually fold in egg yolks.

In a separate bowl, beat egg whites on High speed until stiff and glossy. Fold egg whites into coconut mixture.

Preheat oven to 350 degrees. Divide mixture between muffin cups. Bake for 35 minutes (in water bath) or until firm and golden brown on top.

Remove muffin pan from water and allow to sit at room temperature for 1 hour or until completely cooled. Invert quindim onto a wire rack (run a knife around the inside of the cup to loosen if necessary).

MAKES 12 TARTS

Per tart: 182 calories, 11 g fat, 7 g saturated fat, 45 mg sodium, 19 g carbohydrates, 4 g protein.

VARIATIONS: Add 1 tsp. vanilla extract or the zest and juice of ½ lime. Honey may be used in place of some or all of the sugar.

TIP: If using fresh coconut, you will need the meat of ½ medium-sized coconut.

CANADA
SASKATOON BERRY PIE

MEDIUM · COOK TIME: 45 MINUTES · ACTIVE PREP TIME: 30 MINUTES · INACTIVE PREP TIME: 30 MINUTES

It's easy to assume that the saskatoon berry got its name from Saskatchewan's largest city, but the reverse is actually true. The berry's name comes from an anglicization of *misâskwatômina*, a Cree word meaning "the fruit of the tree of many branches." Saskatoons can grow in the colder parts of the United States, where they're called serviceberries or juneberries. But they thrive the best in Canada's Prairie provinces, where saskatoon berry pie is a regional specialty.

2 c. fresh Saskatoon berries
¾ c. water
¼ c. plus 2 Tbsp. white sugar, divided
2 Tbsp. cornstarch
1 tsp. lemon juice
¼ tsp. salt
Butter, for greasing dish
Double pie crust (see recipe below)
Whole milk, for brushing crust

Combine berries, water, sugar (reserving 1 tsp.), cornstarch, lemon juice, and salt in a large saucepan. Heat over Medium-High heat for about 15 minutes or until the mixture reaches a jam-like thickness. Remove from heat and allow to cool.

Preheat oven to 450 degrees. Grease a 9-inch pie dish. Roll out each portion of the pie crust into a circle large enough to cover the bottom and sides of the pie dish and to extend over the edges. Press the pie crust into the dish and flute the bottom with the tines of a fork.

Pour the cooled berry filling into the pie crust shell and cover with other rolled portion of the dough. Use a sharp knife to trim the edge of the top crust and then pleat the edge with the tines of a fork to seal. Flute the top surface with a fork or use a knife to cut designs to vent. Brush the surface with milk and sprinkle with reserved sugar.

Bake pie for 10 minutes at 450 degrees. Reduce oven temperature to 350 degrees and bake 20 minutes longer or until pie is golden brown. Allow pie to cool slightly before slicing.

For pie crust:
2-½ c. all-purpose flour
¾ tsp. salt
½ c. lard or vegetable shortening
½ c. unsalted butter, very cold

¼ c. ice water

1 egg

Sift together flour and sugar in a large metal bowl. Using a pastry blender, combine flour with lard or shortening, butter, water, and egg to form a rough dough.

Divide dough into two portions. Wrap each portion in plastic wrap and chill for 30 minutes or until ready to use.

MAKES 8 SERVINGS

Per serving: 391 calories, 25 g fat, 13 g saturated fat, 381 mg sodium, 37 g carbohydrates, 4 g protein.

SERVING SUGGESTION: Serve warm with vanilla ice cream.

VARIATION: This pie can be made with blueberries, or a mixture of blueberries and cherries, instead of saskatoon berries. Add 1 Tbsp. of almond extract to better approximate the saskatoon flavor.

TIP: If using frozen berries to make filling, reduce water by 2 Tbsp.

CHILE
ALFAJORES

EASY · COOK TIME: 30 MINUTES · ACTIVE PREP TIME: 30 MINUTES · INACTIVE PREP TIME: 2 HOURS

The first alfajores were thin cylinder-shaped cookies made with honey and almonds, which made their way to Spain via the Moors in the eighth century. They were brought to the Western Hemisphere nearly a millennium later. Today every country in the Spanish-speaking world, from the Philippines to Equatorial Guinea, boasts its own variety of the alfajor. Chilean alfajores are flavored with orange juice and filled with creamy dulce de leche.

1-¼ c. white sugar
¾ c. unsalted butter, at room temperature
2 eggs
3 c. all-purpose flour, plus more for flouring surface
2 tsp. baking powder
1 tsp. salt
¾ c. whole milk
¼ c. orange juice
One 13-oz. can dulce de leche
1 tsp. ground cinnamon (optional)

Combine sugar and butter in the bowl of a stand mixer with a paddle attachment and mix on Medium speed for 3 minutes or until light and fluffy. Add eggs one at a time, mixing after each addition.

Sift together flour, baking powder, and salt. Alternate adding flour mixture, milk, and orange juice, each a little at a time and mixing after each addition. Mix for 2 minutes longer after all ingredients are added. Wrap dough in plastic wrap and refrigerate for at least 2 hours.

Preheat oven to 350 degrees. Line two large baking sheets with parchment paper. Roll dough to a thickness of ¼ inch on a floured surface. Use a round cookie cutter to cut circles from dough. Place dough circles in rows on baking sheets and bake for 10-15 minutes or until light brown. Remove cookies from oven and place on wire racks to cool.

While cookies are cooling, stir together dulce de leche and cinnamon (if using). Once the cookies are completely cooled, spread 1 Tbsp. of dulce de leche over the surface of one cookie. Top with a second cookie and press together to form a sandwich. Repeat with remaining cookies.

MAKES ABOUT 20 ALFAJORES

Per alfajor: 239 calories, 10 g fat, 6 g saturated fat, 182 mg sodium, 34 g carbohydrates, 3 g protein.

SERVING SUGGESTION: Dust with powdered sugar or roll sides in finely grated coconut before serving.

VARIATIONS: Raspberry jam can be used in place of dulce de leche. For additional flavor, add lemon or orange zest, vanilla extract, cinnamon, nutmeg, or cloves to cookie dough. In Argentina and Uruguay, alfajores are dipped in dark chocolate after filling (and are called "Chilean Oreos").

TIP: To make your own dulce de leche, bring 2 c. whole milk, 1 c. white sugar, and ¼ tsp. baking soda to a boil in a heavy saucepan. Reduce heat and simmer, stirring frequently, for 1-½ hours or until mixture is very thick and has darkened in color. Transfer to a separate bowl and allow to cool before using.

COLOMBIA
TORTA ENVINADA

HARD · COOK TIME: 1 HOUR, 15 MINUTES · ACTIVE PREP TIME: 40 MINUTES · INACTIVE PREP TIME: 4 DAYS, 10 MINUTES

The torta envinada (wine cake) is a cousin of the black cake (page 335), with red wine used in place of rum. Like its rum-soaked cousin, torta envinada was introduced to the Western Hemisphere by the British. As the story goes, a group of Welsh immigrants who settled along South America's Caribbean coast brought them along, as the preserved fruitcakes would retain their freshness over the long trip. Today, the torta envinada is still sometimes called the torta negra Galesa (Welsh black cake) by Colombians.

2 c. sweet red wine, divided
1 c. raisins
1 c. prunes
1 c. dried figs
2 c. all-purpose flour, plus more for flouring pan
2 tsp. baking powder

½ tsp. ground cinnamon

½ tsp. ground nutmeg

¼ tsp. ground cloves

¼ tsp. salt

½ c. almonds

¼ c. walnuts

2 c. white sugar

1 c. butter, at room temperature, plus more for greasing pan

2 tsp. vanilla extract

Zest of 1 orange

5 eggs

¼ c. burnt sugar syrup (see Tip)

Chop the raisins, prunes, and figs and cover with 1 c. red wine. Soak fruits for at least 1 day (longer is preferred).

Sift together flour, baking powder, cinnamon, nutmeg, cloves, and salt and set aside. Drain the raisins, prunes, and figs and add to a food processor along with almonds and walnuts. Pulse until finely ground (this is best done in several batches). Set aside.

Combine sugar and butter in the bowl of a stand mixer with a paddle attachment and mix on Medium-High speed for 3 minutes or until light and fluffy. Add vanilla extract and orange zest, followed by 1 egg. Alternate adding flour mixture, a little at a time, and remaining eggs, mixing after each addition. Add the burnt sugar syrup at the end and mix for 1 minute after. Use a wooden spoon to fold the dried fruit and nut mixture into the batter.

Preheat oven to 350 degrees. Grease and flour a 9-inch springform pan. Pour batter into pan, cover with foil, and bake for 1 hour. Remove foil and bake for 15 minutes longer or until a toothpick inserted in center of cake comes out clean. Allow cake to cool in pan for 10 minutes.

Loosen wall belt from pan. Set the cake on a large piece of aluminum foil (if should be large enough to wrap the entire cake). Turn the edges of the foil upward to form a "bowl" around the cake. Slowly pour the remaining wine over the cake and fold the edges of the foil over the cake to enclose it completely, so that the wine saturates the cake and does not leak. Allow the cake to stand at room temperature (do not refrigerate) for at least 3 days before serving.

MAKES 10-12 SERVINGS

Per serving: 561 calories, 21 g fat, 11 g saturated fat, 193 mg sodium, 84 g carbohydrates, 7 g protein.

VARIATIONS: Use a mixture of red wine and rum instead of straight red wine. Add a small amount of instant coffee, dissolved in a few Tbsp. of hot water, to the batter. Fold 1 c. chopped chocolate or candied fruit (such as figs or papaya) into the batter before baking.

TIP: Burnt sugar syrup, also called browning, can be difficult to find in prepared form. To make your own, heat 1 c. brown sugar in a small saucepan over Medium-High heat until completely melted, stirring constantly. Remove from heat, stir in 1 c. boiling water, and set aside until cooled. Syrup will thicken upon standing.

COSTA RICA TRES LECHES CAKE

MEDIUM · COOK TIME: 20 MINUTES · ACTIVE PREP TIME: 30 MINUTES · INACTIVE PREP TIME: 1 HOUR

Costa Rica, along with several other Central American countries, claims the origin of the tres leches (three milks) cake. But history gives the credit to the Nestle company. Canned milk first became available in the 1850s, and in the 1940s its popularity surged in Latin America. One reason was because Nestle, a leading producer of canned milk that had just recently opened production facilities in Mexico, adapted a traditional Latin American cake to use both condensed and evaporated milk and printed the recipe for the cake on its labels.

6 eggs, separated
½ c. white sugar, divided
1 c. all-purpose flour, plus more for flouring pan
1 tsp. baking powder
¼ tsp. salt
Butter or shortening, for greasing pan
One 14-oz. can sweetened condensed milk
½ c. heavy whipping cream, divided
½ c. plus 2 Tbsp. evaporated milk
¼ c. light rum (optional)
1 tsp. vanilla extract
Whipped cream, for serving

For whipped cream:
1 c. heavy whipping cream, very cold
2 Tbsp. white sugar
½ tsp. vanilla extract

With an electric mixer, beat egg whites and ¼ c. sugar on Medium speed until stiff. In a separate bowl, beat together egg yolks and ¼ c. sugar until pale and fluffy.

Sift together flour, baking powder, and salt. Alternate folding flour mixture and egg white mixture, a little at a time, into egg yolk mixture, mixing after each addition.

Preheat oven to 375 degrees. Grease and flour a 9-inch springform pan. Pour batter into pan and bake for 20 minutes or until a toothpick inserted in center of cake comes out clean. Remove cake from oven and loosen wall belt from pan. Allow cake to cool on a wire rack for about 30 minutes.

Combine sweetened condensed milk, ½ c. whipping cream, evaporated milk, rum (if using), and 1 tsp. vanilla extract. Return cake to springform pan. Use a large skewer to prick the cake's surface. Slowly pour about 2 c. of the cream over the top of the cake. Allow the cake to stand until the cream has been absorbed (at least 1 hour).

To make whipped cream: Combine all ingredients in a small bowl or the bowl of a stand mixer. Whip on High speed for 3-4 minutes or until stiff peaks form. Refrigerate until ready to use.

Loosen wall belt and place cake on a serving platter. Spread whipped cream on sides and top of cake in an even layer and serve.

MAKES 8-10 SERVINGS

Per serving: 291 calories, 12 g fat, 7 g saturated fat, 142 mg sodium, 36 g carbohydrates, 8 g protein.

SERVING SUGGESTION: Dust with cinnamon and serve with fresh strawberries.

VARIATIONS: For a coffee-flavored tres leches cake, add 1 Tbsp. instant coffee granules dissolved in a small amount of hot water to the batter. For a chocolate tres leches cake, substitute ¼ c. flour with an equal amount of cocoa powder. For a strawberry tres leches cake, add ½ c. strawberry syrup to the soaking cream.

CUBA
PASTELITOS DE GUAYABA

HARD · COOK TIME: 25 MINUTES · ACTIVE PREP TIME: 30 MINUTES · INACTIVE PREP TIME: 1 DAY, 8 HOURS, 25 MINUTES

The word *pastelito*, or "little pastry," can comprise a wide range of treats, but in Cuba its meaning is a little more specific. Cuban pastelitos are made with puff pastry cut with lard or shortening and a wide range of sweet or savory fillings. But the most familiar is probably guava paste, made from a high-pectin fruit native to the Caribbean, and cream cheese, a product introduced to Cuba from the United States shortly after the Spanish-American War. In Miami, where Cuban bakeries are ubiquitous, the pastelito de guayaba is arguably as popular as it is anywhere on the island of Cuba.

2-½ c. all-purpose flour, plus more for flouring surface
¼ tsp. salt

1-½ c. cold margarine, cut into small cubes
¼ c. rendered lard or vegetable shortening
1 c. cold water, divided
2 c. cream cheese
1 lb. guava paste (see recipe)
2 eggs, beaten
¼ c. white sugar

Sift together flour and salt in a large metal bowl. Place bowl in refrigerator and chill for about 10 minutes.

Using a pastry blender, combine flour with margarine, lard or shortening, and ¾ c. water to form a rough dough. Wrap dough in plastic wrap and chill for 15 minutes.

Turn dough onto a floured surface and roll into a rectangle about 6 inches wide and 18 inches long. Fold sides over center to form a 6 x 6-inch square. Roll out into a rectangle again, and then fold sides over center again. Repeat this process at least four times. Refrigerate dough for 8 hours or overnight.

Divide dough into two portions. Roll each portion into a 12 x 18-inch rectangle. Use a sharp knife to cut each piece into six 6-inch squares. Cut the guava paste and cream cheese into 12 equal slices and lay one slice of each on top of each square. Brush the edges of each square with egg, fold one corner over to form a triangle, and seal the edges. Once the pastry is sealed, use the knife to make a vent in the center of the pastry.

Preheat oven to 350 degrees. Line two baking sheets with parchment paper. Set the pastries on the baking sheet, spaced at least 1 inch apart. Bake pastries for 25 minutes or until golden brown.

While pastries are baking, prepare syrup. Combine sugar and remaining water in a small saucepan and heat over Medium-High heat until sugar is completely melted. After pastries are finished baking, brush them with syrup while still hot.

For guava paste:
2 lbs. fresh guava fruit
2 c. water
3 c. white sugar

Halve guavas and scoop out seeds. Soak the guava seeds in 1 c. water. Bring the other 1 c. water to a boil. Slice the guavas into large pieces and add to boiling water. Reduce heat to Low, cover, and simmer for 30 minutes or until guava has softened. Remove from heat.

Use a fine sieve to strain the water from the guava seeds. Add water to pot and discard seeds.

Puree the guava fruit with the water in a blender or food processor. Add the guava puree to a large saucepan along with an equal amount of sugar (it may not be a full 3 c.). Simmer over Medium-Low heat for 20 minutes or until the mixture is very thick. Remove from heat and stir vigorously for 10 minutes to form a thick paste.

Line a small loaf pan with plastic wrap or wax paper. Pour the guava paste into the pan and allow it to stand for at least 1 day at room temperature. Remove from pan when ready to use.

MAKES 12 PASTRIES

Per pastry: 645 calories, 35 g fat, 13 g saturated fat, 355 mg sodium, 81 g carbohydrates, 9 q protein.

SERVING SUGGESTION: Serve warm with coffee.

VARIATION: Other types of paste, such as mango, may be used in place of the guava paste.

TIP: To greatly simplify this recipe, use pre-made puff pastry and guava paste.

DOMINICA
LIGHT RUM CAKE

EASY · COOK TIME: 35 MINUTES · ACTIVE PREP TIME: 20 MINUTES

Dominica was a French colony in the 1700s, before Great Britain took control of the small island, and French bakers took advantage of Caribbean ingredients like rum and vanilla. This decadent French-style rum cake is much lighter in color than others made in the Caribbean and does not contain the heavy fruits found in black cake (page 335). But it is just as rich, and like other rum cakes it is typically made at Christmas and on other holidays.

1-½ c. almond flour
½ c. all-purpose flour
1 tsp. baking powder
¼ tsp. salt
¾ c. butter, at room temperature, plus more for greasing pan
1 c. white sugar
4 eggs
¼ c. plus 1 Tbsp. light rum, divided
1 tsp. vanilla extract
1-½ c. powdered sugar
2 Tbsp. water

Sift together all-purpose flour, baking powder, and salt. Add butter and sugar to the bowl of a stand mixer with a whisk attachment and beat on Medium speed until light and fluffy. Gradually add almond flour, one spoonful at a time and mixing after each addition. Add eggs one at a time, mixing after each addition. Add all-purpose flour mixture and reduce speed to Low. Add ¼ c. rum and vanilla extract.

Preheat oven to 350 degrees. Grease a 9-inch springform pan. Cut a 9-inch parchment paper circle and place it at the bottom of the pan. Pour batter into pan and bake for 35 minutes or until a toothpick inserted in center of cake comes out clean. Loosen wall belt, remove parchment paper from bottom of cake, and set cake on a wire rack to cool completely.

Sift the powdered sugar into a small bowl. Whisk in remaining rum and water. Once the cake is completely cooled, pour icing on cake and spread over surface using an icing spatula.

MAKES 6-8 SERVINGS

Per serving: 467 calories, 26 g fat, 12 g saturated fat, 233 mg sodium, 50 g

carbohydrates, 7 g protein.

VARIATIONS: Add the juice and zest of one lemon to the icing if desired. For a heavier rum flavor, poke holes in the surface of the cake and brush with rum while cake is cooling.

DOMINICAN REPUBLIC BIZCOCHO DOMINICANO

HARD · COOK TIME: 2 HOURS, 15 MINUTES · ACTIVE PREP TIME: 50 MINUTES

In the Dominican Republic, every special event—whether it's a birthday, anniversary, baby shower, christening, or Holy Communion—is celebrated with a rich, towering white cake. Dominican cakes are characterized by their chiffon-like texture, pineapple filling, and Italian-style meringue frosting (or *suspiro*, from a word meaning "sigh"). It definitely stands as one of the Americas' great cakes.

4 c. all-purpose flour, plus more for flouring pans
3 Tbsp. baking powder
3-½ c. white sugar
2 c. butter, at room temperature, plus more for greasing pans
12 eggs plus 2 egg whites, at room temperature
1 c. freshly-squeezed orange juice
1 Tbsp. plus 1 tsp. vanilla extract
Zest of 1 lime
2 c. pineapple jam (see recipe below)
Suspiro frosting (see recipe below)

Sift together flour and baking powder. Add butter and sugar to the bowl of a stand mixer with a paddle attachment and beat at Medium speed until light and fluffy, about 5 minutes. Alternate adding flour mixture, eggs, and orange juice, each a little at a time and mixing after each addition, followed by vanilla extract and lime zest. Raise speed to High and mix for 2 minutes longer.

Preheat oven to 350 degrees. Grease and flour three 9-inch cake pans. Divide batter between pans and bake for 35 minutes or until a toothpick inserted in center of cake comes out clean. Allow cakes to cool completely before removing from pans.

Pour suspiro frosting into a piping bag or plastic bag with one corner cut. When you are ready to decorate the cakes, set one cake on a serving platter or cake stand and pipe a circle of icing around its perimeter. Spread half of the pineapple jam on top of the cake to fill the circle and set the second cake on top. Repeat the process with the second cake, then top with the third cake. Spread remaining frosting on sides and top of cake in a smooth layer.

For pineapple jam:
1 pineapple, peeled, cored, and finely chopped
1 qt. water
½ c. brown sugar
1 tsp. vanilla extract

Add all ingredients to a large saucepan and bring to a boil. Reduce heat to Low, cover, and simmer for 1 hour, 30 minutes. Remove lid and continue to simmer until most of the liquid has evaporated. Allow jam to cool completely before filling cake.

For suspiro frosting:
1-½ c. white sugar
¼ c. water
¼ tsp. cream of tartar
6 egg whites
¼ c. powdered sugar

Combine white sugar, water, and cream of tartar in a medium saucepan and heat over Medium-High heat until it reaches a temperature of 235 degrees (use a candy thermometer to monitor temperature). Remove from heat and set aside.

Add egg whites to the bowl of a stand mixer with a whisk attachment and beat on Low speed until soft peaks form. Increase speed to Medium and continue to beat until very stiff and opaque.

Increase speed to High and add syrup in a slow stream. Mix for about 5 minutes, add powdered sugar, and continue to mix until frosting has expanded to nearly fill the bowl of the mixer. Refrigerate until ready to use.

MAKES 12-16 SERVINGS

Per serving: 686 calories, 31 g fat, 18 g saturated fat, 264 mg sodium, 97 g carbohydrates, 11 g protein.

SERVING SUGGESTIONS: In the Dominican Republic, bizcochos Dominicanos are elaborately decorated, usually with flowers or ribbons.

VARIATIONS: While pineapple jam is traditional, any flavor of jam can be used in its place. Guava and raspberry are popular choices. Dulce de leche can also be used.

TIP: Make sure that all ingredients are at room temperature before you begin preparing this cake.

ECUADOR
ARROZ CON LECHE

EASY · COOK TIME: 1 HOUR, 20 MINUTES · ACTIVE PREP TIME: 10 MINUTES

Like many Latin American desserts, arroz con leche (rice with milk) originated in Spain. It was first made at some point after the Muslim conquest, when the Moors introduced rice to the Iberian Peninsula. Different versions of rice pudding are popular throughout the world, and different versions of arroz con leche are popular throughout Latin America; in Ecuador the simple and easy dish is cooked with raisins and flavored with orange rind, cinnamon, and vanilla.

1-½ c. short-grain white rice
Water, for rinsing
2 qt. plus 1 c. whole milk

¼ tsp. salt

2 sticks cinnamon

Peel of 1 large orange, pith removed

¾ c. brown sugar

¾ c. raisins

¾ c. sweetened condensed milk

2 Tbsp. butter, at room temperature

2 Tbsp. rum (optional)

1 tsp. vanilla extract

Rinse the rice thoroughly until the water runs clear, and then drain and pat dry. Add the milk, salt, cinnamon sticks, and orange peel to a large saucepan and bring to a boil. Add rice, reduce heat to Low, and simmer for 1 hour or until rice is soft. Remove cinnamon sticks and orange peel.

Stir in brown sugar and raisins. Cook for 20 minutes longer, stirring frequently. Add condensed milk, butter, rum (if using), and vanilla extract. Remove from heat and allow to cool slightly before serving.

MAKES 6 SERVINGS

Per serving: 552 calories, 19 g fat, 11 g saturated fat, 326 mg sodium, 79 g carbohydrates, 16 g protein.

SERVING SUGGESTIONS: Serve either warm or cold; garnish with cinnamon powder, grated chocolate, or caramel sauce.

VARIATIONS: Use coconut milk in place of whole milk, or other fruits or nuts like strawberries, apples, walnuts, or pistachios in place of or in addition to raisins.

TIP: Arroz con leche is often made using leftover cooked rice. If using cooked rice, increase rice to 3 c., decrease milk to 3 c., and decrease cooking time to 20 minutes.

EL SALVADOR
TORTA MARIA LUISA

MEDIUM · COOK TIME: 1 HOUR, 15 MINUTES · ACTIVE PREP TIME: 15 MINUTES · INACTIVE PREP TIME: 10 MINUTES

The torta Maria Luisa (Maria Luisa cake) originated in Caracas, Venezuela in the late nineteenth century and was named for its likely inventor, the celebrated Venezuelan pastry chef Doña María Eugenia López Llamozas. Her original cake contained prune paste, guava jam, and custard encased in an Italian meringue icing. Today it is popular in El Salvador and Colombia as well, though the Salvadoran rendition is much simpler–a basic, orange-flavored sponge cake filled with marmalade and usually left bare but with a dusting of powdered sugar on top.

2-¼ c. all-purpose flour, plus more for flouring pans
2-½ tsp. baking powder
¼ tsp. salt
2 c. white sugar
1-½ c. butter, at room temperature, plus more for greasing pans
9 eggs
Juice and zest of 2 large oranges
Juice and zest of 1 lime
2 c. berry marmalade (see recipe)
Powdered sugar, for garnish

Sift together flour, baking powder, and salt. Add sugar, butter, eggs, and orange and lime zest and juice to the bowl of a stand mixer with a whisk attachment. Mix on Low speed for about 1 minute, then add flour mixture a little at a time. Increase speed to Medium and mix for about 1 minute longer.

Preheat oven to 350 degrees. Grease and flour three 8-inch round cake pans. Divide batter between pans and bake for 30 minutes or until a toothpick inserted in center of cake comes out clean. Allow cakes to cool for 10 minutes before removing from pans. Invert onto a wire rack to finish cooling.

Place one cake layer on a serving platter or cake stand. Spread half of the marmalade over the top of the layer. Top with second layer and spread remaining marmalade on top of the layer. Top with third layer and dust with an even layer of powdered sugar.

For berry marmalade:
2 c. white sugar
1 c. water
1 orange, very thinly sliced
2-½ c. fresh raspberries
½ tsp. butter (optional; helps clarify)

Combine sugar, water, and orange in a large saucepan and bring to a boil over High heat. Reduce heat to Low and simmer for 20 minutes or until orange rind is very tender.

Add raspberries and increase heat to Medium-High. Cook for 25 minutes or until temperature reaches 220 degrees (use a candy thermometer to monitor temperature), stirring frequently.

Remove from heat, stir in butter (if using), and skim foam from the top. Allow marmalade to reach room temperature before assembling cake.

MAKES 12-16 SERVINGS

Per serving: 454 calories, 16 g fat, 9 g saturated fat, 177 mg sodium, 76 g carbohydrates, 6 g protein.

SERVING SUGGESTION: Serve with coffee or tea.

VARIATIONS: Other flavors of jam may be used in place of berry marmalade. Torta Maria Luisa is served iced with suspiro frosting (page 309) for more formal occasions.

TIP: Use a sharp knife or wire to cut the top of each of the first two layers in order to create a perfectly flat surface before spreading marmalade.

GRENADA
NUTMEG ICE CREAM

MEDIUM · COOK TIME: 20 MINUTES · ACTIVE PREP TIME: 10 MINUTES · INACTIVE PREP TIME: 5 HOURS

First introduced in 1843, nutmeg has become so important to Grenada that a cracked nutmeg even appears on its flag. Nearly one out of three Grenadians relies on the nutmeg industry for their livelihood, and 20 percent of the world's supply is produced on the 134-square-mile "Island of Spice." It's not surprising that the "black gold" plays a huge role in its cuisine as well. Nutmeg ice cream is readily available in Grenada, where it is by far the most popular flavor.

2 whole nutmegs, divided
2 c. heavy cream, divided
1-½ c. whole milk
1 dash salt
1 c. white sugar
6 egg yolks
1 tsp. vanilla extract

Use a hammer to crack one nutmeg into pieces. Combine cracked nutmeg, 1 c. heavy cream, and milk in a large saucepan. Bring to a low boil over Medium heat. Remove from heat, cover, and let stand for 30 minutes. Remove nutmeg pieces from mixture.

Grate the remaining nutmeg with a fine grater. Add to a dry skillet and toast over Medium heat just until fragrant, about 2 minutes. Set aside to cool.

Place sugar and egg yolks in the bowl of a stand mixer with a whisk attachment. Mix on Low speed until pale. Slowly add heavy cream mixture in a steady stream while mixing. Return mixture to saucepan and heat over Medium heat for about 10 minutes. Remove from heat and stir in remaining heavy cream, toasted nutmeg, and vanilla. Transfer mixture to a lidded container and chill in refrigerator for at least 2 hours.

Churn mixture in a standard ice cream maker, following manufacturer's instructions. Pour ice cream into a freezer-safe container and freeze for 2 hours longer.

MAKES 1 QUART

Per half-cup: 258 calories, 16 g fat, 9 g saturated fat, 49 mg sodium, 28 g carbohydrates, 4 g protein.

SERVING SUGGESTION: Serve in a small dish and garnish with a cinnamon stick. Nutmeg ice cream is also a good accompaniment for warm desserts, especially apple pie or cobbler.

VARIATION: Add 1-2 Tbsp. of rum or a dash of cinnamon before chilling.

TIP: When grating nutmeg, use a microplane grater. Hold the grater at a 45-degree angle for best results. A nut mill may also be used.

GUATEMALA
BOCADO DE REINA

EASY · COOK TIME: 45 MINUTES · ACTIVE PREP TIME: 10 MINUTES · INACTIVE PREP TIME: 20 MINUTES

King Louis XV of France's queen, Polish princess Marie Leszczyńska (1703-1768), was one of very few French royals known for their frugality. During an economic recession, Queen Marie tried to set an example by having the palace kitchens repurpose leftovers. One of the dishes her chefs created in response made its way across the Atlantic to become one of Central America's beloved desserts. This story answers the age-old question of how a dish made from stale bread received a name that means "the Queen's bite."

8-10 slices white bread (preferably stale), torn into pieces
½ c. raisins
¼ c. orange juice
1 c. whole milk
1 c. white sugar
2 eggs, beaten
1 very ripe banana, mashed
1 Tbsp. ground cinnamon
1 tsp. vanilla extract
Butter or shortening, for greasing pan

Soak raisins in orange juice. Combine milk and sugar in a medium saucepan and heat over Medium-High heat just until sugar has dissolved. Remove from heat and allow to stand until cooled.

In a large bowl, mix together milk mixture, eggs, banana, cinnamon, and vanilla extract. Add bread and allow to stand for 5-10 minutes or until completely saturated. Drain raisins and fold into bread mixture.

Preheat oven to 350 degrees. Grease an 8-inch springform pan. Pour bread mixture into pan and bake for 45 minutes. Allow cake to cool slightly before loosening wall belt and slicing.

MAKES 6 SERVINGS

Per serving: 265 calories, 3 g fat, 1 g saturated fat, 120 mg sodium, 58 g carbohydrates, 5 g protein.

SERVING SUGGESTION: Serve with whipped cream or vanilla ice cream.

VARIATIONS: Milk and sugar can be replaced with one 14-oz. can sweetened condensed milk (more common in Guatemala today). For a chocolate bocado de reina, replace raisins with chocolate chips and omit orange juice.

GUYANA
CUSTARD BLOCK

MEDIUM · COOK TIME: 10 MINUTES · ACTIVE PREP TIME: 20 MINUTES · INACTIVE PREP TIME: 4 HOURS

In Guyana, "dessert" usually means "custard." The only matter of dispute is whether it's better baked or frozen. While European-style baked custard is enormously popular, custard in frozen form is unique to the English-speaking South American country. Less creamy and more icy than ice cream or gelato, and cut into squares instead of scooped, Guyanese custard block can be made with whole eggs (as here) or with custard powder.

One 14-oz. can sweetened condensed milk
One 12-oz. can evaporated milk
6 eggs
1 tsp. vanilla extract
½ tsp. ground nutmeg
½ tsp. ground cinnamon

Combine condensed and evaporated milk in a medium saucepan and bring to a boil over Medium-High heat. Reduce heat to Low.

Crack eggs into a medium bowl and beat with a wire whisk. Add a small amount of milk mixture to eggs (about ¼ c. at a time), whisking vigorously after each addition. Return egg and milk mixture to pan along with vanilla extract, nutmeg, and cinnamon and continue to cook on Low, whisking constantly, until the custard becomes thick enough to coat the whisk.

Pour the custard into a shallow rectangular dish (ice cube trays or ice pop molds can also be used). Freeze for at least 4 hours. Cut into squares to serve.

MAKES 8-12 SERVINGS

Per serving: 276 calories, 11 g fat, 6 g saturated fat, 158 mg sodium, 36 g

carbohydrates, 11 g protein.

VARIATIONS: Cloves, almond extract, or other flavorings can be added to custard block. Replace sweetened condensed milk with an equal amount of whole milk and ¼ c. brown sugar.

TIP: If available, 3 Tbsp. of custard powder can be used in place of eggs. After heating milk, whisk together custard powder and ½ c. milk and add to pan. To make your own custard powder, combine ½ c. powdered milk, ¼ c. cornstarch, 1 Tbsp. vanilla sugar, and a dash of powdered yellow food coloring.

HAITI
BLAN MANJE

EASY · COOK TIME: 10 MINUTES · ACTIVE PREP TIME: 10 MINUTES · INACTIVE PREP TIME: 6 HOURS

Blancmange, a milk pudding of Arab origin (page 127) eaten in various forms throughout Europe, has its Haitian equivalent in blan manje. The names of both desserts mean "white dish," in French and in Haitian Creole. Unlike other versions, blan manje incorporates a decidedly Caribbean ingredient, coconut milk, and two very Latin American staples, evaporated milk and condensed milk.

One 12-oz. can evaporated milk
Two 15-oz. cans full-fat coconut milk
One 14-oz. can sweetened condensed milk
½ c. white sugar, divided
¾ c. warm water
2 Tbsp. plus 1-½ tsp. gelatin
½ tsp. vanilla extract
Cooking spray, for spraying pan

Combine evaporated milk, coconut milk, condensed milk, and sugar in a large saucepan. Dissolve gelatin in water and stir into milk mixture. Cook over Medium-Low heat until sugar is completely dissolved (do not bring to a boil). Remove from heat and stir in vanilla extract.

Spray the inside of a 9-cup gelatin mold or Bundt pan. Pour milk mixture into pan. Refrigerate blan manje for at least 6 hours (overnight is preferable). Invert onto a serving platter just before serving.

MAKES 8-10 SERVINGS

Per serving: 415 calories, 21 g fat, 17 g saturated fat, 137 mg sodium, 51 g carbohydrates, 9 g protein.

SERVING SUGGESTION: Top with toasted shredded coconut.

VARIATION: For a fruit blan manje, add a can of fruit cocktail, cherries, pineapple, or other canned fruit (drained) to the mold before pouring milk mixture. You will need a slightly larger mold if including fruit.

TIPS: After pouring into the mold, cover the blan manje with plastic wrap to keep a film from forming on the top. Make sure that the wrap covers the surface of the blan manje. To remove the blan manje from the mold more easily, dip the mold in a hot water bath (very briefly) to loosen it from the sides.

HONDURAS
TORREJAS

EASY · COOK TIME: 25 MINUTES · ACTIVE PREP TIME: 10 MINUTES

Fans of French toast will love torrejas, which is similar in many ways to the familiar American breakfast staple. But in Latin America, torrejas is more often eaten as a dessert and is especially popular at Easter and Christmas. Countless variations on this basic dish exist throughout the Caribbean and Central America. Adding prunes and raisins to the syrup makes it Honduran.

One 12-inch loaf baguette bread, thickly sliced (preferably pan de manteca or pan de dulce)
3 eggs
Vegetable oil, for frying
2 c. water
2 c. white sugar
Juice and zest of 1 orange
1 Tbsp. allspice berries
4 whole cloves
1 stick cinnamon
½ c. prunes, chopped
¼ c. raisins

With an electric mixer, beat eggs on High speed until soft peaks form. Dip each slice of bread in egg to coat both sides.

Heat a small amount of oil in a large skillet over Medium-High heat. Fry bread slices in batches until golden brown on both sides, about 5 minutes. Set toast slices on a wire rack to cool.

Add water, sugar, orange juice and zest, allspice, cloves, and cinnamon stick to a large saucepan and bring to a boil. Reduce heat to Medium-Low, add prunes and raisins, and simmer for 5-10 minutes.

When ready to serve, dip each toast slice in syrup until fully saturated. Ladle remaining syrup over toast slices to serve.

MAKES 4-6 SERVINGS

Per serving: 667 calories, 8 g fat, 1 g saturated fat, 594 mg sodium, 143 g carbohydrates, 9 g protein.

SERVING SUGGESTION: Dust with powdered sugar.

VARIATIONS: Add a few Tbsp. of rum to syrup. Use honey in place of sugar when making the syrup (you will not need as much) or use milk in place of water.

TIP: Allow the toast slices to cool before dipping them into the syrup. If they are too hot, syrup that is also hot will make them soft and mushy.

JAMAICA
SWEET POTATO PUDDING

MEDIUM · COOK TIME: 2 HOURS, 15 MINUTES · ACTIVE PREP TIME: 30 MINUTES

Several of Jamaica's desserts are shared with the American South. One example is hummingbird cake, the recipe for which was used in publicity materials by Jamaica's tourism agency ten years before the magazine *Southern Living* popularized it in the United States. Another is sweet potato pudding, which is much like a crustless sweet potato pie (even though their origins are probably unrelated). Unlike its American counterpart, this Jamaican dessert is made using boniatos (Caribbean sweet potatoes), which have purple skins, white flesh, and a mild flavor.

3 lbs. boniatos (Caribbean sweet potatoes), peeled and grated
Two 15-oz. cans full-fat coconut milk, divided
1 c. brown sugar
3 Tbsp. burnt sugar syrup, divided
1 Tbsp. plus 1 tsp. vanilla extract, divided
1 Tbsp. rum
2 c. all-purpose flour
1 tsp. ground ginger
¾ tsp. ground cinnamon, divided
½ tsp. ground nutmeg
¼ tsp. plus 1 dash salt, divided
¼ c. raisins (optional)
Butter, for greasing pan

Working in batches, pulse grated sweet potatoes and coconut milk in a blender until smooth. (Use only enough coconut milk to make a smooth puree, and make sure to reserve at least ½ c.)

In a large mixing bowl, stir together sweet potato puree, brown sugar, 2 Tbsp. burnt sugar syrup, 1 Tbsp. vanilla extract, and rum. Sift together flour, ginger, ½ tsp. cinnamon, nutmeg, and ¼ tsp. salt. Slowly stir flour mixture into sweet potato mixture, a little at a time, until fully incorporated. Fold in raisins (if using).

Preheat oven to 350 degrees. Grease a 9-inch springform pan. Pour batter into pan and bake for 2 hours or until a toothpick inserted in the center of the pudding comes out mostly clean.

Whisk together ½ c. coconut milk, 1 Tbsp. burnt sugar syrup, 1 tsp. vanilla extract, and 1 dash salt. Spread coconut milk mixture evenly over the surface of the pudding. Return to oven and bake for 15 minutes longer.

Remove pudding from oven and allow to cool completely before loosening wall belt and slicing.

MAKES 10-12 SERVINGS

Per serving: 445 calories, 21 g fat, 19 g saturated fat, 80 mg sodium, 61 g carbohydrates, 6 g protein.

SERVING SUGGESTION: Serve at room temperature or chilled, plain or with whipped cream or vanilla ice cream.

VARIATION: While less authentic, orange sweet potatoes can be used in place of boniatos. Reduce brown sugar by ¼ c. if using orange sweet potatoes.

TIP: Burnt sugar syrup, also called browning, can be difficult to find in prepared form. To make your own, heat 1 c. brown sugar in a small saucepan over Medium-High heat until completely melted, stirring constantly. Remove from heat, stir in 1 c. boiling water, and set aside until cooled. Syrup will thicken upon standing.

MEXICO
CAPIROTADA

EASY · COOK TIME: 1 HOUR, 25 MINUTES · ACTIVE PREP TIME: 10 MINUTES · INACTIVE PREP TIME: 20 MINUTES

Originally a savory dish made with meat, onion, and tomatoes, capirotada was introduced to Mexico by Spanish conquistadores. Today it is a dessert often associated with Lent, as the cheese provides a filling and protein-rich meat substitute, and particularly with Good Friday. Over time, religious symbolism was attached to its ingredients; the bread and syrup represent the body and blood of Christ, the cloves and cinnamon sticks the nails and wood of the cross, and the melted cheese the Holy Shroud.

4 large dinner rolls (preferably stale), sliced
3 c. water
One 8-oz. cone piloncillo, or 1 c. dark brown sugar
4 whole cloves
2 sticks cinnamon
¼ c. butter, at room temperature, plus more for greasing dish
2 c. grated cheese (such as Oaxaca, Manchego, Monterey Jack, or Colby)
½ c. raisins
½ c. slivered almonds

Combine water, piloncillo or brown sugar, cloves, and cinnamon sticks in a large saucepan. Bring to a boil, reduce heat to Medium-Low, and simmer for 30 minutes. Remove from heat and allow to cool.

Preheat oven to 350 degrees. Arrange the bread slices in a single layer on a baking sheet and brush with butter. Toast for 10-15 minutes or until dry. (If using stale bread you can skip toasting.) Allow bread to cool completely.

Grease a 9 x 9-inch square glass baking dish. Arrange half of the bread slices on the bottom. Top with half of the raisins and half of the almonds, followed by half of the cheese. Pour half of the syrup on top and allow to stand for 10 minutes. Repeat with the remaining bread, raisins, almonds, cheese, and syrup.

Cover the baking dish with aluminum foil. Bake for 30 minutes, remove foil, and bake for 15 minutes longer or until cheese is melted. Allow capirotada to cool slightly before serving.

MAKES 8 SERVINGS

Per serving: 397 calories, 20 g fat, 10 g saturated fat, 343 mg sodium, 47 g carbohydrates, 11 g protein.

SERVING SUGGESTION: Sprinkle with nonpareils or jimmies and serve warm or chilled. If desired, pour a small amount of heavy cream on top before serving.

VARIATIONS: Replace raisins with other fresh or dried fruits, such as prunes, figs, or bananas, and almonds with other nuts, such as pecans or peanuts.

NICARAGUA
PIO QUINTO

HARD · COOK TIME: 1 HOUR, 10 MINUTES · ACTIVE PREP TIME: 30 MINUTES · INACTIVE PREP TIME: 5 HOURS, 30 MINUTES

The Pio Quinto (Pío V) cake was named for sixteenth-century pope Pius V, although his connection to the cake (if any) is not known. Nicaragua's most popular cake at Christmastime, Pio Quinto is similar to the tres leches cake (page 302), except that the delicious sponge cake is soaked in a rum syrup instead of milk and topped with custard instead of whipped cream. The custard used here is starch-bound, meaning that it uses cornstarch as a thickener. For this reason, it's important to bring it to a boil at high heat so that it can retain its thickness.

1 qt. plus ½ c. whole milk, divided

6 sticks cinnamon, divided

6 c. white sugar, divided

2 Tbsp. cornstarch

6 eggs, separated, plus 4 egg yolks, divided

¾ tsp. plus 1 dash salt, divided

3 Tbsp. butter, at room temperature, divided, plus more for greasing dish

2 Tbsp. vanilla extract, divided

½ c. raisins

12 prunes

1 c. white rum

1 qt. plus 2 c. water

6 whole cloves

2 c. all-purpose flour

1 Tbsp. plus 1 tsp. baking powder

2-½ tsp. ground cinnamon, plus more for dusting

Place 1 qt. milk in a large saucepan and add 2 cinnamon sticks. Bring to a boil over Medium-High heat. In a separate large saucepan, combine 1 c. sugar, cornstarch, 4 egg yolks, and 1 dash salt. Whisking vigorously, add ¼ c. of the infused milk mixture, followed by the rest of the milk mixture in a steady stream. Bring to a boil over Medium heat, whisking constantly, until mixture is thick enough to coat the whisk.

Remove from heat, add 2 Tbsp. butter and 2 tsp. vanilla extract, and stir until butter is melted. Pour custard into a bowl and cover with plastic wrap (so that wrap covers the actual surface of the custard). Refrigerate for at least 4 hours.

Place raisins and prunes in a small bowl and cover with rum. Add water, 3-½ c. sugar, remaining cinnamon sticks, and cloves to a large stockpot and bring to a boil over Medium-High heat. Boil for about 30 minutes or until syrup is reduced by one-quarter. Remove cinnamon sticks and cloves. Strain prunes and raisins, reserving rum, and add to syrup. Set aside.

Sift together flour, baking powder, and cinnamon. Add egg whites and ¾ tsp. salt to the bowl of a stand mixer with a whisk attachment and beat on Low speed until frothy, about 2 minutes. Increase speed to Medium and beat until soft peaks form, about 2 minutes longer. Increase speed to High and add sugar, a little at a time. Beat for 3 minutes or until mixture is stiff and glossy. Add remaining egg yolks, reduce speed to Low, and add flour mixture, a little at a time, followed by remaining ½ c. milk and vanilla extract.

Preheat oven to 350 degrees. Grease a 9 x 13-inch baking dish. Pour batter into dish and bake for 30 minutes or until a toothpick inserted in center of cake comes out clean.

Once syrup is completely cooled (and while cake is still warm), strain the raisins and prunes from the syrup and stir in reserved rum. Poke holes in the surface of the cake with a skewer or fork. Pour the syrup over the cake and allow it to stand until syrup is completely absorbed.

Spread custard over the surface of the cake in an even layer. Arrange prunes and raisins in a pattern on the custard's surface and dust with cinnamon. Refrigerate cake for 1 hour before serving.

MAKES 12 SERVINGS

Per serving: 774 calories, 10 g fat, 5 g saturated fat, 250 mg sodium, 160 g carbohydrates, 10 g protein.

VARIATIONS: Coconut milk may be used in place of whole milk. Dried fruits can be omitted if desired. For a chocolate Pio Quinto, replace cinnamon in cake batter with cocoa powder. Some versions of Pio Quinto replace some of the flour with fine white cornmeal.

TIP: To make custard lighter and more spreadable after refrigerating, beat it on Low speed with an electric mixer for 1-2 minutes.

PANAMA
SOPA DE GLORIA

MEDIUM · COOK TIME: 55 MINUTES · ACTIVE PREP TIME: 30 MINUTES

Sopa de gloria (or "glorious soup") isn't literally a soup, but it's soft and moist enough to require a spoon. It resembles another beloved Panamanian dessert, sopa borracho ("drunken soup"), with an extra custard layer added on top. It's a mainstay at Panamanian weddings and quinceañeras, but simple enough for any special occasion.

6 eggs, separated, plus 3 egg yolks, divided
3-½ c. white sugar, divided
2 c. all-purpose flour
2 tsp. baking powder
2-½ c. whole milk, at room temperature, divided
2 tsp. butter, at room temperature, plus more for greasing pan
One 14-oz. can sweetened condensed milk
One 12-oz. can evaporated milk
2 tsp. vanilla extract
1 c. chopped almonds (optional)
2 c. water, plus more for boiling
1 Tbsp. ground cinnamon
1 c. rum (light or dark)

Add egg whites to the bowl of a stand mixer with a whisk attachment and beat on Low speed until frothy, about 2 minutes. Increase speed to High and add 1-½ c. sugar, a little at a time. Beat for 3 minutes or until mixture is stiff and glossy. Add 6 egg yolks, one at a time.

Sift together flour and baking powder. Reduce speed to Low and add flour mixture, a little at a time, followed by ½ c. milk.

Preheat oven to 350 degrees. Grease a 9 x 13-inch baking dish. Pour batter into dish and bake for 30 minutes or until a toothpick inserted in center of pudding comes out clean. Set cake aside to cool completely.

Bring water to a boil in the bottom of a double boiler. Reduce heat to Low and whisk together 3 egg yolks and butter in the top of the double boiler. Slowly add 2 c. whole milk, sweetened condensed milk, and evaporated milk. Whisk egg yolk mixture constantly until it forms a thick custard (this will take at least 10 minutes). Remove from heat, stir in vanilla extract, and set aside until custard cools completely. Fold in almonds (if using).

Add 2 c. sugar, water, and cinnamon to a large saucepan. Bring to a boil, reduce heat to Medium-Low, and simmer uncovered for 15 minutes. Remove from heat and stir in rum.

To assemble sopa de gloria, cut the sponge cake into 2-inch squares. Arrange squares in the bottom of a large bowl (a glass trifle bowl is ideal). Ladle warm syrup on top of cake, a little at a time, until syrup is mostly absorbed. Spoon custard on top in an even layer and refrigerate until ready to serve.

MAKES 12 SERVINGS

Per serving: 616 calories, 16 g fat, 7 g saturated fat, 146 mg sodium, 98 g carbohydrates, 14 g protein.

SERVING SUGGESTION: Serve chilled and top with dried fruit (such as raisins or prunes) or Jordan almonds. Sopa de gloria can be assembled and served in individual ramekins instead of a single bowl.

VARIATIONS: Port or muscat wine or sherry may be used in place of or in addition to rum. Walnuts or raisins may be added to the custard in place of almonds. If desired, assemble the dessert in layers of cake and custard.

TIPS: Making sopa de gloria one day in advance will allow time for its flavors to meld and strengthen. When making syrup-drenched cake desserts, it is very important not to pour hot syrup onto a hot cake. Wait until the cake cools and pour the syrup while hot or wait until the syrup cools and pour onto hot cake.

PARAGUAY
DULCE DE MAMÓN

EASY · COOK TIME: 2 HOURS, 30 MINUTES · ACTIVE PREP TIME: 20 MINUTES · INACTIVE PREP TIME: 1 HOUR

When Paraguay was first invaded by Europeans five hundred years ago, the Guaraní were the most populous tribe in the region, with hundreds of thousands of members. Centuries of oppression, violence, and disease decimated their numbers, but they remain the leading indigenous group in Paraguay and hold a great influence over the small nation's culture. Papaya and other tropical fruits are central to Guaraní cuisine, and dulce de mamón (sweet papaya) is one of their most distinctive dishes.

2-½ lbs. slightly unripe papaya (about 2-3 small papayas)
1 Tbsp. baking soda
4 c. white sugar, divided
½ c. water, divided, plus more for boiling and rinsing
2 Tbsp. lemon juice, divided
Peel of 1 sour orange, or of 1 lemon and 1 lime, pith removed

Peel papayas, cut into quarters lengthwise, and remove seeds. Slice each quarter into 1-inch thick slices. Rinse papaya slices with cold water.

Place papaya slices in a large stockpot and add enough water to cover. Bring to a boil over High heat and continue to boil for 5 minutes. Remove from heat. Drain fruit and rinse again with cold water. Return to pot.

Once again, add enough water to cover along with baking soda. Stir until baking soda is dissolved and allow to stand for 1 hour. Drain and rinse with cold water once again.

In a heavy skillet, combine 2 c. sugar, ¼ c. water, and 1 Tbsp. lemon juice. Cook over Medium-Low heat for approximately 8-10 minutes or until the syrup has caramelized and is a deep golden brown. Transfer syrup to stockpot and repeat with remaining sugar, water, and lemon juice.

Add papaya and citrus peel to pot along with syrup and add enough water to cover. Bring to a boil over High heat, reduce heat to Low, and simmer uncovered for 2-3 hours or until liquid is reduced by half. When ready, the dulce de mamón will be a deep orange color. Allow to cool completely before serving.

MAKES 6-8 SERVINGS

Per serving: 487 calories, 0 g fat, 0 g saturated fat, 551 mg sodium, 129 g carbohydrates, 1 g protein.

SERVING SUGGESTIONS: Serve at room temperature or chilled, alone or topped with cold milk.

VARIATIONS: Add vanilla extract, cloves, or a cinnamon stick to the syrup.

PERU
CREMA VOLTEADA

MEDIUM · COOK TIME: 1 HOUR, 45 MINUTES · ACTIVE PREP TIME: 20 MINUTES · INACTIVE PREP TIME: 4 HOURS, 30 MINUTES

Crema volteada ("flipped cream"), also known as Peruvian flan, bears many similarities to the Spanish dessert upon which it is based (page 92). Its chief difference is that it receives the Latin American treatment with condensed and evaporated milk, giving this custard a creamy, rich flavor and mouthfeel. It is typically baked in a ring-shaped savarin mold instead of individual custard cups.

1 c. white sugar
¼ c. water
2 Tbsp. plus 1 tsp. vanilla extract, divided
6 eggs
One 14-oz. can sweetened condensed milk

One 12-oz. can evaporated milk
Zest of 1 lemon

Heat sugar and water in a small saucepan over Medium-Low heat until a smooth, golden-brown syrup is formed, stirring constantly. It should take at least 15 minutes for the sugar to completely liquefy. Add 1 tsp. vanilla extract and stir.

Pour syrup into an 8-inch savarin mold and tilt the mold so that the bottom and sides are coated with syrup. Place the mold inside a deep glass baking dish and fill dish with hot (but not boiling) water. Set aside to allow water to warm mold while crema volteada is being prepared.

Add the eggs, sweetened condensed milk, evaporated milk, and 2 Tbsp. vanilla extract to a blender and mix for 2 minutes or until very smooth. Stir in lemon zest and pour into the mold.

Preheat oven to 300 degrees. Bake crema for 1 hour, 30 minutes or until golden brown on top. Remove mold from water and allow to sit at room temperature for 30 minutes or until completely cooled. Cover with aluminum foil and refrigerate for at least 4 hours.

To serve, invert the crema volteada onto a serving platter (run a knife around the inside of the mold to loosen it if necessary). The syrup at the bottom of the mold will create a caramel sauce to coat the crema.

MAKES 10-12 SERVINGS

Per serving: 305 calories, 9 g fat, 5 g saturated fat, 132 mg sodium, 48 g carbohydrates, 9 g protein.

SERVING SUGGESTION: Serve chilled with fresh strawberries or blueberries.

VARIATION: For a crema volteada peruana, add 2-3 c. cooked quinoa to blender with eggs and milk. Cooking time will need to be reduced by at least 30 minutes.

SAINT KITTS AND NEVIS SUGAR CAKE

EASY · COOK TIME: 10 MINUTES · ACTIVE PREP TIME: 10 MINUTES

While it's called "sugar cake," this Caribbean treat is more like coconut rock candy, with a hard outer shell and a softer center. Sugar cake is usually colored with pink or bright red food coloring, though a full spectrum of jewel tones is not uncommon. Brightly colored sugar cake is a specialty of the Kittitian and Nevisian carnival, known as Sugar Mas, and is also a popular Diwali treat with the islands' Hindu minority.

4 c. white sugar
1 c. water
4 c. desiccated coconut
2 tsp. grated fresh ginger
½ tsp. cream of tartar
1 tsp. almond extract
Liquid food coloring of choice (optional)
Cooking spray, for coating baking dish

Add sugar and water to a large saucepan and bring to a boil over High heat. Continue to boil until temperature reaches 235 degrees (use a candy thermometer to monitor temperature). Stir in coconut, ginger, and cream of tartar and continue to cook until the coconut has mostly absorbed the syrup.

Remove from heat and stir in almond extract and food coloring (if using). Coat an 8 x 8-inch glass baking dish with cooking spray. Press coconut mixture into dish. Allow to cool completely before cutting into 16 squares to serve.

MAKES 16 SERVINGS

Per serving: 564 calories, 37 g fat, 32 g saturated fat, 22 mg sodium, 64 g carbohydrates, 4 g protein.

VARIATIONS: Some versions of sugar cake use brown sugar. Cinnamon or vanilla extract can be used in place of ginger or almond extract.

TIP: For a very special presentation, divide the coconut mixture before adding food coloring and dye the two parts different colors (or leave one part white). Press the two colors into the dish in two separate layers to make a two-toned sugar cake.

SAINT LUCIA BANANA CAKE

EASY · COOK TIME: 45 MINUTES · ACTIVE PREP TIME: 20 MINUTES

It's difficult to believe that bananas are not native to the Caribbean since they have thrived there since being introduced from the Canary Islands in 1516. At many points in St. Lucia's history the singular crop has sustained the island nation's economy. It has been said that you haven't had a banana until you've had one grown in St. Lucia, and those who have will agree that the Saint Lucian variety is far sweeter than nearly any other.

2-¾ c. all-purpose flour, plus more for flouring pans
1 tsp. baking soda
1 tsp. ground cinnamon
½ tsp. ground nutmeg
½ tsp. ground allspice
4 eggs
¾ c. plus 2 Tbsp. vegetable oil
¾ c. brown sugar
2 very ripe bananas, mashed
Juice and zest of 1 orange
½ c. finely chopped pineapple

½ c. finely chopped walnuts
½ c. butter, at room temperature, plus more for greasing pans
1 c. cream cheese, softened
4 c. powdered sugar
2 tsp. banana extract (optional)
Crushed banana chips, for garnish

Sift together flour, baking soda, cinnamon, nutmeg, and allspice. Combine eggs and oil in the bowl of a stand mixer with a whisk attachment and beat on Medium speed until smooth. Add brown sugar and beat for 2 minutes longer, followed by bananas and orange juice and zest. Add flour mixture a little at a time. Fold in pineapple and walnuts.

Preheat oven to 350 degrees. Grease and flour two 8-inch round cake pans. Divide batter between pans and bake for 45 minutes or until a toothpick inserted in center of cake comes out clean. Allow cakes to cool completely before removing from pans.

To make icing, beat butter and cream cheese with an electric mixer until smooth. Gradually add powdered sugar, followed by banana extract (if using) and continue to mix until creamy. Refrigerate until ready to use.

To assemble cake, spread an even layer of icing on top of one cake layer. Top with second layer and spread an even layer of icing on top. Spread remaining icing on sides of cake. Sprinkle with banana chips.

MAKES 12 SERVINGS

Per serving: 637 calories, 38 g fat, 13 g saturated fat, 240 mg sodium, 71 g carbohydrates, 7 g protein.

VARIATIONS: Use raisins or other dried fruit in place of pineapple and/or walnuts. Add ¼ c. spiced rum to icing (reduce butter by ¼ c.).

SAINT VINCENT AND THE GRENADINES BLACK CAKE

HARD · COOK TIME: 2 HOURS, 30 MINUTES · ACTIVE PREP TIME: 1 HOUR · INACTIVE PREP TIME: 1 WEEK, 3 DAYS

Black cake, a descendant of the English plum pudding, is not specific to Saint Vincent and the Grenadines. In fact, if there was a single dessert that truly united the entire Caribbean, this would be it. On virtually every island (and in the Caribbean diaspora), it is customary to begin the process of making the Christmas black cake shortly after the New Year begins. Some cooks soak their dried fruit for a year in advance! This recipe makes three cakes; given the time and effort involved in its preparation (and its long keeping time), baking black cake in large quantities makes a lot of sense.

12 c. (about 4 lbs.) dried fruit (raisins, prunes, currants, or dried cherries or figs, in any proportions)
1-½ c. candied orange peel
3 c. port wine or cherry brandy
4 c. dark rum, divided
2 c. all-purpose flour
1 Tbsp. plus 1 tsp. baking powder
2 tsp. ground cinnamon
½ tsp. ground nutmeg
¼ tsp. ground cloves
2 c. butter, at room temperature, plus more for greasing pans
2 c. brown sugar
Juice and zest of 1 lemon
Juice and zest of 1 lime
1 Tbsp. vanilla extract
1 tsp. almond extract
½ c. burnt sugar syrup

Working in batches, grind dried fruit and candied orange peel in a food processor until it reaches a paste-like consistency (add a small amount of wine or brandy if needed). Place the fruit pulp in a jar and add the wine or brandy and 3 c. rum. Stir, close jar, and allow to stand undisturbed for at least 1 week (longer is preferred).

Sift together flour, baking powder, cinnamon, nutmeg, and cloves. Combine butter and brown sugar in the bowl of a stand mixer with a whisk attachment and beat on Medium speed until fluffy. Add eggs one at a time, followed by lemon and lime zest and juice and vanilla and almond extracts. Add flour mixture a little at a time and turn off mixer once flour is fully incorporated.

Drain fruit (if necessary) and gently fold into batter using a spatula. Stir in burnt sugar syrup one spoonful at a time.

Preheat oven to 275 degrees. Grease three 8-inch round pans and line with parchment paper. Divide batter between pans. Bake for 1 hour, then reduce temperature to 225 degrees and bake for 1-½ to 2 hours longer or until a toothpick inserted in center of cake comes out mostly clean.

Remove cakes from oven and set aside to cool. Brush the surfaces of the cakes with remaining rum, repeating every 10 minutes until the cakes are completely cool. Once cakes have cooled completely, remove from pans and wrap with plastic wrap. Allow to stand for 3 days before serving.

MAKES ABOUT 30 SERVINGS

Per serving: 476 calories, 13 g fat, 8 g saturated fat, 100 mg sodium, 71 g carbohydrates, 4 g protein.

SERVING SUGGESTION: Serve alone or with vanilla ice cream.

TIPS: Some cooks prefer to soak the fruit before macerating; either way is effective. If pressed for time, boiling the fruit in wine for 20 minutes before macerating will yield satisfactory (but not ideal) results. Burnt sugar syrup, also called browning, can be difficult to find in prepared form. To make your own, heat 1 c. brown sugar in a small saucepan over medium-high heat until completely melted, stirring constantly. Remove from heat, stir in 1 c. boiling water, and set aside until cooled. Syrup will thicken upon standing. Black cake gets its signature dark color primarily from burnt sugar syrup; adding more or less will impact the color of the cake.

SURINAME BOJO

EASY · COOK TIME: 45 MINUTES · ACTIVE PREP TIME: 20 MINUTES

Suriname has the distinction of being the only Dutch-speaking country in South America, but it also stands as one of the world's most ethnically diverse small countries. Many Surinamese people are descendants of Indian, Chinese, and Indonesian immigrants, and all of these cultures have left a mark on Suriname's cuisine. Bojo (boyo), a type of flourless cake known as pone in Anglophile countries, is most likely a composite of many ethnic desserts made with South American ingredients like cassava and coconut.

2 lb. cassava, peeled
¼ c. dried mango or papaya, coarsely chopped
¼ c. raisins
Juice and zest of 2 oranges
1 c. desiccated coconut
½ c. full-fat coconut milk
4 eggs
1-½ c. light brown sugar
¼ c. plus 1 Tbsp. butter, at room temperature, divided, plus more for greasing pan
1 Tbsp. vanilla extract
1 tsp. almond extract
½ tsp. ground cinnamon

Combine dried mango or papaya, raisins, and orange juice and set aside to soak. Use a food processor or the small holes of a box grater to grate cassava as finely as possible. With a dish towel or cheesecloth, strain any excess liquid from the grated cassava.

Place cassava, coconut, and coconut milk in a food processor or blender and pulse for 5 minutes to form a thick paste. This may need to be done in batches.

With an electric mixer, beat eggs and brown sugar on Medium speed until light and fluffy. Add ¼ c. butter, vanilla and almond extracts, and cinnamon. Fold in soaked mango or papaya and raisins.

Preheat oven to 350 degrees. Grease a 9-inch springform pan and pour batter into pan in an even layer. Slice the remaining butter thinly and pat the top of the cake. Bake cake for 45 minutes or until a toothpick inserted in center of cake comes out clean. Allow cake to cool completely before loosening wall belt and slicing.

MAKES 8-10 SERVINGS

Per serving: 512 calories, 27 g fat, 21 g saturated fat, 94 mg sodium, 65 g carbohydrates, 6 g protein.

SERVING SUGGESTION: Top with nonpareils or a dollop of whipped cream, and serve warm, at room temperature, or chilled with hot tea. In Suriname, bojo is sometimes eaten with cheese, such as Gouda, Edam, or Limburger.

VARIATIONS: Use rum In place of orange juice for soaking fruit. Fruit can also be omitted.

TIP: Frozen and thawed grated cassava can be used in place of fresh cassava. You will need about 2-½ c. of grated cassava for this recipe.

TRINIDAD AND TOBAGO SOURSOP ICE CREAM

EASY · ACTIVE PREP TIME: 10 MINUTES · INACTIVE PREP TIME: 4 HOURS, 20 MINUTES

The soursop, or guanabana, is a tropical fruit closely related to the cherimoya that is difficult to find in fresh form in the United States, though it is ubiquitous in the

Caribbean. It has a prickly green skin and creamy white flesh with large seeds. Its complex earthy flavor can be compared to a cross between pineapple and papaya, with hints of strawberry, banana, and apple. Soursop ice cream is enjoyed throughout the Caribbean but is most popular in Trinidad and Tobago.

4 c. soursop pulp, with seeds removed
One 14-oz. can sweetened condensed milk
1 c. heavy whipping cream
2 tsp. lime juice (optional)
1 tsp. vanilla extract (optional)

Place soursop pulp in a blender and pulse until extremely smooth. Add the condensed milk to the blender, followed by whipping cream, lime juice, and vanilla extract (if using). Transfer mixture to a lidded container and chill in refrigerator for at least 2 hours.

Churn mixture in a standard ice cream maker, following manufacturer's instructions. Pour ice cream into a freezer-safe container and freeze for 2 hours longer.

MAKES 1 QUART

Per half-cup: 345 calories, 12 g fat, 7 g saturated fat, 107 mg sodium, 57 g carbohydrates, 7 g protein.

SERVING SUGGESTION: Garnish with cherries or grated coconut. Soursop ice cream is frequently served with black cake (page 335) in the Caribbean.

VARIATIONS: Add about ¼ c. of ginger juice to mixture while blending. Use mature ginger for the most juice and strongest flavor. For a coconut version, replace condensed milk with 1 c. full-fat coconut milk and 1 c. white sugar.

TIP: If you do not have an ice cream maker, place mixture in a freezer-safe container and place in freezer for at least 4-6 hours or until frozen, stirring with a fork every 30 minutes.

UNITED STATES
APPLE PIE

MEDIUM · COOK TIME: 1 HOUR · ACTIVE PREP TIME: 40 MINUTES · INACTIVE PREP TIME: 30 MINUTES

Nothing's more American than apple pie, right? Actually, neither the dessert nor its chief ingredient is native to the United States. The first recorded recipe for apple pie dates to fourteenth-century England, and the varieties of apple used for baking were introduced to the New World by European settlers. (The crabapple, the only native American species, was used to make cider but was too sour for baking.) But the apple pie became a manufactured symbol of the United States in the twentieth century, when the phrase "as American as apple pie" came into use. A traditional American apple pie uses a 9-inch double crust cut with butter and is flavored with cinnamon, nutmeg, and lemon juice.

8 apples (preferably Braeburn, Gala, or Golden Delicious)
4 c. all-purpose flour, divided
¾ c. white sugar, divided
½ tsp. salt
1-¾ c. cold butter, cut into cubes, divided
1 egg, separated
¼ c. water
½ c. brown sugar
Juice and zest of 1 small lemon
1 tsp. ground cinnamon
½ tsp. ground nutmeg

Sift together flour (reserving 2 Tbsp.), ½ c. white sugar, and salt in a large bowl. Add 1-½ c. butter and mix with two knives until butter pieces are mostly chopped and mixture is crumbly. Add egg yolk and water and stir to form a firm dough. Knead dough until smooth, divide into two equal portions, wrap in plastic wrap, and refrigerate for 15 minutes.

Turn one dough portion onto a floured surface and roll into a 12-inch circle of even thickness. Press dough circle into a 9-inch pie pan and prick several times with the tines of a fork. Cover with aluminum foil and place in freezer for 15 minutes longer.

Preheat oven to 350 degrees. Pull back foil, fill the pie shell with pie weights (or dry beans), replace foil, and bake for 10 minutes. Remove weights and foil and set aside to cool.

Peel, core, and quarter apples, then slice into ¼-inch thick pieces. Transfer apples to a large bowl and add 2 Tbsp. flour, ¼ c. white sugar, brown sugar, cinnamon, and nutmeg and toss to coat. Add apple mixture to the baked pie crust. Slice the remaining butter thinly and pat the surface of the apples.

Turn remaining dough portion onto a floured surface and roll into a 12-inch circle of even thickness. Cover pie with second crust. Use a sharp knife to trim the edge of the top crust and then pleat the edge with the tines of a fork to seal. Flute the top surface with a fork or use a knife to cut designs to vent. Brush the surface with beaten egg white.

Bake pie at 350 degrees for about 50 minutes or until golden brown on top. Allow to cool before slicing.

MAKES 10-12 SERVINGS

Per serving: 481 calories, 18 g fat, 11 g saturated fat, 234 mg sodium, 77 g carbohydrates, 6 g protein.

SERVING SUGGESTION: Serve warm or at room temperature with a scoop of vanilla ice cream or a slice of melted cheese (popular in New England and the Midwest) on top.

URUGUAY
CHAJÁ

HARD · COOK TIME: 2 HOURS · ACTIVE PREP TIME: 45 MINUTES

A cake named after a turkey-sized wild fowl native to the Southern Cone, the chajá was invented in 1927 by Orlando Castellano, owner of the Confitería Las Familias in Paysandú, Uruguay. Today the bakery still makes (and exports) thousands of the beloved cakes every year, but its recipe is such a well-kept secret that no single employee knows it in its entirety. This recipe comes very close to Castellano's original.

6 eggs plus 4 egg whites, separated
½ tsp. cream of tartar
3-¼ c. white sugar, divided
2-½ tsp. vanilla extract
¼ tsp. plus 1 dash salt, divided
2 c. heavy whipping cream, very cold
2 c. butter, at room temperature, plus more for greasing pans
1-½ c. all-purpose flour, plus more for flouring pans
2 tsp. baking powder
Two 15-oz. cans sliced peaches, in heavy syrup
1 c. water
One 13-oz. can dulce de leche
Fresh peach slices, for garnish

Place 4 egg whites and cream of tartar in the bowl of a stand mixer with a whisk attachment. Mix on Medium speed until soft peaks form. Add 1 c. sugar one spoonful at a time, followed by ½ tsp. vanilla extract and 1 dash salt, pausing after each addition to scrape down the sides of the bowl. Continue to mix until mixture is thick and glossy, and sugar is completely dissolved.

Preheat oven to 200 degrees. Cover a rimmed baking sheet with parchment paper. Use a rubber spatula to spoon the meringue in the center of the baking sheet and spread to the edges, reserving about ½-inch around the edge. Bake meringue for 1-½ hours or until completely dry. Remove from oven and set aside to cool. Once meringue is completely cooled, use a knife or spatula to break the meringue into pea-sized pieces.

In a medium mixing bowl, combine whipping cream and ¼ c. sugar. Beat on High speed with an electric mixer until stiff peaks form. Cover and refrigerate the Chantilly cream until ready to use.

In a large mixing bowl, whisk together eggs, 1 c. sugar, butter, and 2 tsp. vanilla extract until smooth. Sift together flour, baking powder, and ¼ tsp. salt. Add flour mixture to egg mixture, a little at a time, stirring after each addition.

Preheat oven to 350 degrees. Grease and flour three 8-inch round cake pans. Pour batter into pans and bake for 25 minutes or until a toothpick inserted in center of cake comes out clean. Allow cake layers to cool before removing from pans.

Drain and finely chop the canned peaches, collecting and reserving syrup. Combine peach syrup, water, and 1 c. sugar in a heavy saucepan. Heat over Medium-High heat, stirring constantly, until sugar is completely dissolved. Remove from heat and set aside.

To assemble cake, set the first cake layer on a cake stand or platter and brush with peach syrup. Spread half of the dulce de leche over the cake's top surface, followed by one-quarter of the meringue pieces, a thin layer of Chantilly cream, and half of the chopped canned peaches. Place the second layer on top and repeat. Top with the third layer and brush entire cake with peach syrup. Spread the remaining Chantilly cream over the top and sides of the cake and sprinkle top and sides with remaining meringue pieces. Garnish with fresh peach slices.

MAKES 12-16 SERVINGS

Per serving: 671 calories, 41 g fat, 24 g saturated fat, 245 mg sodium, 76 g carbohydrates, 5 g protein.

VARIATIONS: Add 2 Tbsp. rum or peach-flavored vodka to the syrup. Some variations of chajá use an angel food cake instead of a sponge cake as a base. Others omit the dulce de leche and use a mascarpone-based cream filling in its place.

TIPS: Chajá can be simplified by using a packaged cake mix, pre-baked meringue cookies, and prepared whipped cream.

VENEZUELA
BIENMESABE

HARD · COOK TIME: 45 MINUTES · ACTIVE PREP TIME: 50 MINUTES

The name of this extremely sweet and indulgent cake translates to "it tastes good to me." What else do you need to know? Bienmesabe originated in Spain, but Venezuelan bienmesabe is much different from the Spanish dessert from which it descended. While Spanish bienmesabe is made with honey and ground almonds, Venezuelan bienmesabe has coconut as its primary flavor and is almost always made with rum or another liqueur. The rich custard and fluffy meringue layers are optional in the Spanish dessert, but in Venezuelan bienmesabe they are mandatory.

13 eggs, separated and divided
5-¾ c. white sugar, divided
One 15-oz. can full-fat coconut milk, divided
1 c. sweetened shredded coconut
⅓ c. cornstarch
Butter, for greasing baking dish
2 tsp. vanilla extract, divided
1-¼ c. all-purpose flour
1 tsp. baking powder
4-½ c. whole milk
2-¼ c. water, divided
¼ c. light rum
1 tsp. cream of tartar
1 dash salt

Whisk together 8 egg yolks, ¾ c. sugar, coconut milk (reserving ½ c.), shredded coconut, and cornstarch. Heat whole milk and ¾ c. sugar in a large saucepan over Medium heat just until sugar dissolves (do not bring to a boil). Remove from heat.

Stir about ¼ c. of milk mixture into egg yolk mixture to temper. Add egg yolk mixture to milk mixture in saucepan and cook over Medium-Low heat until custard thickens. Transfer custard to a bowl and cover with plastic wrap (so that wrap covers the actual surface of the custard). Refrigerate until ready to use.

Preheat oven to 350 degrees. Grease a 9 x13-inch baking dish. (You may find it helpful to coat the dish with parchment paper as well.) Beat 5 whole eggs, ¾ c. sugar, and 1 tsp. vanilla extract with an electric mixer on Medium speed until pale and fluffy. Sift together flour and baking powder and add to wet ingredients a little at a time. Pour batter into baking dish and bake for 30 minutes or until a toothpick inserted center of cake comes out clean. Remove from oven and allow to cool in pan completely before inverting onto a wire rack.

In a small saucepan, combine 2 c. water and 2 c. sugar. Bring to a boil over High heat. Remove from heat, allow to cool slightly, and add reserved coconut milk and rum. Set aside.

Place 8 egg whites and cream of tartar in the bowl of a stand mixer with a whisk attachment. Mix on Medium speed until soft peaks form. Add 2 c. sugar one spoonful at a time, followed by 1 tsp. vanilla extract and salt, pausing after each addition to scrape down the sides of the bowl. Continue to mix until mixture is thick and glossy and sugar has completely dissolved.

Preheat broiler to High. With a long, sharp knife or wire cake cutter, slice cake crosswise to make two equal halves. Place one half on a large baking sheet and brush with half of syrup. Spread half of the custard on top. Set the second layer on top of the first, brush with remaining syrup, and top with remaining custard. Spread the meringue on top of cake. Broil for about 2-3 minutes or until meringue is golden brown.

MAKES 12-16 SERVINGS

Per serving: 581 calories, 21 g fat, 15 g saturated fat, 147 mg sodium, 94 g carbohydrates, 10 g protein.

SERVING SUGGESTION: Serve chilled with strong coffee.

VARIATIONS: Use ladyfingers in place of cake (you will need about 1 lb. of ladyfingers for each layer). Dip the ladyfingers in syrup (do not saturate) and layer with custard and meringue. Refrigerate at least 4 hours before serving to allow flavors to meld.

CATEGORICAL INDEX

Made in the USA
Las Vegas, NV
10 December 2023

82484187R30195